GETTING READY TO LEARN

Getting Ready To Learn describes how educational media have and are continuing to play a role in meeting the learning needs of children, parents, and teachers. Based on years of meaningful data from the CPB-PBS Ready To Learn Initiative, chapters explore how to develop engaging, playful, and developmentally appropriate content. From Emmy-Award-winning series to randomized controlled trials, this book covers media production, scholarly research and technological advances surrounding some of the country's most beloved programming.

Shelley Pasnik is Director of the Center for Children and Technology and a vice president of the Education Development Center.

GETTING READY TO LEARN

Creating Effective, Educational Children's Media

Edited by Shelley Pasnik

Routledge
Taylor & Francis Group

NEW YORK AND LONDON

First published 2019
by Routledge
52 Vanderbilt Avenue, New York, NY 10017

and by Routledge
2 Park Square, Milton Park, Abingdon, Oxon, OX14 4RN

Routledge is an imprint of the Taylor & Francis Group, an informa business

© 2019 Taylor & Francis

Disclaimer: The contents of chapters 1, 2, 4, 9, 12, 13, 14, 15, and 16 were developed under a grant from the Department of Education. However, those contents do not necessarily represent the policy of the Department of Education, and you should not assume endorsement by the Federal Government. The project is funded by a Ready To Learn grant (PR/AWARD No. U295A150003, CFDA No. 84.295A) provided by the Department of Education to the Corporation for Public Broadcasting.

Library of Congress Cataloging-in-Publication Data
A catalog record for this title has been requested

ISBN: 978-1-138-57258-4 (hbk)
ISBN: 978-1-138-57260-7 (pbk)
ISBN: 978-0-203-70197-3 (ebk)

Typeset in Bembo
by Swales & Willis Ltd, Exeter, Devon, UK

CONTENTS

FOREWORD

Dr. Alice Wilder and Sir Ken Robinson

All children deserve, and have the right, to sustain the joyful love of learning that is the hallmark of early childhood. As this book so clearly shows, children's television and digital media have unique roles in enriching the learning experiences of all young children, not least in the critical early years of their lives.

In his recent book, *You, Your Child and School*, Ken notes that every newborn baby is a seething bundle of possibilities. From the moment they're born, children continue to go through a miraculous metamorphosis. As they grow, they change physically in size, strength, and appearance. They evolve emotionally as their brains and neural systems become more sophisticated. They develop cognitively as their knowledge and understanding of the world increases. They grow socially in their ability to relate to other people. They develop spiritually as they find meaning, purpose, and compassion in their lives.

None of this is inevitable. How they develop, and what they become, has much to do with the environments in which they grow and learn. What sorts of communities and environments help children learn best, and what can children's television and media contribute?

There are differences between learning, education, and school. *Learning* is acquiring new skills and understanding; *education* is an organized approach to learning; a *school* is any community of learners. Children love to learn, but they don't all enjoy education, and some have a hard time with conventional schools.

Newborn babies learn at a prodigious pace. Take language: In their first 24 months or so, they go from being inarticulate bundles of cries and gurgles to being able to speak. Why do babies learn to speak? They have a natural capacity for it, and they love to learn. As they go through life, they'll pick up all sorts of skills and knowledge just for the love of learning—because they want to, and they can. As they go through formal education, children can begin to lose interest or confidence in learning, often because of the rituals and pressures of conventional schooling.

As a child, Alice didn't especially enjoy school and never thought of herself as a "learner." She remembers two transformational moments when a love of learning took firm hold of her. The first was during her freshman year at Skidmore College, when Mary Ann Foley, a professor of psychology, said these six words to her: *I like the questions you ask.* That was the first time anyone had said anything positive to Alice about the way she saw the world. She realized at that moment that she did have a distinctive point of view and that when she was engaged with questions that interested her, she wanted to learn more. That exchange inspired a lifelong commitment to ensuring that kids of all ages are inspired to love learning and to see themselves as lifelong learners. She realized that we all have opportunities to tell others about the strengths we see in them, just as Mary Ann Foley did with her.

Her second transformational moment was watching the 1988 fantasy movie *Big*, starring Tom Hanks. Hanks plays a 12-year-old boy named Josh, whose wish to become "big" unexpectedly comes true and he finds himself stuck in the body of a 30-year-old man. Josh lands a job at a prestigious toy company after the president sees him playing and recognizes how important it is for someone with the outlook of a child to help drive decisions. In a board meeting, the executives pass around a toy, which they claim will be "the next big thing." Josh, whose inner 12-year-old is the target audience for the toy, takes one look at it and says, "What's so fun about that?" That's when Alice had her second light-bulb moment.

She left the movie wanting to know how she could play the part of Josh in real life, how she could be that person in the room who says, "I don't get it. What's so fun, relevant, or understandable about that?" From then on, she had a clear vision of the sort of job she wanted. *Big* provided her with role models for a career in sparking transformational learning moments for children everywhere, making learning appealing, relevant, and joyful. You may have had such sparks of inspiration in your own life, transformational moments when a passion for learning and achievement was kindled and ignited. Understanding the power of such moments is one key to creating the kind of learning environments that all children need and deserve, in schools, in the home, and in our communities. As the many examples in this book illustrate, children's television and digital media can be a powerful, inspiring resource for transformational learning.

Natural learning is driven by curiosity and the sheer pleasure of discovery. One reason why children's appetite for learning can dull as they get older is the pressure of formal education and testing. Great educators know that their first task is to keep the flame of curiosity alive in young people by making learning pleasurable as well as challenging. Children's television and media are rooted in engaging the interests and imaginations of children, and in sustaining their interest through captivating ideas, stories, and characters.

Learning abstract concepts can be difficult; children's media can make such concepts concrete through stimulating visuals, animation, music, and sound. They draw upon a vivid variety of forms and techniques to help children understand ideas and information in ways that complement other ways of learning.

Learning is as much a social as an individual process. As with learning to speak, children learn by watching how other people behave and act. Their own ideas and actions are affected not only by what they hear people say but by what they see them do. Children's media can offer significant role models through the characters and stories they present. Characters who are curious, creative, take initiative, and are kind to others can have a positive impact on how kids act in their own lives. One of many examples from the Ready To Learn Initiative in action features *Super Why!*, which introduced kids to inspirational characters they wanted to emulate. When researchers went into lower income schools, four-year-old kids shouted, "I want to be like him—Super Why, with the Power to Read!" Such is the power of the medium.

For people of all ages, one of the most compelling forms of teaching and learning is telling stories. Stories set ideas in context and, most importantly, they engage us emotionally in events and ideas at a personal level. Children's media can present relevant, comprehensible, age-appropriate stories that engage the feelings and thoughts of young people in ways that make learning "sticky." And what is learning, if it's not sticky?

Kids *love* to learn and be challenged. Children's media can provide scaffolding—striking a balance between too easy and too hard—that can introduce young people to content through progressive levels of complexity to propel their learning even further. Digital devices offer another example of media's ability to spark transformational learning moments. *Pause* and *rewind* buttons enable kids to pause for a question, take a moment to think and reflect, and rewind to hear or watch again in order to master the content at their own pace.

Finally, learning happens anywhere and everywhere, not only at desks in conventional classrooms. Children's television and digital media can spark learning *beyond* the screen—at home, at a museum, or anywhere learning takes place—inspiring a child to use what they learned online, *offline*. For example, *Super Why!* Reading Camps are weeklong programs taught by Head Start teachers. One morning, a parent dropped off her four-year-old daughter and said, "I don't know what you are doing during this camp, but last night my daughter was calling out letters (of the alphabet) all the way home and throughout our house!"

In all of these ways, children's love of, and pleasure in, learning can be greatly enhanced by thoughtful, well-crafted children's media, which combine absorbing images, ideas, stories, and characters on screen. It can be endlessly extended by the support of caring individuals who help children discover their own strengths and interests as learners and foster their natural sense of awe and curiosity in the ever-changing world around them.

Dr. Alice Wilder is an Emmy Award-winning educational psychologist who knows the only way to make quality products that appeal to kids and support their learning is to ask them. *Blue's Clues, Super Why!, Tumble Leaf, Creative Galaxy*, and *The Stinky & Dirty Show* are just a few she has helped develop.

Sir Ken Robinson, Ph.D., is an internationally recognized leader in the development of creativity, innovation, and human potential. He advises governments, corporations, education systems, and some of the world's leading cultural organizations. He is the author of *The Element*, which has been translated into 23 languages, and most recently, *You, Your Child and School: Navigate Your Way to the Best Education*, written with Lou Aronica.

ACKNOWLEDGMENTS

A book like this happens because many people give their time, share their knowledge, and make a commitment to make it happen. I am grateful to all who did just that on behalf of this one.

The Ready To Learn Initiative runs in five-year cycles, and this book was produced smack dab in the middle of year three of the current cycle, which, arguably, is the crunchiest of crunch times. Amazingly, writing teams pulled off the 16 chapters while continuing to do the demanding work of the initiative; they wrote while simultaneously carrying out research studies, producing television series and games, and keeping family workshops going throughout the country, not to mention ably attending to the parts of their lives outside of work. As the brief contributor biographies make clear, this is an accomplished group of professionals. What may be implied by the bio sketches, I will affirm: These are hard-working people who consistently tilt toward generosity and learning, whether it's kids who are doing the learning, or themselves.

The authors are members of various institutions, and this book had the good fortune to have the support of each of those, especially from the Education Development Center, SRI International, PBS, and the Corporation for Public Broadcasting (CPB). When asked, these larger organizations created intellectual and legal pathways, helping to smooth the process of working with some of the biggest brands in children's media (that, to my great relief and to the benefit of this book, approached copyright and licensing with an open hand). Heartfelt thanks to PBS and CPB legal counsel, and to EDC's intellectual property guide, Lisa Ballew.

Thanks, too, to everyone who attended to countless nitty-gritty publishing tasks, such as image preparation and copyediting—chief among them, EDC's Alice Kaiser. Alice brought an abundance of conscientiousness, as well as calm, keeping in place a head-spinning number of credits, files, and figures. Thanks also to EDC's John Parris, Bronwyn Taggart, Hemali Patel, and Rebecca Driscoll; PBS's Stefanie Wilcox and Kayla Springer; and nSightWorks's Alex Elder.

And then there are PBS's David Lowenstein and CPB's Pam Johnson, who approach all aspects of the Ready To Learn work with incredible diligence and care—and this book was no exception. This book would not exist without them.

There are many other people who did not make it onto the author roster but who have contributed mightily to the shape and success of Ready To Learn research, production, and leadership over the years. This includes people too numerous to name, though, from my corner of the initiative, call-outs are required to Carlin Llorente and Bill Penuel, who were shoulder-deep in the research beginning in 2006; to CPB's Barbara Lovitts, who followed not long after; and to Peggy O'Brien, who got many of us involved in the first place.

On the federal side, enormous thanks also go to the U.S. Department of Education's Office of Innovation and Improvement, the capable steward of the Ready To Learn Television Grant Program. Brian Lekander occupies his role as program officer in just the right ways: judiciously, insightfully, and never veering from sound reason and Congressional intent. Thanks, too, to the U.S. Congress for its foresight in establishing the program and for understanding that America's kids and families require consistency if they are to thrive.

Dr. Alice Wilder and Sir Ken Robinson wrote a pitch-perfect frame for this book. I would feel sheepish about how little time they had to write, but I knew that for these two it was less about writing and more about channeling: They needed only to be who they are—creators who have a knack for solving a worthy problem, and who want nothing less than to give kids the tools to learn how to do the same.

And last, thanks to the many babies who were born during these last two decades, including one Sabine June Pasnik McClure, adding to the rhythm and cadence of the multi-year grant cycles. From production to research, the homes of many folks working on the Ready To Learn Initiative became fuller as these little people entered them, strengthening our resolve to create more equitable futures for all children, not just our own.

CONTRIBUTORS

Alexandra Adair is a former middle-school English language, arts, and humanities teacher, in both public and private schools in New York City. Currently, Alexandra is a doctoral candidate and presidential magnet fellow at the CUNY Graduate Center in the Educational Psychology program. Before beginning the Ph.D. program, she received her master's degree in psychology at the New School for Social Research, where she conducted research on attachment, print exposure, emotional intelligence, empathy, and theory of mind. Her interests include the impact and use of media and technology in the home learning environment, school readiness assessment, and early childhood science.

Kea Anderson studies out-of-school learning as a senior education researcher at SRI International. Her work focuses on improving access to high-quality STEM learning experiences for children, youth, and families from under-resourced communities. She has been studying and supporting the Community Collaboratives since their inception and was delighted to collaborate with PBS and CPB for a chapter on them in this book. Kea's love of science learning comes from a childhood full of discovery. She learned by watching her mother approach everything, from gardening to raising aquarium fish, systematically—carefully observing and patiently changing one thing at a time, until—Eureka!

Dylan Arena is co-founder and chief learning scientist at Kidaptive, whose mission is to empower learners of all ages by creating a vibrant ecosystem of personalized learning experiences. Dylan helps guide that mission by establishing new partnerships, determining what success looks like for each partner, and overseeing all issues related to learning, assessment, and reporting. Dylan spent 11 years at Stanford University studying cognitive science, game-based learning, and next-generation assessment while earning a bachelor's degree in symbolic systems, a master's degree in philosophy, a master's degree in statistics, and a Ph.D. in learning sciences and technology design.

Kim Berglund is a 15-year veteran of children's media and early childhood education. Kim began her career at Disney TV Animation, Nickelodeon, and finally PBS KIDS, where she spent eight years as the curriculum director for the Ready To Learn Television Grant Program. After PBS, she served as the program director for Stanford University's Development and Research in Early Math Education (DREME). She is now the founder of Chicken Fiddle Media, which specializes in the development and production of children's media, working with companies, such as GoldieBlox, Age of Learning, and Netflix. Kim has a B.A. from Dartmouth College and an Ed.M. from the Harvard Graduate School of Education.

Shannon K. Bishop is the director of content at PBS KIDS Digital where she oversees development and launches for leading PBS KIDS series digital portfolios. Under the CPB-PBS initiative, Bishop has focused on designing science inquiry experiences for children two to eight, pioneering production of PBS KIDS' first adaptive games. She continues to evolve PBS KIDS Digital's approach to play, gaming, and education and guides strategic experimentation involving new platforms.

Sarah D. Blodgett is a doctoral student in literacy education at Boston University's School of Education. She teaches courses in educational technology and is a research assistant for the Ready To Learn Initiative at Boston University in collaboration with CPB/PBS. She is a former elementary and preschool teacher with a specialization in exploring literacy and science with young children. She joined Boston University's Ready To Learn team in 2015 as a literacy and science education specialist.

Lori Brittain is the senior director of strategy and operations for PBS Education. Lori has over 20 years of experience managing and advising on the design and implementation of programs that empower educators to support children of all ages. In her role at PBS, she collaborates with all levels within the organization to drive executive decision-making and operationalize strategic goals for a number of initiatives including content and community engagement, school readiness, and professional learning. Lori is an avid reader, the proud mother of one son, Noah, and frequently enjoys live music and travel with her husband.

Gregory K. W. K. Chung is associate director for technology and research innovation at the National Center for Research on Evaluation, Standards, and Student Testing at the University of California, Los Angeles (CRESST/UCLA).

His current work at CRESST involves designing telemetry and game-based interventions, evaluating technology innovations, and developing innovative assessment formats for use in technology-enhanced learning applications. Greg has extensive experience in the design, development, and implementation of technology applications for learning and assessment purposes.

Michael Conn-Powers is a research associate at Indiana University, an adjunct assistant professor in the School of Education, and director of the Indiana Institute on Disability and Community's Early Childhood Center. His previous positions have included early interventionist, preschool teacher, state administrator, university professor, and consultant. Over the past five years, Dr. Conn-Powers has been extensively involved in research and product development in the areas of early intervention, service coordination, school readiness, and universal design. Dr. Conn-Powers has also been involved with designing and implementing Indiana's First Steps (Part C) child and family outcome evaluation system.

Jean B. Crawford is senior manager of parent and teacher content, Ready To Learn at PBS. She oversees the development of print and digital resources designed to help parents and educators engage with young children to build early math, literacy, and science skills. She joined the Ready To Learn team in 2003 as Director of PBS' award-winning website for parents. Prior to that, she was director of AOL's content area for parents, and an editorial director at Time-Life Books, where she led the development of an innovative 12-volume book series for children that threaded math concepts through stories and activities.

Claire Christensen is an education researcher at SRI International. She studies young children's learning from educational media. Her work includes formative and summative evaluations of media for science, math, and social-emotional learning in early childhood. Dr. Christensen holds a B.A. from Illinois State University and an M.A. and Ph.D. in community and prevention research from the University of Illinois at Chicago.

Sara DeWitt joined PBS in 1999 to grow the new interactive learning presence for children. As vice president of PBS KIDS Digital, DeWitt oversees the pbskids.org website, streaming video services, educational gaming apps, and digital experiences for parents, working to make PBS KIDS content engaging and accessible to widely diverse audiences. Previously, DeWitt worked as a preschool teacher and studied media habits of children in rural areas. She holds a B.A. and an M.A. in English from Stanford University, and a certificate from the University's children, society, and public policy curriculum. She is a military spouse and mom to two boys.

Ximena Domínguez, Ph.D., is director of early STEM research at Digital Promise. Her research examines child-level factors and classroom-level processes that influence young children's learning and STEM readiness, with the goal of informing early childhood education practices at home and school. Her work involves partnerships with educators and families from disadvantaged backgrounds and in culturally and linguistically diverse communities. Her portfolio of work includes research and development projects, evaluation efforts, and assessment development initiatives—all focused on early STEM and exploring the unique affordances of developmentally appropriate technology for early teaching and learning.

Nell K. Duke is a professor in literacy, language, and culture and in the combined program in education and psychology at the University of Michigan. Her work focuses on early literacy development, particularly among children living in poverty. Duke has been named one of the most influential education scholars in the U.S. in *EdWeek*. Her recent books include *Inside Information: Developing Powerful Readers and Writers of Informational Text through Project-based Instruction* and *Beyond Bedtime Stories: A Parent's Guide to Promoting Reading, Writing, and Other Literacy Skills from Birth to 5, Second Edition*. Her Twitter handle is @nellkduke.

Cosimo Felline earned an undergraduate degree in physics from the University of Cagliari, Italy, and a Ph.D. in nuclear physics from Florida State University, with a focus in computational models. Cosimo has been employed at PBS since 2009, as a web developer, software developer manager, and currently as data science developer, where he contributes to the development of the Learning Analytics Platform.

Michael Fragale is vice president, education and children's content, at the Corporation for Public Broadcasting (CPB). He leads CPB's strategic education initiatives and content investments. He directs the Ready To Learn Television Grant Program from the U.S. Department of Education, providing strategic counsel on operations, policy, and engagement. He has developed public media grant projects on topics such as early learning, distance learning, dropout prevention, STEM education, and adult literacy. Fragale is the former director of content and strategy for the PBS Adult Learning Service. Prior to his work at CPB, he was an academic program manager for SAS Institute, a leading business intelligence and analytics software company.

Elisa Garcia is an early childhood researcher with the Ready To Learn project at SRI International. Her research interests focus on how the home and classroom contexts promote the academic and socioemotional development of ethnically and linguistically diverse children. Dr. Garcia has worked on evaluations of the effectiveness of preschool and elementary programs and contributed to research projects studying the development of early vocabulary, math, and executive functions. Prior to joining SRI, she worked at a policy think tank in Washington, D.C., and taught English in Spain. Dr. Garcia earned her Ph.D. from the Stanford Graduate School of Education.

Sarah Nixon Gerard is an education researcher at SRI International. She studies the impact of learning interventions on young children, focusing on interventions that involve technology and educational media. She is especially interested in research projects that develop and evaluate systems of learning across school and home contexts for economically disadvantaged children. Previously, Gerard taught pre-kindergarten in Washington, DC. She holds a B.A. from American University and a master's in public policy from Georgetown University.

Marion Goldstein is a research scientist at the Education Development Center. Her work promotes developmentally appropriate uses of technology to support young children's learning in pre-K–12 classrooms, at home, and in informal contexts. Her R&D efforts enhance low-income families' access to high-quality learning opportunities, identify strategies to strengthen learning for all children, and contribute to the development of digital tools shown to enhance STEM learning and accommodate a variety of instructional needs. She holds a B.A. from the University of Pennsylvania, an M.A. from New York University, and an Ed.D. in educational technology from Teachers College, Columbia University.

Carol Greenwald is the award-winning senior executive producer and director of children's media at WGBH Boston. The recipient of five Emmys and a George Foster Peabody award, Carol has produced some of the best-loved children's shows on television, including the top-rated *Curious George* and the beloved *Arthur* (and its spin-off, *Postcards from Buster*), as well as *The Ruff Ruffman Show, Martha Speaks, Time Warp Trio,* and *Long Ago and Far Away*. In addition to the development and production of innovative children's programming, Carol oversees the development of websites, games, and outreach initiatives related to her projects.

Jaime Gutierrez is a research associate at the Center for Children and Technology, a part of the Education Development Center in New York, NY. He has a deep knowledge of early childhood learning through his experiences teaching young children. He has worked in a variety of early childhood education settings, focusing on children aged three to seven. His main research interests are in study design and implementation, qualitative research, STEM education, and the use of technology as a tool to support learning for young children and adults, with a focus on working with families and educators in low-income communities.

Naomi Hupert has worked at the intersection of technology, literacy, and STEM content areas for over 20 years. Her work focuses on the use of technology as a tool to support learning for children and the adults who work with them and aims to provide all students with engaging and challenging academic instruction. She brings a special focus on improving outcomes for students who struggle to meet grade-level academic benchmarks due to inadequate access to quality instruction, disabilities, or other challenges to learning, and engages digital resources to support this population of students and their families.

Pamela Johnson is executive director of the CPB-PBS Ready To Learn Initiative, a school readiness program that teams public media content with community collaboration to support improved educational outcomes for children, especially those from low-income families. This work is conducted in partnership with PBS KIDS, the U.S. Department of Education, PBS member stations, and other content, engagement, and research collaborators. Prior to joining CPB, Pam was vice president for education and engagement at WNED/Buffalo, New York where she spearheaded ThinkBright TV, the Buffalo Professional Development and Technology Center, PBS TeacherLine NY, and Reading Rainbow's national outreach and web efforts.

David Lowenstein, MPA, is the senior director of the CPB-PBS Ready To Learn Initiative, where he oversees strategy and operations for Ready To Learn at PBS and helps manage teams responsible for content development, educator and family engagement, and relationships with contributing producers. Prior to joining PBS, David was a national urban fellow at the Sesame Workshop and co-authored a policy brief entitled Game Changer: Investing in Digital Play to Advance Children's Learning and Health. Early in his career, David worked for the Hip-Hop Summit Action Network, the Minority Media and Telecom Council, National Urban League, Education Technology Think Tank, and U.S. congressman Major Owens.

Anne E. Lund, M.S., is the director of curriculum and content for PBS KIDS and the CPB-PBS Ready To Learn Initiative. In this role, she works closely with content producers, reviewing assets on all media platforms to ensure that the content and curriculum accurately reflects the show's premise and learning objectives. Lund has spent years in children's media specializing in educational curriculum development and media research, working on projects for media outlets and research groups, including Nick, Jr., and the Sesame Workshop, and serving as director of research and curriculum for Disney Junior's *Little Einsteins*. She also has experience as an elementary school teacher and preschool director.

Lawrence S. Mirkin, B.A., M.F.A., Yale University, is an award-winning independent television producer/writer. His programs for children include: *Fraggle Rock, The Jim Henson Hour, What's Your News, Hi, Opie!*, and for Portfolio Entertainment, the Ready To Learn season of *The Cat in the Hat Knows a Lot About That!* His productions have appeared on PBS KIDS, NBC, Sprout, Netflix, and HBO in the U.S.; CBC, CTV, and TVO in Canada; and various stations around the world, winning or nominated for many honors including the Emmy, the Gemini, the Ace, the Prix Jeunesse, the Youth Media Alliance Award, and the International Emmy.

Savitha Moorthy, Ph.D., is the director of STEM equity research at Digital Promise. Her work focuses on STEM education, and on understanding how media and technology resources can be integrated into STEM teaching and learning experiences. The majority of Savitha's projects are situated in early childhood education contexts and involve partnerships with educators, families, and developers. Her projects are aimed at making education more equitable for traditionally disadvantaged populations, including low-income families, English Language Learners, and children, families, and teachers in diverse, urban school districts.

Aaron Morris, Ed.M., is the director of family and community learning, working collaboratively with education professionals at PBS Stations and the producers of PBS KIDS' media properties to create impactful in-person learning experiences for children and families that meaningfully leverage PBS KIDS content and resources. An alumnus of the Harvard Graduate School of Education, Aaron joined PBS KIDS in 2012 as a content manager on the PBS KIDS Digital team. Prior to joining PBS, Aaron worked as a research assistant at the MIT Media Lab in support of the Scratch teams work with formal and informal educators.

Lisa O'Brien, Ed.D., is a lecturer in literacy education at Boston University where she teaches courses in elementary literacy instruction. Her research focuses on providing all children equitable opportunities to learn and includes studies of family literacy program effects, transformative technology integration practices, and relations between knowledge, comprehension, and text types. She is a former head preschool teacher, an elementary classroom teacher, and reading specialist/literacy leader in a K–4 school. She joined Boston University's Ready To Learn team in 2010 as a literacy education specialist.

Jeanne R. Paratore, Ed.D., is professor emerita of literacy education at Boston University. She is a former classroom teacher, reading specialist, and Title I director. In 1989, she founded a family literacy program, which continues to serve immigrant parents and their children. In 2010, she began her work with

Ready To Learn, focusing on integrating PBS KIDS programming with evidence-based instruction in literacy, mathematics, and science. Her publications relate to family literacy, classroom literacy instruction, and integrating high-quality digital media within early childhood instruction. In 2007, she was elected by her peers to the Reading Hall of Fame.

Charles B. Parks is a programmer and data analyst at UCLA CRESST. His current work involves analysis of digital learning objects, machine learning, and the development of feature-detection algorithms. He has previous experience in designing and building educational games for use in classroom studies. His research interests are in designing effective and engaging educational games and developing measurement tools for game telemetry.

Shelley Pasnik is a vice president at the Education Development Center where she directs the Center for Children and Technology and oversees the early childhood practice area. She has helped shape national policy, developed public education campaigns, and guided the production of children's educational services, collaborating with the U.S. Department of Education, PBS, the Corporation for Public Broadcasting, the Bill & Melinda Gates Foundation, Apple, Google, MIT Media Lab, IBM, Carnegie Hall, the National Science Foundation, and the Sesame Workshop, among others. A spokesperson for the thoughtful integration of digital media and equitable futures for all families, she is regularly featured in news outlets, including *The Washington Post, Christian Science Monitor, EdWeek*, and NPR.

Elizabeth J. K. H. Redman, Ph.D., is a senior researcher at UCLA CRESST. Her current research is focused on STEM games, game-based assessment, and the creation of gameplay measures from telemetry data to understand players' in-game performance and behavior. She holds graduate degrees in education from the University of California, Los Angeles.

Jeremy D. Roberts is director of learning technologies for PBS KIDS Digital, where he works closely with award-winning content properties such as *Curious George, Dinosaur Train*, and *The Cat in the Hat Knows a Lot About That!* to deliver innovative educational media and real-world experiences to kids aged two to eight across multiple platforms including web, phone, tablet, whiteboards, video, and reality itself. Roberts also helps to oversee the development of playful learning experiences utilizing newer and promising technologies for learning including personalized and adaptive content, voice and facial recognition, conversational user experiences, and more.

Jennifer Rodriguez, Ed.M., is the director of digital learning at PBS KIDS where she has worked for the past ten years designing play experiences to help teach literacy, math, science and inquiry, and SEL skills and practices. She holds a master's in technology in education from Harvard University and is the proud mother of three kids. Jennifer and her colleagues are hard at work making adaptive and universally designed games and apps to better personalize learning for America's kids.

Deborah Rosenfeld, Ph.D., is a research associate at the Education Development Center. She has a deep knowledge of early childhood mathematics through her experiences teaching young children, studying their teachers' knowledge and beliefs about early childhood mathematics, and working with teachers to develop knowledge of mathematical development. Her current work uses technology and media to engage children in narratives and games that leverage their natural curiosity and strengths as learners to develop their mathematical understanding, computational thinking skills, and promote their persistence in solving problems.

Daisy Rutstein, Ph.D., is a senior education researcher in SRI International's Education Division. Dr. Rutstein's work focuses on the application of Evidence-Centered Design to develop assessments. She moves through the different stages of the development process, including the initial conception of the assessment, the development of items, the creation of a complete assessment, and the validation of the assessment. Dr. Rutstein is the lead developer of assessments on several projects in computer science, mathematics, and science, moving from pre-K to high school.

Alejandra Salinas, Ph.D., is a clinical associate professor of mathematics education at Boston University where she teaches courses in mathematics content and methods, with a specialization in STEM teaching in urban schools. She is also the practicum director for mathematics education. Her broad research interest is the improvement of teacher quality in mathematics. In 2010, she joined the Ready To Learn team as a mathematics and science education and professional development specialist.

Sara Schapiro is the vice president of education at PBS. In this role, she leads PBS' efforts to deepen partnerships across the education sector by engaging directly with educator communities and launching new initiatives that empower and support students, educators, parents, and member stations. Prior to her role at PBS, Schapiro helped found Digital Promise, an independent, bipartisan non-profit organization whose mission is to spur innovation and improve all Americans' opportunity to learn. Schapiro previously worked for the New York City Department of Education, Chicago Public Schools, the New Jersey Department of Education, and Pearson.

Katerina Schenke is a senior researcher at UCLA CRESST. Her research is on understanding how and under what circumstances students are motivated toward learning, how we can measure motivation and engagement through digital games, and how we can develop models of assessment that are informative to students and teachers. She received her Ph.D. in Education in 2015 from the University of California, Irvine, and has published in journals such as *Computers and Education*, the *Journal of Educational Psychology*, and *Learning and Instruction*.

Megan Silander, Ph.D., is a senior research associate at Education Development Center, where she conducts research for the Ready To Learn project. Her research focuses on the use of digital tools and media to increase capacity to support children's learning, both in and out of school. One strand of this work focuses on under-resourced families' use of media and technology to support their children's learning in the home. A second strand focuses on effective means of incorporating digital tools into instruction to improve student learning.

Linda Simensky is vice president of children's programming at PBS. Before joining PBS, she was in charge of original animation for Cartoon Network, where she oversaw development and series production of *The Powerpuff Girls*, among other programs. She began her career at Nickelodeon, where she helped build the animation department and launch the popular series *Rugrats, Doug*, and *Rocko's Modern Life*. Simensky also teaches Animation History at the University of Pennsylvania.

Devon Steven is director of community engagement for Ready To Learn at CPB. She manages a network of public media stations and local partners that collaborate to support children, families, and educators in low-income communities. She was previously associate director for PBS KIDS marketing and communications at PBS, where she led campaigns for *The Cat in the Hat Knows a Lot About That!* and *Wild Kratts*. She graduated cum laude from The George Washington University and holds an Ed.M. in technology in education from the Harvard Graduate School of Education and an executive certificate in non-profit management from Georgetown University.

Sara S. Sweetman, Ph.D., is an assistant professor of education in the College of Education and Professional Studies at the University of Rhode Island (URI) and directs URI's School of Education's Guiding Education in Math and Science Network (GEMS-Net), a school-university partnership focused on translating research into practice for continual improvement in teaching and learning. Dr. Sweetman's interests in research, teaching, and practice involve engaging the community in fun and meaningful science learning through manipulation of materials and social interactions. She has been an advisor on a variety of children's productions, including *Sesame Street* and Ready To Learn.

Phil Vahey is director of strategic research and innovation at SRI Education. Vahey's research examines the design and use of technology-based systems that enhance the learning of conceptually difficult STEM concepts, as well as how to scale up the use of these systems. His early childhood research focuses on the use of media and games for making ideas in math, science, and computational thinking more accessible for preschool children. Prior to joining SRI, he received his Ph.D. in learning sciences from UC Berkeley.

Regan Vidiksis, M.S. Ed., is a research associate at the Education Development Center. Her research focuses on advancing effective strategies to promote young children's learning of early science, math, and computational thinking and to support teachers in integrating technology into early childhood settings in developmentally appropriate ways. Prior to EDC, Vidiksis was a preschool special educator and developmental evaluator, providing individualized services to young children and families in school, community, and home-based settings. Through all of her work, she aims to support the development of meaningful and equitable learning and teaching experiences for all.

INTRODUCTION

Shelley Pasnik

This book is about a long-standing federal investment in public media's ability to enrich the social-emotional and academic lives of young children and the adults who care for them. As the title and cover convey, this investment is not in food subsidies or housing assistance, childcare vouchers, or universal pre-school, treatment for adverse childhood experiences, or any of the other supports that benefit families, especially those living in neighborhoods with limited financial resources. Instead, this investment takes an entirely different form: well-crafted stories and games filled with endearing characters. The Ready To Learn Television Grant Program, funded by Congress and adminis-tered by the U.S. Department of Education since 1995, enables the Corporation for Public Broadcasting (CPB) and PBS to make much of the free, educational media that exists in this country for children ages two to eight. Some of children's most beloved fictional friends—including Emmy and Max (*Dragon Tales*), Lionel and Leona (*Between the Lions*), Maya and Miguel (*Maya & Miguel*), Martha and Helen (*Martha Speaks*), Super Why and Wonder Red (*Super Why!*), Peg and Cat (*Peg + Cat*), Agents Otto and Olive (*Odd Squad*), Nick and Sally (*The Cat in the Hat Knows a Lot About That!*), and Ruff Ruffman and Blossom (*The Ruff Ruffman Show*)—exist in whole or in part because of the Ready To Learn Initiative.

What does a generation of fictional characters and the worlds they occupy have to do with children's learning and growing? Plenty, it turns out.

Enlivening the Circles of Care

Many children growing up in the United States—too many children—have it far from easy. The CPB-PBS Ready To Learn Initiative, like any federally funded program, operates within a broader context, which includes intractable social, health, and economic disparities. The following points are likely well-known to readers but are relevant foregrounding for this volume:

- Two out of five children live in low-income families (Koball & Jiang, 2018).
- Achievement gaps between children from low-income communities and their more affluent peers are larger than ever and often exist by the time children enter kindergarten (Duncan & Magnuson 2011; Morgan, Farkas, Hillemeier, & Maczuga, 2016).
- Two out of three children have all parents in the workforce (National Kids Count, 2018), and one out of two children live in "childcare deserts" (Malik & Hamm, 2017).
- One out of two children is not enrolled in a preschool program (National Center for Education Statistics, 2017).
- Nearly one out of five children has special health care needs (Child Trends, 2016).
- Preschool expulsion is a trending social problem, and African-American boys are disproportionately affected (Malik, 2017).
- Children's early experience lays the foundation for their lifelong thinking skills and approach to learning (Gopnik, Meltzoff, & Kuhl, 1999; Sackes, Trundle, Bell, & O'Connell, 2011; Shonkoff & Phillips, 2000).

Young children need much more than disjointed care arriving in unpredictable spurts if they are to learn and thrive; they need ever-expanding circles of care that remain reliable and responsive. The Ready To Learn Initiative is about enlivening the circles of care that surround young kids and the adults in their lives—what CPB and PBS representatives often refer to as a *learning ecosystem*. It does so not by simply serving up sets of make-believe characters that appear on game and video screens but by creating a consistent, trusted "place" where families and educators can go when they want and as often as they need. Ready To Learn-supported media, when filled with light, humor, a healthy amount of challenge, and a feeling of being cared for, touch far more than our nation's youngest media consumers. The initiative is a bigger promise of early learning and exploration that radiates out beyond any one individual PBS program. It envelops community-service organizations involved in formal collaborations with local public media stations upon which families rely, and it pulls in parents, teachers, daycare providers, grandparents, and millions of other adults doing the daily work of nurturing children and readying them for school and life.

The Expectation of Proof

Merely asserting that the CPB-PBS Ready To Learn Initiative is consequential, as I just did, is insufficient, however. Since 2005, the U.S. Department of

Education has made research and evaluation a requirement of all Ready To Learn Television Grant Program proposals. This call for evidence of effectiveness—scientific proof—asks for more than goodwill and good intentions. Rather than settling for producers' assertions of effectiveness, program administrators have ensured that educational resources produced with funding from Ready To Learn are subjected to rigorous, independent evaluation. Beginning in 2006 and continuing through the current grant, I have led an evaluation team focused on determining the efficacy of the CPB-PBS Ready To Learn Initiative, an effort that has yielded dozens of studies. All the while, I have encountered co-workers, peers, and strangers alike, many of whom have spent their professional careers dedicated to young children's healthy development in essential domains like food, shelter, education, childcare, safety, physical and mental health, and they have often wondered aloud what meaningful difference "supplemental experiences" like videos and games can make in children's lives.

In part, this book is a response to that collective wondering. From quick and early formative research that includes handfuls of children to rigorous, randomized controlled trials with participant numbers in the hundreds, each Ready To Learn grant-funded study is guided by a specific set of research questions centered on children's learning and that generate findings unique to those questions. Taken together though, these studies seek to answer the more pragmatic questions that trail all federal initiatives: "Does it work?" and the blunter, "Is the investment worth it?"

Unlike the pockets of experimentation taking place in university research labs or within the commercial marketplace, the Ready To Learn Initiative has an obligation to demonstrate both its production and research value precisely because it is publicly funded and operates nationally at-scale. As a result, this book is meant to speak to a broad spectrum of readers, including private and government-sector media producers and app developers wanting to know and possibly replicate how high-quality educational resources get made. Likewise, it presents research findings for the benefit of educators, policymakers, media organizations, child advocates and all others wanting to understand the potential of engaging with digital resources. This comingling of contents—half production, half research, and the interplay between them—is by design and central to the success of the initiative. I encourage readers to draw their own conclusions about its merit and effectiveness, interrogating, borrowing from, and otherwise using all the authors have shared.

What This Book Contains

A quick scan of chapter headings will give readers a general sense of the book's contents; what follows, therefore, are descriptions of where each chapter is located within the broader terrain of the CPB-PBS Ready To Learn Initiative as well as some way-finding information for those who prefer thematic clusters.

History, Vision, and National Systems

The first two chapters, written by members of the core Ready To Learn leadership teams at PBS and CPB, provide expansive views of the initiative, its relationship to the larger educational and civic mission of the public media system, and the general approach PBS KIDS takes toward media production for young children and families.

- **Chapter 1** contains a historical overview of the CPB-PBS Ready To Learn Initiative, tracing its evolution over multiple grant cycles. Each of the three authors—David Lowenstein, Pam Johnson, and Michael Fragale—has helped direct PBS and CPB's efforts for many years, which means they not only experienced multiple grant cycle arcs but served as influential architects of grant proposals to the U.S. Department of Education. From their invocation of Fred Rogers' "meaningful expression of care" to keeping pace with technological changes over a 20-year history, they tell a story of lasting impact.

- Likewise, in **Chapter 2**, Sara DeWitt and Linda Simensky give a first-hand account of media production at a national level. How PBS KIDS approaches content development, conceptually and structurally, both reinforces and is reinforced by the Ready To Learn Initiative's mandate to support all children's learning, especially those living with few economic resources. And it is this mutuality—PBS's national platform and the initiative's infusion of resources specifically for families contending with poverty—that comes through in their writing. Even more, it is expressed in the children's media properties they greenlight for broadcast, on the web, as apps, and in all places children can be found having digital learning experiences.

People and Places

A cross-section of the book focuses on audience and place. As Chapters 3, 4, and 13 make clear with their descriptions of parents and homes, teachers and classrooms, and community leaders and neighborhoods, audience is not a passive construction within the Ready To Learn Initiative, nor is place static.

- The essential roles parents and other caregivers have in supporting children's early learning are present throughout much of this volume, but, in **Chapter 3**, Megan Silander and Elisa Garcia give their roles full treatment from a research perspective. Their points of entry are two studies: One a more conventional study of children's learning with media resources in which parental involvement was central, and the other is a national survey of more than 1,400 parents about learning at home. There is no shortage of talk about parents—what they need and do, how they should be supported; this study repositions the microphone, amplifying parents' direct experiences, especially with early science at home.

- Similarly, **Chapter 4** presents CPB-PBS Ready To Learn Initiative efforts to support formal classroom learning by helping teachers integrate digital resources into ongoing instructional activities and strengthening their classroom practice overall. While this is a topic that has been explored in some detail over the past decade, e.g., through Chip Donohue's work at the Erikson Institute and as evidenced by the National Association for the Education of Young Children's position statement on young children and interactive media, there is a practicality and potential scale that grounds the CPB-PBS Ready To Learn Initiative's work with teachers. The chapter is co-authored by PBS's Sara Schapiro, Jean Crawford, and Lori Brittain, along with Boston University Wheelock College Department of Education and Human Development's Jeanne Paratore, Alejandra Salinas, Lisa O'Brien, and Sarah Blodgett.
- And, because of its direct engagement with individual communities, **Chapter 13** is where readers will find the soul of the CPB-PBS Ready To Learn Initiative as it describes how local efforts are taking root in neighborhoods in Jackson, Mississippi; Las Vegas, Nevada; Detroit, Michigan; Lexington, Kentucky; and elsewhere throughout the country. The chapter's narrative blends the perspectives of three people each with distinct affiliations and therefore roles: PBS's Aaron Morris, CPB's Devon Steven, and SRI's Kea Anderson. While commercial media companies are increasingly producing TV series and mobile apps that claim to be and sometimes are educational, the public media system's network of local stations remains unmatched. These stations work shoulder-to-shoulder with local community partners, many of them providing a broad array of services families and educators need.

Producing for Learning

Several Chapters—5, 9, and 12—lift the curtain that regularly shrouds and therefore preserves the mystery of what it takes to make children's media. Although the production processes are accessibly described in these chapters, the hard work and multiple revision cycles required to produce each new show and digital game are evident. Ultimately, the shared message of these production chapters is this: Producing for the CPB-PBS Ready To Learn Initiative is markedly different than producing for other contexts. From script writing to instructional design, it takes creativity, stamina, and importantly, a willingness to enter into a full collaboration with educational advisors.

- In **Chapter 5**, Kim Berglund describes the story of *Peg + Cat*, a children's property built entirely from scratch and that focuses on early math learning.

Math is an area of limited prior attention, but it is critical to young children's later academic success. The property emphasizes ordinal numbers, spatial relationships, 3D shapes, and other preschool math topics while also meeting the CPB–PBS Ready To Learn Initiative's interest in transmedia, which required conceptualizing a new property across platforms from the outset rather than moving sequentially from broadcast to web to hands-on materials.

- In **Chapter 9**, the composition of the writing team mirrors that of production, including two staff members from PBS, Anne Lund and Shannon Bishop, a seasoned media producer, Larry Mirkin, and curriculum advisor, Sara Sweetman. As with Berglund's chapter, the team takes up a similar goal of early learning with a media property, though the focus is science inquiry, and the starting point is an existing, high-profile brand, *The Cat in the Hat Knows a Lot About That!* The result is a new season of Seussian stories where physical science and engineering practices are woven throughout episodes and games. Also, preschoolers come away with kid-sized role models, Nick and Sally, who engage in scientific practices suitable for any backyard exploration; parents can discover The Cat is just as much their guide when it comes to leading with curiosity as he is for their children.
- **Chapter 12** rounds out the trio of production chapters as it describes a children's media property, *Molly of Denali*, still in development and the emphasis it places on young children's learning with informational text. All three productions have faced, or are facing, the dilemma of limited prior models to varying degrees: Math is an uncommon children's media topic (*Peg + Cat*), science practices are rarer still (*The Cat in the Hat Knows A Lot About That!*), and informational text is virtually unheard of (*Molly of Denali*). In a Q&A format fitting the newness of their collaboration, the three authors—curriculum advisor, Nell Duke; senior executive producer, Carol Greenwald; and PBS KIDS senior director of content and curriculum, Anne Lund—reveal how the series has two stars. It features everyday informational text and Molly, an Alaska native girl who is relatable to all kids, especially those living in rural communities who have been rarely and inaccurately depicted in past children's media productions.

Making the Case: Evidence and Impact

Nearly half of this book is expressly about the research that is foundational to the CPB–PBS Ready To Learn Initiative. As a result of the federal research requirement, the initiative has generated a much fuller body of research than what appears here, both in terms of type (e.g. literature reviews, formative studies, case studies, context studies, experimental studies) as well as topic (e.g., literacy, math, parental involvement, classroom integration, community implementation). For the sake of consistency, all of the research-oriented chapters included in this volume are written by current or past members of the Education Development-SRI International (EDC-SRI) summative evaluation team and these chapters tilt toward the more recent studies we have completed. Readers will be well served to seek out the longer line of research the Ready To Learn Initiative has produced, including independent research done by established and emerging scholars (e.g., Hurwitz, 2018) as well as studies led by researchers formally supported by grant resources (e.g., Linebarger, 2015; Neuman & Dwyer, 2011; Tiu, McCarthy, & Linlin, 2015; Wartella, Lauricella, & Blackwell, 2016; many of these studies are available at pbslearningmedia.org/readytolearn).

Below is a walk-through of research highlights that are both unique to the CPB-PBS Ready To Learn Initiative and relevant to broader questions about children's learning and the supports adults and resources can bring.

Early math learning, the 2010–2015 Ready To Learn Television Grant Program's readiness area, is the main subject of two chapters and is referenced in several others within this volume.

- Whereas Berglund's chapter tells the production origin story of *Peg + Cat*, **Chapter 6** describes two studies which explored the transmedia property's effectiveness. Not only do Deborah Rosenfeld and Daisy Rutstein review study designs and resulting mathematical learning, they also describe the related challenge of measuring that learning in the form of reliable assessments, an area of ongoing and future research.
- In **Chapter 8**, Savitha Moorthy and Ximena Domínguez take a thematic cut through the same *Peg + Cat* studies as well as several other context studies that predated them, drawing attention to two topics central to children's learning with media: the thoughtful selection of content and adults' intentional use of media resources to support early learning. This chapter adds to the body of knowledge about systemic barriers low-income families face when it comes to interacting with their children and what can be done about it. Their conclusion: Curation and mediation need not be the exclusive tools of economically advantaged families.

Literacy and children's language development is the second pair of research-focused chapters, summoning the early days of the Ready To Learn Television Grant Program when readiness was nearly synonymous with traditional reading and emergent reading skills. These chapters are not nostalgic in tone or purpose but instead lay important groundwork for the informational text studies still to come with *Molly of Denali* and other PBS, CPB, and partner-led efforts in the 2015–2020 grant.

- In **Chapter 7**, for instance, there are reverberations of Chapter 4 as Phil Vahey, Regan Vidiksis, and Jamie Gutierrez examine the integration of digital technologies into early childhood classrooms. It is not surprising, but it bears repeating that the authors conclude that there is a need for professional development and further coaching if there is to be a meaningful uptake of digital resources in schools.
- Likewise, in **Chapter 11**, Naomi Hupert and Alexandra Adair use the findings from multiple studies, as well as the interventions that led to those findings, to draw attention to media's potential to support young children's language development. This holds true when the study is expressly about literacy and also when it is about another domain, like math.

Finally, although young children have been engaging in scientific exploration for as long as there have been children, as a field of study and as a line of media resources, these still are early days. At the time this volume was being written, a series of science studies were underway by EDC, SRI, UCLA CRESST, and Rockman et al, Inc., exploring public media's support for early science learning. Among others, in 2018–2019, the research team is undertaking studies of *The Cat in the Hat Knows a Lot About That!*, *The Ruff Ruffman Show,* and other resources still in development.

- More than a placeholder for the study results still to come, **Chapter 10** takes up this newer area of early science learning with direct, actionable advice for media producers, a complement to the PBS KIDS Science Learning Framework that gives additional ballast to Chapter 9. Marion Goldstein, Claire Christensen, Sarah Gerard, and Megan Silander have been engaged in pioneering work involving public media properties outside of the CPB-PBS Ready To Learn Initiative as well as properties receiving its support, and are well poised to present "What Media Producers Can Do" call-outs throughout the chapter.

Innovative Digital Tools, Real People

On the surface, the last set of contributions—Chapters 14, 15, and 16—appear to be fine-grained examinations of the technical systems and structures undergirding Ready To Learn–funded media productions, both large and small, e.g., building and then revising a navigation bar for a science game about force and motion; mining no fewer than 256 levels of gameplay data from a single production; devising an intelligent backend data platform. In actuality, these chapters not only describe how the initiative is pushing the limits of personalized and adaptive technological capacity, in this case, PBS's as well as its partners, WGBH and Kidaptive, but is doing so to serve greater numbers of children, however diverse and multi-layered their individual needs.

- In **Chapter 14**, Jennifer Rodriguez and Michael Conn-Powers plumb the necessity of universal design for learning. Their chapter is two parts practical—it presents a universal design for learning checklist and also walks through a decision-by-decision case study of a digital game—and one part inspiration as the authors imagine a future where all productions will be accessible to all kids.
- **Chapter 15** picks up the universal design for learning checkpoints introduced in the chapter before it and applies them to a single production. As described by the team of authors, which includes PBS's Jennifer Rodriguez and Jeremy Roberts and Kidaptive's Dylan Arena, the goal is a learning game that is personalized and adaptive. Readers may find encouraging, the authors' honest appraisal of how far they have and haven't got.
- Lastly, **Chapter 16** rounds out the volume by making a further push toward data science to inform children's learning outcomes. PBS's Jeremy Roberts and Cosimo Felline are joined by UCLA CRESST's Charles Parks, Greg Chung, Elizabeth Redman, and Katerina Schenke. Though there is a machine-learning quality to the experimental work they describe, and the chapter is data-laden, their purpose is clear: The CPB-PBS Ready To Learn Initiative's future remains with the people it serves.

References

Child Trends. (2016). A State Multi-Sector Framework for Supporting Children and Youth with Special Health Care Needs. Bethesda, MD: Child Trends. Retrieved from: www.childtrends.org/wp-content/uploads/2018/05/PackardConceptua-Framework_ChildTrends_May2018.pdf.

Duncan, G. J., & Magnuson, K. (2011). The Nature and Impact of Early Achievement Skills, Attention Skills, and Behavior Problems. In G. J. Duncan & R. J. Murnane (Eds.), Whither Opportunity (pp. 47–69). New York: Russell Sage.

Gopnik, A., Meltzoff, A. N., & Kuhl, P. K. (1999). The Scientist in the Crib: Minds, Brains, and How Children Learn. New York: Harper Collins.

Hurwitz, L. (2018). Getting a Read on Ready To Learn Media: A Meta-Analysis Review of Effects on Literacy. *Child Development*, 1–18.

Koball, H., & Jiang, Y. (2018). Basic Facts about Low-Income Children: Children under 18 Years, 2016. New York: National Center for Children in Poverty, Columbia University Mailman School of Public Health.

Linebarger, D. L. (2015). *Super Why!* to The Rescue: Educational Television, Preschoolers, and Early Literacy Skills. *International Journal for Cross-Disciplinary Subjects in Education*, 6(1), 2060–2068.

Malik, R. (2017). New Data Reveal 250 Preschoolers are Suspended or Expelled Every Day. Washington, DC: Center for American Progress. Retrieved from: www.american progress.org/issues/early-childhood/news/2017/11/06/442280/new-data-reveal-250-preschoolers-suspended-expelled-every-day/.

Malik, R. and Hamm, K. (2017). Mapping America's Child Care Deserts. Washington, DC: Center for American Progress.

Morgan, P. L., Farkas, G., Hillemeier, M. M., & Maczuga, S. (2016). Science Achievement Gaps Begin Very Early, Persist, and are Largely Explained by Modifiable Factors. *Educational Researcher*, 45(1), 18–35.

National Center for Education Statistics (NCES). (2017). Preschool and Kindergarten Enrollment. Washington, DC: NCES. Retrieved from: https://nces.ed.gov/programs/coe/indicator_cfa.asp.

National Kids Count. (2018). Analysis of Data from the U.S. Census Bureau, 2008–2016 American Community Survey. Baltimore, MD: The Anne E. Casey Foundation. Retrieved from: https://datacenter.kidscount.org/data/tables/5053-children-ages-6-to-12-with-all-available-parents-in-the-labor-force#detailed/1/any/false/870,573,869,36,868,867,133,38,35/any/11463,11464.

Neuman, S. B. & Dwyer, J. (2011). Developing Vocabulary and Conceptual Knowledge for Low-income Preschoolers: A Design Experiment. *Journal of Literacy Research*, 43(2), 103–129.

Saçkes, M., Trundle, K. C., Bell, R. L., & O'Connell, A. A. (2011). The Influence of Early Science Experience in Kindergarten on Children's Immediate and Later Science Achievement: Evidence from the Early Childhood Longitudinal Study. *Journal of Research in Science Teaching*, 48(2), 217–235.

Shonkoff, J. P. & Phillips, D. A. (Eds.). (2000). From Neurons to Neighborhoods: The Science of Early Childhood Development. Washington, DC: National Academies Press.

Tiu, M., McCarthy, B., Linlin, L. (2015). *Odd Squad*: Learning Math with PBS KIDS Transmedia Content at School and Home: A Report to the CPB-PBS Ready To Learn Initiative. San Francisco, CA: WestEd.

Wartella, E., Lauricella, A., & Blackwell, C. (2016). The Ready To Learn Program: 2010–2015 Policy Brief. Evanston, IL: Northwestern University.

1

READY TO LEARN AND PUBLIC MEDIA

Improving Early Learning Outcomes for America's Children

David Lowenstein, Pamela Johnson, and Michael Fragale

Introduction

There is an often-told story in public media lore about the time in May 1969 when Fred Rogers, creator and host of the beloved and influential children's television series *Mister Rogers' Neighborhood*, testified before the Senate Subcommittee on Communications. The Nixon Administration was eager to cut the appropriation for the newly formed Corporation for Public Broadcasting, and Fred Rogers was asked to talk about how the cut would impact his work (Rogers, 1969). Most people focus on the end of the story when subcommittee chairman Senator John O. Pastore, clearly moved by Rogers' remarks, said, "Looks like you just earned the 20 million dollars." While that was a seminal moment in the history of federal funding for public broadcasting, what makes it more remarkable is how Rogers made his case. His persuasive argument was not about the need to produce a daily, half-hour television show. Rather, he talked about the need to provide, what he called, "a meaningful expression of care" that helped very young children deal with "the inner drama of childhood" and taught them that their "feelings are mentionable and manageable." Fred Rogers' method for helping young children, especially those most in need, happened to be through a television show, but it was the need he was meeting, not the medium, that carried the day.

The 1991 report, *Ready To Learn: A mandate for the nation*, written by Ernest Boyer, the president of The Carnegie Foundation for the Advancement of Teaching, was the initial spark that led to the creation of the Ready To Learn Television Act legislation that lives on today. However, like Fred Rogers, Boyer's interest was in meeting a demonstrated need; in this case the need to improve school readiness for young children after a five-year decline. Boyer was advocating for ways to ensure that all children enter school prepared to succeed.

One way was to provide access to resources through what he called "ready to learn television" (Boyer, 1991).

The idea of media not as a goal, but rather a tool to meet needs and achieve goals goes back even further to the founding principles of public broadcasting itself. The Public Broadcasting Act of 1967, the legislation that established the Corporation for Public Broadcasting (CPB), laid out a broad vision for educational media. The intent was to address a gap that commercial media was not filling. In fact, a 1988 amendment to the Act included stronger, more specific language that declared, "It is in the public interest to encourage the development of programming that involves creative risks and that addresses the needs of unserved and underserved audiences, particularly children and minorities."

Built on this foundation, the work of CPB and PBS aligns with Ready To Learn to meet needs and provide solutions; to serve people and experiment with new ideas. The mission remains evergreen, while the process of fulfilling that mission evolves to meet changes in needs, technology, and media consumption habits. Every five years, the Ready To Learn Television Grant Program, authorized by Congress and administered by the U.S. Department of Education, serves as a catalyst for continual learning, experimentation, improvement, and disruption.

Today, Rogers' "meaningful expression of care" and Boyer's "mandate for the nation" lives on in places like the Hilltop neighborhood of Tacoma, Washington, where a mom and her six-year-old daughter take advantage of an innovative rent-subsidy program run by the local housing authority. While the mom attends a mandatory job training program, the girl is in another classroom, her attention fixed on a computer screen, watching a character named Peg and her friend Cat solve problems using math. Later, the young girl will follow Peg and Cat through an adventure in a digital game, only this time the girl will be the one solving the problems. Characters not only drive fictional stories; they also guide children's learning.

Scenes like this play out every day across the U.S. in child care centers, homes, libraries, health clinics, and other places where young children are. Video content, digital games, and hands-on activities created with Ready To Learn funds, featuring PBS KIDS characters and facilitated by local public media stations support young children and the adults in their lives.

Educational Priorities across Time

With Ready To Learn's focus on the school readiness needs of young children, the U.S. Department of Education has historically identified particular early learning priorities. Each competitive solicitation of the federal Ready To Learn Television Grant Program has emphasized a particular area of focus. Across time, there has been an enduring emphasis on the reading and language development needs of preschoolers, and these literacy priorities have recently expanded to include an emphasis on early math and science learning (see Figure 1.1).

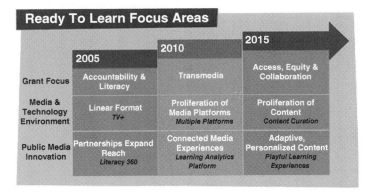

Ready To Learn Focus Areas

	2005	2010	2015
Grant Focus	Accountability & Literacy	Transmedia	Access, Equity & Collaboration
Media & Technology Environment	Linear Format *TV+*	Proliferation of Media Platforms *Multiple Platforms*	Proliferation of Content *Content Curation*
Public Media Innovation	Partnerships Expand Reach *Literacy 360*	Connected Media Experiences *Learning Analytics Platform*	Adaptive, Personalized Content *Playful Learning Experiences*

FIGURE 1.1   Ready To Learn Focus Areas Chart highlighting leading priorities established during the past five-year grant cycles (Courtesy of PBS; The PBS logos and wordmarks are trademarks of the Public Broadcasting Service and used with permission; and CPB)

National Assessment of Educational Progress (NAEP) scores are a useful barometer of America's educational needs. With scores from NAEP released every two years, education policy leaders are able to review national academic achievement data and trends based on NAEP assessments of the fourth and eighth grades in reading, mathematics, and writing. Recent analysis by the Brookings Institute and Brown Center found that NAEP scores in both reading and math from 2009 to 2015, as well as the preceding period of 1998–2009, have been generally "flat since 2009, not deviating by more than a single scale score point." The authors point-out that before 2009, reading scores stayed flat, while math scores experienced solid increases. However, these gains in math did not continue into 2009–2015 (Brookings Institute, 2018).

Given this backdrop, it is understandable that Ready To Learn's initial years featured a broad focus on children's literacy development, which ultimately crossed two, five-year grant rounds to public media (i.e., 1995–2000 and 2000–2005). These grants enabled PBS and partners to expand existing children's TV series such as *Arthur, Clifford the Big Red Dog, Reading Rainbow,* and *Sesame Street,* while also developing new literacy properties, including *Dragon Tales* and *Between the Lions.* To extend the use of this media in communities, local PBS stations delivered awareness and training workshops to childcare providers and parents on the effective use of these literacy series and partnered with First Book to distribute millions of related children's books for free to families and schools in low-income communities.

However, when it came to the 2005–2010 grant cycle, Ready To Learn's focus on literacy was significantly heightened by new policy directions and thought-leadership generated by the National Reading Panel. At the request of

Congress in 1997, the panel's charge was to determine the effectiveness of different instructional approaches used to teach children to read. Administered by the National Institute of Child Health and Human Development (NICHD) at the U.S. Department of Health and Human Services, the panel included experts in the field of reading and children's development. In April 2000, these literacy thought-leaders published the report *Teaching children to read*, which emphasized research-based practices in fundamental areas of literacy instruction including phonemic awareness, phonics, fluency, vocabulary, comprehension, independent reading, computer-assisted instruction, and teacher professional development (NICHD, 2000). Soon after this effort in 2002, The National Early Literacy Panel was convened to conduct a synthesis of the scientific research on the development of early literacy skills in children ages zero to five, and on home and family influences on early literacy development (National Institute for Literacy, 2008).

These reports played a major role in shaping the No Child Left Behind's federal literacy policies and initiatives. Education leaders at CPB and PBS were similarly influenced by insights from both panels and used their evidence-based guidance as a springboard for new approaches to children's television production and outreach. In the 2005–2010 grant cycle, the CPB-PBS Ready To Learn Initiative proposed and then successfully helped to develop an award-winning collection of PBS KIDS properties that leveraged known best practices in early reading education, including *Super Why!, Martha Speaks, The Electric Company, Sesame Street*, and *Between the Lions*.

While literacy has remained a major through line for Ready To Learn over the last two decades, the Department of Education expanded the program's priorities to include math education as part of the 2010–2015 grant cycle. Based on the increased national attention to the role of early math in fortifying children's long-term academic success, this direction afforded CPB and PBS a first-time opportunity to help develop two new PBS KIDS math properties, *Peg + Cat* and *Odd Squad*, which provided local PBS member stations and their partners a strong foundation for providing children with engaging content from their preschool years into the early elementary grades (see Chapter 5 for a detailed description of the production process that led to *Peg + Cat*).

Fast forward to the current 2015–2020 grant cycle, in which the Department of Education opened new doors for the development of original content to support early science learning. For CPB and PBS, this is creating new pathways for producing multiplatform media that focuses on core science concepts, science inquiry, and engineering practices. *The Ruff Ruffman Show, The Cat in the Hat Knows a Lot About That!, Ready Jet Go!*, and a new preschool science property aim to help our nation's youngest learners cultivate a positive mindset toward science, giving them ample opportunities to think and act like scientists (see Figure 1.2). Additionally, CPB and PBS are taking

Ready To Learn Timeline

1995-2000

Dragon Tales and Between the Lions

- Companion parent programs, online activities and outreach plans

2000-2005

Maya & Miguel and Postcards from Buster

- Performance indicators on the effectiveness of training parents and teachers in diverse populations
- Emphasis on teaching young English-language learners
- Continued funding for Sesame Street, Reading Rainbow, Clifford the Big Red Dog, Dragon Tales, Between the Lions and Arthur
- Launch of the first PBS website for parents and the "Form The Start" website for teachers

2005-2010

Martha Speaks, Super WHY!, WordWorld and The Electric Company

- Extension of content beyond television screens to websites, computer games, books, magazines and outreach programs
- Continued funding for digital content from Sesame Street and Between the Lions
- New outreach methods targeting low-income communities, such as summer camps and online courses for caregivers, were developed through the PBS KIDS Raising Readers campaign
- Independent researchers demonstrated that Ready To Learn content helps children from low-income families improve critical early literacy skills and helps close the achievement gap with their peers

2010-2015

Peg + Cat and Odd Squad

- Independent researchers demonstrated that Ready To Learn content helps children from low-income families improve critical early math knowledge and enhances family engagement
- Continued funding for digital content from Wild Kratts, Curious George, Sid the Science Kid, Dinosaur Train, The Cat In The Hat Knows a Lot About That!, Martha Speaks, The Electric Company, Fetch with Ruff Ruffman, Fizzy's Lunch Lab, Cyberchase, and Super WHY!

80 episodes with a math-based curriculum

135 educational online games

100 educational activities

New, innovative parent & teacher tools

FIGURE 1.2 The Ready To Learn Initiative Timeline outlining the major children's media and engagement resources developed by the CPB-PBS Ready To Learn Initiative from 1995 to 2015[1]

public media's literacy work to the next level, through an original property called *Molly of Denali*, which focuses on informational text (see Chapter 12 for a detailed description).

Ready To Learn as a Catalyst for Innovation

Public media's commitment to harnessing the power of television and digital media for the public interest has been undergirded by Congress and the U.S. Department of Education for the past 25 years through the Ready To Learn Television Grant Program. The grant has provided the funding and strategic direction that's enabled public media to innovate with how children's educational media is produced and delivered, how it's utilized across learning environments, and how caregivers can use it to support and assess children's learning.

The Ready To Learn Television Grant Program has fueled public media's vision to see every new technology as an opportunity for learning. Public media also has utilized the Ready To Learn grant to experiment with various approaches for delivering content and engagement experiences over the years. Early efforts during Ready To Learn grants in 1995–2000 and 2000–2005 focused on making engaging TV episodes of PBS KIDS shows and allowing kids to "play the shows" through related Flash-based learning games on pbskids.org. Efforts during the 2005–2010 grant included new literacy-themed television shows and a curated website, PBS KIDS Island, which featured related digital games, as well as opportunities for kids to participate in hands-on activities at week-long PBS KIDS summer camps organized by PBS member stations and their local community partners.

More recent efforts have taken advantage of new methods for delivering content including tablets, smartphones, and mobile-friendly websites and apps, and new understandings of how to support kids' media engagement across various learning environments. During the 2015–2020 Ready To Learn Television Grant Program, for example, children are engaging with the characters and stories from their favorite shows through streaming video on the *PBS KIDS Video App*, through digital games on the *PBS KIDS Games App*, through related classroom activities that their teachers can access on PBS LearningMedia, through activities that caregivers can find on the PBS KIDS for Parents website, and through month-long workshops at their local public media stations that bring families together weekly to play with the media and engage in joyful learning experiences. All of the content and engagement experiences map to PBS KIDS Learning Frameworks that have been designed by curriculum advisors and provide producers with guidance on the skills, practices, and age-appropriate habits of mind that their content should support for children between the ages of two and eight.

Advances in technology are being utilized in this 2015–2020 round of the grant to not only innovate on how content is delivered, but also to enhance the content itself, providing children with opportunities to personalize their learning experiences and giving PBS KIDS producers the ability to create digital games that adapt to a child's individual learning and engagement needs (see Chapter 15 for a description of personalized and adaptive learning efforts).

Research findings from past Ready To Learn grants revealed that while an individual television episode, digital game, or hands-on activity can advance learning, children actually learn more when they combine watching a PBS KIDS show, playing related digital games, and engaging in related real-world hands-on activities that extend the learning away from the screen (McCarthy et al., 2013, 2012, 2015; Pasnik & Llorente, 2013; Penuel et al., 2009). This transmedia approach to content and engagement development was the primary goal of Ready To Learn 2010–2015, and research results from this time revealed that not only did PBS KIDS content improve children's school readiness, but children learned even more when their parents or teachers fully understood what their children were experiencing, had confidence in their ability to support their children's engagement with the media, and when adults dedicated time to interacting with their kids using the media. These lessons have been a catalyst for new approaches to helping young children learn by supporting and engaging their caregivers. Professional development resources, like the Ready To Learn–funded teaching tips and videos developed in collaboration with the Boston University School of Education, and PBS TeacherLine courses that incorporate the teaching tips described in Chapter 4, provide preservice and in-service early childhood educators with standards-aligned guidance for how to effectively utilize quality media in classroom and childcare settings.

The CPB-PBS Ready To Learn Initiative has endeavored to increase parental involvement in children's learning through mobile apps designed to foster engagement between children and their caregivers. The *PBS KIDS Play & Learn App* and the *Play & Learn Science App* foster co-play experiences between parents and their young children around early math, literacy, and science concepts. The apps also include tips for activities that parents can do with their kids in a variety of locations. In addition, the Ready To Learn Television Grant Program has funded the research and development of the PBS KIDS Learning Analytics Platform, which is designed to analyze gameplay data to determine whether the games are effectively meeting children's learning and engagement needs (see Chapter 16 for a description of the Learning Analytics Platform's use of evidence and analysis).

From Broadcast TV to the Digital Age: A Dynamic Media Landscape

The founders of the Ready To Learn Act in Congress sought to harness the reach of public television to help prepare our nation's youngest and most vulnerable learners – kids in underserved, impoverished communities – for success in school and in life. Television ownership was ubiquitous then and remains so now, even in the most rural and under-resourced communities, and families can watch high-quality PBS KIDS content on their local PBS station for free. As our nation entered the twenty-first century, however, new technologies presented new opportunities for learning but also new challenges for how to provide equitable access to these technologies for children and families despite growing disparities in income. While research indicates that television is still how most young children consume media, leaders at the U.S. Department of Education who have administered the Ready To Learn grant over the past 20 years have tasked the Ready To Learn Initiative's grantees with creating educational children's content on multiple media platforms and reducing barriers for underserved kids and families to access that content.

Public media has responded to this dual task by researching how children, especially underserved kids, consume media. This requires testing content on a variety of platforms and hardware and ensuring that the content is accessible, not only on the latest high-end gadgets but more importantly on the tablets, smartphones, and browsers that are used by kids in low-income communities. PBS member stations that receive Ready To Learn grant funding also play a significant role in reducing access barriers for kids and families, both by purchasing technology and forming partnerships with local community organizations offering mobile media labs and tech centers in schools and libraries. Local public media stations also offer a free 24/7 PBS KIDS channel and streaming service, which ensures that kids can access Ready To Learn–funded content anytime, anywhere.

The Ready To Learn Television Grant Program also supports public media's research and design efforts to make content accessible for children with disabilities and to create media that gives voice and choice to learners. Testing Ready To Learn–funded digital content in schools and childcare centers that support underserved children with developmental challenges, including the Kennedy Krieger Institute, provides valuable feedback and informs product design and iteration (see Chapter 14 for a description of how public media is operationalizing universal design for learning approaches).

With a media landscape that is in a constant state of change, the need for public media to stay knowledgeable about the landscape and the related changes in children's media habits is critical for ensuring the wide reach and high impact of Ready To Learn–funded content. For instance, as more children transitioned away from visiting websites and started accessing content through mobile apps that bundle games and streaming video, the free *PBS KIDS Games App* and free

PBS KIDS Video App were launched. As of 2018, these two apps have been downloaded 29 million times (May 2011–May 2018; App Figures) and in 2017, PBS KIDS videos have been streamed 3 billion times (January–December 2017; Google Analytics) across desktop, mobile, and over-the-top platforms. Evolving technology has also necessitated changes to the way public media produces digital content. As the majority of web browsers no longer support Flash-based content, public media has moved toward the creation of content using HTML5 and has pioneered the use of an open-source software called SpringRoll that allows PBS KIDS producers to create media once and publish it in multiple places (e.g., producing a *Ready Jet Go!* game that can be published on pbskids. org, in a *Ready Jet Go!* mobile app, and in the *PBS KIDS Games App*).

Public media also has experimented with ways to utilize the reach and popularity of PBS KIDS content on television to engage kids in digital and hands-on, real-world learning experiences. During the 2010–2015 Ready To Learn Television Grant Program, producers of *The Electric Company* at the Sesame Workshop created short animated stories at the end of each live-action television episode. These animated shorts ended with a cliffhanger and a call-to-action for kids to visit pbskids.org to help *The Electric Company* defeat their nemesis. Through the use of analytics, PBS and CPB noticed a significant increase in traffic to the website during those times when characters on the television series were encouraging children to go online, validating this approach to transmedia storytelling.

Encouraging children and families who watch PBS KIDS television to extend the learning through digital and real-world activities is a mainstay of Ready To Learn. Approaches include live-action interstitials with astronomer Amy Mainzer that model at-home earth science experiments between and after episodes of *Ready Jet Go!*; animated interstitials between and after TV episodes of *The Cat in the Hat Knows a Lot About That!* which showcase free mobile apps for families to download that allow kids to play and learn with Nick, Sally, and the Cat; and television spots produced by local public media stations that run before and after the episodes and highlight local engagement experiences for the whole family.

Innovations in Community Engagement

While the chief priority of the federal Ready To Learn Television Grant Program has always been to produce high-quality, research-based content and ensure its wide-scale national distribution to all American households, CPB and PBS have similarly placed great emphasis on family and community engagement through local PBS stations and their partners. This intentional coupling of national and local assets is a hallmark trait of the public media system that excels at providing both a wide reach and a deep service to our target audience: children in home, school, and out-of-school settings. For public media, this national–local infrastructure helps to support a highly interdependent way of delivering on its educational mission and has resulted in its own set of engagement innovations that live at the intersection of content, community, and collaboration.

2005–2010: Geo-Targeting Communities and New Approaches to Engagement

Some of the most dynamic innovations in community engagement were seeded during the 2005–2010 Ready To Learn Television Grant Program, when CPB, PBS, and local public media stations headed out into uncharted territory through a new approach to outreach that involved the geo-targeting of under-resourced neighborhoods via ZIP Code tracks to deliver last-mile services to children from low-income communities. This was a first for local stations that served as Ready To Learn Initiative community sites, and there was much to learn with respect to mastering this new ZIP Code-based outreach method, cultivating appropriate partners, and carrying out the highly focused work of content implementation in a specific neighborhood. During this time, Ready To Learn also launched its first community-based public awareness campaign designed to cultivate a pro-literacy spirit or culture within targeted ZIP Code tracks. Under the guidance of CPB and PBS communication staff and media consultants, local billboards encouraged children and families to learn together, and these high-visibility literacy messages were further amplified through television and radio spots that aired on both local public media and commercial stations.

There were other notable innovations in the 2005–2010 grant round that grew as a direct extension of this deeper approach to community engagement. For example, producers of the literacy series *Super Why!* from Out of the Blue Enterprises collaborated with CPB and PBS to develop a week-long Summer Reading Camp that brought *Super Why!*'s fun approach, early reading goals, and characters to children in a dynamic new way through local stations and their partners. Similarly, producers of *Martha Speaks* from WGBH created a unique Reading Buddies program designed to engage older elementary students with their younger peers in promoting and practicing book reading and vocabulary development. In both cases, these CPB-PBS Ready To Learn Initiative resources were designed as robust experiences that engaged children in dosage-rich, hands-on learning. As these programs took flight in communities across the country, more such programs followed as producers at the Sesame Workshop developed and presented an innovative stage show to amplify the reading fun and priorities of *The Electric Company*, along with expanded learning programs for summer and after-school time. Taken in total, these innovations offered fresh new engagement models that made it possible for local PBS stations and their partners to double-down on the delivery of a more comprehensive approach to children's learning in the community, an approach that also made a stronger impact on children.

2010–2015: Innovations with Math Transmedia, New Partnership Models

During the 2010–2015 grant cycle, CPB and PBS invited local PBS stations and their partners to submit proposals to serve as Transmedia Demonstration Stations. As part of this vision, not only did stations continue with their focused work in specific underserved communities, but they also implemented a dynamic set of new math engagement resources, which included *Peg + Cat's* 100th Day of School Events, the *Odd Squad* "Be the Agent" Summer Camp, and a comprehensive set of PBS KIDS Summer and After-school Adventures. As part of this effort, partners including the National Summer Learning Association and Every Hour Counts provided professional development and technical support related to out-of-school time learning to local stations. These resources introduced children to early math concepts and leveraged the highly sequenced and curated learning power of transmedia content.

At the same time, CPB and PBS leaders observed that certain stations were excelling at forming or joining dynamic new community networks and were bringing meaningful new approaches to working with like-minded community stakeholders in highly intentional ways. For example, in Cleveland, Ohio, public station WVIZ/PBS ideastream was an active member of the Broadway P-16 network and was collaborating with diverse partners in the city's Slavic Village neighborhood to implement Ready To Learn–funded transmedia resources. In Tacoma, Washington, KBTC was cultivating an innovative partnership with the Tacoma Public Schools, the Tacoma Housing Authority, the Children's Museum of Tacoma, and other community stakeholders in order to reach and influence high-need children and their families. Also, WCTE in Cookeville, Tennessee, negotiated a unique shared-staff agreement with the Putnam County School System that enabled a classroom teacher to work as a Ready To Learn Initiative project manager at the station while also building strong working relationships with leading school programs and departments, along with other county-wide organizations.

2015–2020: Network of Community Collaboratives for Early Learning and Media Focused on Science and Literacy

Fast forward to the Ready To Learn 2015–2020 grant cycle when the public media system is placing significant bets on an integrated vision that seeks to maximize the combined effects of content, community, collaboration, personalized learning, and research that builds upon insights and lessons from the prior ten years. As we write this chapter, 16 Community Collaboratives for Early Learning and Media are successfully underway, and 14 more community collaboratives soon will be selected for funding during the final two years of the 2015–2020 grant.

Excitement continues to build for the innovative community engagement model in which local stations serve as educational media experts and work side-by-side with partners in honing and contextualizing Ready To Learn–funded media with children and families. As part of this approach, the station and its partners conduct formative needs assessments, follow human-centered design principles, and develop customized annual plans that support local priorities. This work is guided by technical assistance and resource trainings from Education Development Center, SRI International, CPB, and PBS, using specially developed needs-assessment tools and the first-ever set of family and community engagement measures designed to help stations consistently survey participants and partners about their experiences and learnings from media. From a community innovation standpoint, this growing network of community collaboratives is helping to bring new engagement practices to light, fortifying the capacity of local stations and partners, and taking public media's community and dual-generation family engagement efforts to a new level. These collaboratives are also providing families and educators with a variety of evidence-based, field-tested engagement experiences, including a series of PBS KIDS Family & Community Learning workshops, and a number of camps and professional development trainings (see Chapter 13 for a fuller description of this community work).

Assessing Impact on Children's Learning

As many chapters in this book richly describe, one of the most important aspects of the federal Ready To Learn Television Grant Program is its emphasis on the rigorous research and evaluation of new children's media and educational resources that have been developed within each five-year grant cycle. Across nearly two decades, this priority has enabled CPB and PBS to commission well over 150 reports and studies by highly qualified educational evaluators.

In the current 2015–2020 grant round, public media has engaged the Education Development Center and a consortium of well-respected researchers from SRI International, Rockman et al, and UCLA-CRESST to implement the Ready To Learn Initiative's multi-year research agenda for evaluation. The consortium's formative research informs the iterative design and production process for new content and engagement resources, including early concept reviews, tests of digital games in the early stages of production, and outlines and scripts for new and existing properties. Its modestly sized content studies demonstrate the promise of Ready To Learn media and resources to impact child learning and family engagement and lay the foundation for later large-scale pilot and summative evaluations. These efficacy studies, which are embedded in station communities, are designed to measure the impact of the Ready To Learn's model of content, community, and collaboration on the target audiences: children, families, and educators.

In past grant cycles, other leading researchers and organizations have joined public media in reviewing and assessing the impact of Ready To Learn–funded content and engagement materials on young children, including the American Institutes for Research, the University of Michigan, the University of Pennsylvania, and WestEd.

Reflecting on This Work

Public media's more than 20-year involvement with Ready To Learn gives us the opportunity to take stock and reflect on how together, CPB, PBS, children's media producers and technologists, local PBS stations and their communities, educational researchers, the U.S. Department of Education, and Congress have continued to deliver on the original mandate to help all children enter school "Ready To Learn." Taken as a whole, this significant body of work continues to reach millions of children with content and services that support the early learning needs of all children, including roughly 54% of America's three- to five-year-olds who are not enrolled in formal preschool (Annie E. Casey Foundation, 2017). Our work has also informed an evolution in the way CPB and PBS approach content creation, dissemination, engagement, and evaluation. Over the past two decades we have moved from a broadcast-centric model in which primacy was given to the creation and distribution of video content, to a model focused on platforms and devices, to the current iterative design process informed by research and by where, when, how, and by whom the resources will be used.

As Figure 1.3 illustrates, collaboration from the earliest stages among producers, researchers, end users, local stations, and community partners is integral to the creation of content that is intentionally built to have a positive impact on young children's learning. In an enduring yet adaptable way, the missions of public broadcasting and Ready To Learn align in a symbiotic relationship that results in the creation of engaging, high-quality children's media and content that provides a backbone for learning in all communities across the country.

The rapid pace with which technology changes often exceeds the ability of our institutions to leverage its many affordances. The Ready To Learn Television Grant Program, however, helps public media remain at the forefront of pioneering efforts to harness the benefits of new media technologies and community engagement approaches to help prepare all children for success in school and in life. The Ready To Learn funding that Congress appropriates and the strategic direction provided by the U.S. Department of Education's Office of Innovation and Improvement help ensure that public media continues to navigate the rapidly changing social and media landscapes to meet the most pressing needs of our youngest learners, especially in under-resourced communities.

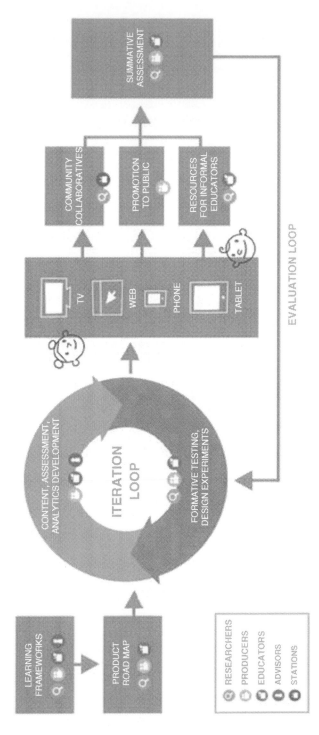

FIGURE 1.3 Content Development and Evaluation Loop that PBS and CPB use to guide production and answer questions of efficacy (Courtesy of PBS and CPB)

Note

1 Sources and permissions for Figure 1.2 are as follows: *Dragon Tales* TM and all related characters, logos and design elements are owned and licensed by Sesame Workshop. © 2018 Sesame Workshop. All Rights Reserved.; *The Electric Company* ® and all related characters, logos, and design elements are owned and licensed by Sesame Workshop. © 2018 Sesame Workshop. All Rights Reserved.; WordWorld image courtesy of *WordWorld* © 2018 General Word LP, All Rights Reserved.; *Super Why!* image courtesy of *Super Why!* © 2018 Out of the Blue Enterprises LLC. All Rights Reserved.; *Maya & Miguel images* courtesy of Scholastic Entertainment Inc. © 2018 Scholastic Entertainment Inc.; *Postcards from* Buster image courtesy of TM/© 2004, 2018 WGBH Educational Foundation & Marc Brown Studios.; *Between the Lions* image courtesy of © 2018 WGBH/Sirius Thinking. BTL TMs WGBH; and *Peg + Cat* and *Odd Squad* images courtesy of *Peg + Cat* © 2013 Feline Features, LLC, All Rights Reserved. *Odd Squad* © 2014 The Fred Rogers Company, All Rights Reserved.

References

Annie E. Casey Foundation. (2017). *Kids count data book. State trends in child well-being.* Baltimore, MD: Annie E. Casey Foundation.

Boyer, E. L. (1991). *Ready To Learn: A mandate for the nation.* Princeton, NJ: The Carnegie Foundation for the Advancement of Teaching.

Brookings Institute. (2018). *What to look for in the 2017 NAEP results.* Washington, DC: Brookings Institute. Retrieved February 23, 2018, from www.brookings.edu/blog/brown-center-chalkboard/2018/02/23/what-to-look-for-in-the-2017-naep-results/.

McCarthy, B., Li, L., Atienza, S., Sexton, U., & Tiu, M. (2013). *PBS KIDS mathematics transmedia suites in preschool homes and communities. A report to the CPB-PBS Ready To Learn Initiative.* San Francisco, CA: WestEd.

McCarthy, B., Li, L., & Tiu, M. (2012). *PBS KIDS transmedia mathematics suites in preschool homes. A report to the CPB-PBS Ready To Learn Initiative.* San Francisco, CA: WestEd.

McCarthy, B., Li, L., Tiu, M., Atienza, S., & Sexton, U. (2015). *Learning with PBS KIDS: A study of family engagement and early mathematics achievement. A report to the CPB-PBS Ready To Learn Initiative.* San Francisco, CA: WestEd.

National Institute for Literacy. (2008). *Developing early literacy: A report of the national early literacy panel.* Washington, DC and Louisville, KY: National Center for Family Literacy, National Institute for Literacy.

National Institute of Child Health and Human Development. (2000). *National reading panel teaching children to read: An evidence-based assessment of the scientific research literature on reading and its implications for reading instruction.* Washington, DC: U.S. Department of Health and Human Services, National Institute of Child Health and Human Development.

Pasnik, S., & Llorente, C. (2013). *Preschool teachers can use a PBS KIDS transmedia curriculum supplement to support young children's mathematics learning: Results of a randomized controlled trial. A report to the CPB-PBS Ready To Learn Initiative.* New York, NY and Menlo Park, CA: Education Development Center and SRI International.

Penuel, W. R., Pasnik, S., Bates, L., Townsend, E., Gallagher, L. P., Llorente, C., & Hupert, N. (2009). *Preschool teachers can use a media-rich curriculum to prepare low-income children for school success: Results of a randomized controlled trial.* New York, NY and Menlo Park, CA: Education Development Center and SRI International.

Rogers, F. (1969). *Videotaped appearance before U.S. Senate subcommittee on communications on May 1, 1969.* Washington, DC: Corporation for Public Broadcasting. Retrieved May 2018 from www.cpb.org/aboutpb/mrrogers.

2

FROM MISSION TO SCREENS

The PBS KIDS Approach to Content

Sara DeWitt and Linda Simensky

Introduction

Children's content on PBS began with two programs that redefined children's television and heavily influenced the following five decades of content. *Mister Rogers' Neighborhood* and *Sesame Street*, premiering in 1968 and 1969, respectively, introduced children's television that went beyond entertainment to incorporate learning goals into storytelling. The programs were also two of the first children's shows to launch without commercial advertising, showcasing how content could be created away from the pressures of attracting sponsorship revenue and still draw large and diverse audiences. PBS quickly became a destination for households with young children, and these two series solidified the idea that television could be educational, informative, and accessible to children from all backgrounds.

Today educational children's programming is available across networks, streaming services, and platforms, but the PBS KIDS production process remains different from most of the industry. As PBS President Paula Kerger stated in her 2018 annual address to the Television Critics' Association, following days of presentations from other networks, "We're in a slightly different business than any other media organization that has stood on this stage over the last two weeks. We just happen to use the same tools."

From the outset, the PBS KIDS production model considers the full complement of experiences that will accompany a television show in a child's life. As early as the pitch/proposal process, the PBS KIDS team is looking for concepts that will support each part of the early childhood "learning ecosystem," including:

- What kids watch on-screen (long- and short-form narrative video)
- What kids play on-screen (digital games on a desktop, tablet, or connected TV device)

- How kids interact with their parents/caregivers (co-play in digital games, offline play, activities, conversations)
- How kids engage with formal and informal educators (digital games, digital activities, and simulations, offline play, hands-on activities, conversations, and discussions, reading books)

In addition to providing critical funding for the creation of new shows, games, and resources, The CPB-PBS Ready To Learn Initiative has supported and improved the PBS KIDS production process over the past 20 years. As Chapter 1 makes clear, the Ready To Learn Initiative serves all young children, with a particular focus on children living in communities where there are limited financial resources. In this chapter, we'll describe the mechanics of how content is created to serve the needs of our wide audience, including research that helps confirm the educational impact and audience-appropriate engagement of programs and digital games, as well as R&D on new platforms and services. (See Chapters 9, 12, and 16 for descriptions of production and data analysis currently underway.)

In order to best understand some of the groundbreaking work happening within the Ready To Learn Initiative, one must first understand the PBS KIDS production process and how it shepherds the original idea for a series into a world that children can explore at home, in schools, during playtime, and on almost any digital platform they access.

Linda is the head of children's programming and Sara oversees digital development; we work very closely to determine which series and games are distributed across PBS KIDS stations and digital platforms. This sounds like a lot of responsibility (and it is!) but have you ever spent hours debating whether dinosaurs can ride trains? Our jobs are also a lot of fun.

Bringing Ideas to Life through Television Series Production

PBS KIDS maintains a robust series development and production pipeline and Ready To Learn has helped PBS put several series, such as *Peg + Cat* and *Odd Squad*, into production.

PBS is a distributor of content, working on behalf of stations across the U.S. It is not designed to operate in the way a cable channel does, where the channel finds, purchases, and fully owns properties before producing them. Rather, PBS acts as a commissioner and American distributor, finding properties of interest, working with the creators and producers on developing the ideas, and then greenlighting the series, partially funding them, and overseeing the production. To finance the series, producers count on international sales, revenue from additional video-on-demand platforms, licensing and merchandising, and grants. The Ready To Learn Initiative has been crucial in inspiring new directions for programming and funding series that otherwise might not have been produced.

Series creators, production teams, and educational experts work together to imagine and build worlds designed to introduce viewers to specific characters, ideas, and topics. The development and production process PBS KIDS uses is similar to the way other companies work, with a major difference. The PBS KIDS approach to integrating the educational curriculum is much more extensive and methodical, making development and production a lengthier process. Based on Linda's experience developing series for Nickelodeon and Cartoon Network, a series with an educational focus can take up to a full year longer.

The PBS KIDS audience is children between the ages of two and eight. To determine what children need to know at this age to succeed in school and in life, the PBS KIDS content department posed this question to several experts in different curricular areas. In 2012, the PBS KIDS content team worked with these advisors to develop a "Whole Child" curriculum focusing on all the areas important for viewers including science, technology, engineering and mathematics (STEM), literacy, social-emotional learning and executive function, social studies and community, and health, among other areas.

As we consider new areas of focus, we assemble different teams of advisors to help build curriculum-specific frameworks that cover the foundational skills and learning progressions for children in the two- to eight-year-old target age group.

Refining the Idea

Network executives work with creators on developing the story, relationships, and curriculum together from the start, so that the learning goals are as integral to the narrative as the characters.

The PBS KIDS team is not pressured to be trend-followers in the industry, but instead can chart unexplored territory, finding new approaches to areas that have not been covered in children's shows. We count on our advisors to help us determine where the gaps in the curriculum are and we then let producers know what areas we want to target. For example, when an advisor reviewed the PBS KIDS literacy offerings, she identified nonfiction reading as a gap. This led the PBS team to consider informational text as a potential curriculum in the 2015–2020 Ready To Learn Television Grant Program, which included the general topic of literacy. Eventually, our interest in informational text led to the development of a new property.

Once the PBS KIDS development team finds a curricular area we think is important to cover for a Ready To Learn grant, we then build it into a request for proposals (RFP) for producers and series creators who have expressed an interest in working with us. We have found that an RFP allows us to see many different creative and educational approaches to a topic. With this process, we can choose the directions that work best for the PBS KIDS team and our viewers. This also allows us to solicit ideas from a wide range of potential show creators.

A typical RFP includes details about the need for the series, what sort of topics PBS KIDS is looking for, a look at the curriculum and advisors, and information about what the pitch must include. The properties that producers submit are then reviewed by the entire PBS KIDS team, along with our partners from the Corporation for Public Broadcasting and the educational advisors working on the RFP. PBS KIDS might send an RFP to more than a hundred producers and creators, and then can look at as many as 50–60 show pitches to find one idea to take to pilot or series. For the informational text pitch, we sent the RFP to 108 recipients. Through review meetings, we worked the list down to 14 potential ideas, then nine, then five, and finally to two projects that were produced as pilots.

After taking those two pilots through focus group testing with children between the ages of four and six, along with their parents, we selected *Molly of Denali* from WGBH in Boston to go into series production to launch in 2019. (See Chapter 12 for a description of the development process for this new series.)

Creators and Series Ideas

New series ideas can come from any number of sources. Content creators are frequently writers, producers, book illustrators, animation artists, or directors with ideas that they believe will fit the PBS KIDS audience and will be meaningful to their lives. The creators of a series are the visionaries, the ones who envision the detailed imaginary world of the series, and define its sensibility and humor. In putting together a show, it is as crucial to find the right creator as it is to find the right idea. The PBS KIDS development team focuses on finding creators who are both talented and inspired and are drawn to the idea of producing mission-driven programming. The creator of a series must have the experience, skills, enthusiasm, and passion for telling stories for the target age group and for communicating ideas effectively in a narrative format. The pitch must then stand out from the other ideas.

The initial idea for *Peg + Cat* came from Jennifer Oxley, an animator, filmmaker, and creative director of animated preschool programs. She teamed up with Billy Aronson, a writer she had worked with previously, to develop the *Peg + Cat* idea. Oxley's work on other preschool series was well-regarded. The *Peg + Cat* pitch was notable for its overall appeal; it resembled a children's book and even read at points like a narrative. Even more interesting to us was that Oxley, an artist, was able to capture her love of math in the pitch. (See Chapter 5 for a description of how *Peg + Cat* was developed.)

Odd Squad creators Tim McKeon and Adam Peltzman both had extensive careers in writing for children's series. McKeon, living in Los Angeles, had written and developed shows for the Cartoon Network and the Disney Channel, while Peltzman, in New York, had written extensively for Nick Jr. They were from the same hometown in Massachusetts and reconnected at a wedding, where they decided to try working together. A PBS KIDS RFP in 2010 gave them the chance to blend their creative sensibilities and the result was the pitch for *Odd Squad*. The pitch was notable for its humorous take on math, TV procedurals, and spy shows; it was part *Spy Kids*, part *Law and Order*, and part *Airplane!*

Given that PBS KIDS is mission-driven, the ideas that are considered are reviewed with the viewer in mind, not toy companies, advertisers, or Nielsen ratings. We specifically consider the needs of our lower-income audience. In service of this goal, producers are asked to avoid shows that present fantastical problems and solutions; stories where the problem can be solved with magic or through a purchase. Rather, PBS tries to offer actual kid-related issues and real-world solutions. The takeaway from each story must be clear and usable in day-to-day life. Early on in our interest in developing a math-focused show, many creators presented math as being a magical skill. Ultimately, we chose *Peg + Cat*, where math was presented as a useful skill that could help solve actual problems one might encounter. The problems could still be presented as funny or silly, as long as the solutions could be used in real-life situations. *Odd Squad* features a fictional world where all problems are odd and are solvable by math. Again, the world is fantastical and whimsical, but the tools the agents use to solve a problem—like identifying patterns to predict outcomes or using measurements to compare objects—are tools that viewers can apply to problems in real life.

In the course of developing so many series, we have started to establish a list of qualities we look for in a series proposal, including:

- A cast of unique and captivating characters
- Characters who are relatable and empathetic, aspirational, and well thought out
- A range of characters with diverse backgrounds
- Stories that are compelling and original, and age-appropriate with regards to stories, humor, and curriculum
- Humor that is smart, character-based, and observational
- Unique and contemporary designs that fit in with the other PBS KIDS shows visually but are not too similar to them
- An innovative feel, technologically and visually
- Voices and music that are fun and appealing to a wide range of viewers and are not overly loud, squeaky, or obnoxious-sounding

The Ready to Learn Difference: Research and Advisors

Ready To Learn–funded projects require testing to determine that they are producing their intended results. While every series has educational experts attached, grant-funded content requires an even greater involvement by outside advisors who help develop and/or consult on the educational goals. These advisors are instrumental in reviewing materials at all points during development and production. Ultimately, any episode or piece of content, e.g., game, app, or hands-on material, must be shown to be effective if tested with an audience.

As the program idea is refined, educational experts help design the curriculum framework for the series. When the PBS KIDS development team was considering using informational text as a topic for a Ready To Learn literacy series, we contacted Nell Duke, who is considered to be the preeminent expert on the subject. She presented an enlightening webinar on informational text to the PBS KIDS, CPB, and the Ready To Learn Initiative team. This discussion inspired the group to see how the topic could work as a series for PBS KIDS. Duke went on to serve as the curriculum advisor for the series, *Molly of Denali*, and is embedded in the production as an advisor across all content platforms.

Advisor feedback extends beyond a single expert. The producers of *Molly of Denali* work not only with Duke, but with cultural, science, and social studies experts reviewing specific information within the larger context of informational text. In the case of *Molly*, the producers also tapped advisors able to consult on matters of Alaskan culture, language, and heritage.

Once a script for a pilot is written, the producers use storybook research to test a story. The pilot story is sketched out in a loose storyboard format resembling a children's book and is presented to test audiences, usually in a classroom or preschool setting. This phase determines whether viewers understand the story and the takeaway lesson. Using the results from this testing can help clarify issues or focus the story. We then use the pilot and testing to confirm that the story and characters are also appealing.

In the event that segments of the pilot are difficult for the intended audience to understand, the advisors can explain how to use the curriculum more effectively or in a more age-appropriate way. This development process can be lengthy, especially if the pilot or series idea needs reworking before production starts.

When a Ready To Learn–funded property becomes a series, the producers, programming executives, and advisors all give notes at each step of the production process. Because of the involvement of the advisors and the need to get the information right, development and production take more time for PBS KIDS shows than they would for other networks. Ready To Learn series-funded research can add time as well. Chapter 9 offers a detailed description of *The Cat in the Hat Knows a Lot About That!* and the differences between Seasons two and three, where Season three received Ready To Learn grant funding.

As soon as a few episodes of a series are completed, research teams begin the process of testing the episodes to make sure they work as intended. Testing series such as *Odd Squad* and *Peg + Cat* has helped the PBS KIDS Programming team understand the audience better and has sharpened producers' focus on age skew and comprehension. When these reports are completed, the findings are applied to future episodes in production and even to other series. For example, with *Peg + Cat*, we tested an episode called "The Golden Pyramid Problem" that introduces children to different 3D shapes. Central to the plot of the episode is a "magic" cylinder that allows Peg and Cat to travel from place to place. The cylinder and its features are named several times throughout the story; it appears on-screen for an extended period of time; and there is a simple, catchy song about the magic cylinder that repeats the name of the shape over and over. Test results showed that while no child was able to identify a cylinder before watching the episode, 17 out of 58 children were able to correctly name it afterwards—a gain that was found to be statistically significant. Repetition is key: The more often we can represent a word or a principle in dialogue, in a simple song, and with clear and focused visuals, the stronger the reinforcement and the more likely it is that the learning goal will stick.

PBS KIDS Digital Content Production

Each PBS KIDS television property is developed with the goal of engaging children in specific learning objectives as they watch their favorite shows, all while considering how a child might explore those concepts through play. A high compliment for any PBS KIDS show is discovering that children want to "play the show" in their own living rooms or backyards. Our analysis of game-play data confirms that millions of children continue to "play the show" through digital games and apps as well. This section will discuss the development of games and other digital content for PBS KIDS series.

Approach

The PBS KIDS approach to digital game development differs from most commercial networks in that games are not approached merely as show promotion or advertising tools. The PBS KIDS team views each game or digital experience as an opportunity to introduce, reinforce, and extend the curriculum goals of each series in new ways.

We believe that this approach has been a major driver in the success of PBS KIDS digital products through the years. With an average of 12 million unique visitors per month, PBS KIDS is regularly one of the most-used children's digital destinations. Our games are also widely used and displayed within classrooms and libraries across the country, not just as safe content for children, but as content that can help children learn key skills.

Game Ideas and Curriculum Development

The digital development for a series begins almost as soon as the characters and concept take shape. Often as early as the series scripting phase, creators, production teams, and curriculum experts work together to craft game ideas that are natural and organic to the show's characters and worlds. PBS KIDS is intentional about including the show creator in the early phases of digital development because the creator's inspiration and passion for the content needs to come through whenever their characters are presented to our audience—whether that is in a video or a game. Because not all creators have game development experience, the PBS KIDS team often helps creators find a digital producer who can help translate their vision into gameplay ideas.

What drives those game ideas is a combination of 1) situations and problems that stem from the show's narrative world, and 2) the learning goals the team hopes to achieve through gameplay. Within that process, the team considers which core learning goals from the series can be best introduced, practiced, or assessed through digital experiences. While educational advisors are almost always included in the early ideation stages of game development, Ready To Learn projects also benefit from expert advice and counsel throughout the production process.

The PBS KIDS team works closely to determine which game mechanics and digital experiences can best allow the audience to learn and practice key skills, exploring where the curriculum can be extended by the unique interactions digital technologies can offer. For example, input options such as microphones, cameras, and drawing tools can allow a pre-reader to answer questions or move their bodies within the digital gameplay experience. The *Curious George* game "Bubble Pop" uses the microphone so that children can clap their hands to count and pop virtual bubbles, while the *Ready Jet Go!* "Space Explorer" app uses a camera so that players can move their tablet to see different areas of the night sky. These inputs allow children to engage in natural preschool body play patterns while learning new skills.

Because digital games provide an interaction channel and can respond to audience choices and reactions, digital games related to a series also have the power to evaluate how well the target audience understands the concepts presented. The Ready To Learn team within PBS KIDS Digital sometimes categorizes digital experiences based on how they support different moments within a child's learning process. Some games, such as *The Cat in the Hat Knows a Lot About That!* "Slidea-Ma-Zoo," help present and model concepts to children, while others, like *Daniel Tiger's* "Day and Night" routines app, allow children to practice or experiment with those concepts, and still others, like *Curious George* "Blast Off" can assess a child's understanding of a concept based on how well that child succeeds in the game. (See Chapters 15 and 16 for additional descriptions of game development and analytic tools.)

Most games on pbskids.org and within the PBS KIDS Games app are created as standalone experiences that do not require a broader knowledge of the series. That said, each series production team aims to create a collection of games that, when combined, can best support the series' learning goals and world experience overall. The hope is to create a transmedia experience across all platforms so that regardless of the entry point (game or video), children have a consistent and satisfying experience with the series.

Playtesting and Research

All games on PBS KIDS are taken into playtesting sessions multiple times during the production process. Playtesting takes place in preschools and elementary school classrooms that represent the diverse populations of children that access our content. The PBS KIDS content team leads the experience, noting children's body language, comments, and whether they can successfully complete game challenges. Open-ended questions can lead to interesting insights that are not visible in gameplay data. For example, in playtesting sessions for games introducing the scientific inquiry process, the facilitators noted whenever children verbalized the inquiry process:

> "I got an idea!"
> "How is this gonna work?"
> "I think it's going to do this... [pointing to items on the screen] And then this... And then that and then BOOM!"

Playtesting is a critical step for recognizing which gameplay mechanics may be too easy or too difficult for a child, whether the game has adequate instructional language and prompts, and how successful the overall game concept will be.

The Ready To Learn Initiative also supports key formal research studies, helping the team test and prove the efficacy of the digital content development. For example, the 2014 study, *Learning Math with Curious George: PBS KIDS Transmedia and Digital Learning Games in the Preschool Classroom* (McCarthy, Tiu, & Li, 2014), confirmed that the *Curious George* digital games met their intended curriculum goals, while broader data analysis trials like the ones described in Chapter 16 can help the team identify ways to better support learning by continually improving gameplay experiences. While such research funding and support is not available for all properties, the findings from Ready To Learn research trials inform and guide digital production across all PBS KIDS series.

Distribution: Maximizing Access Everywhere Possible

A key piece of the PBS KIDS mission is to experiment and innovate with media that can support learning. Research and development on new platforms and with new technologies is critical to 1) staying relevant with our audiences, 2) being accessible to the widest possible audience, and 3) maximizing the learning potential of PBS KIDS content. As mentioned above, the team regularly explores how new and available technologies (microphone inputs, cameras, wearables, etc.) might improve engagement or learning outcomes.

For PBS KIDS, innovation does not always mean working with cutting edge technologies and platforms. The team's creative thinking also focuses on how we can best deliver engaging, educational content on older and lower-powered platforms that may be more prevalent in the lives of lower-income audiences.

For example, while 78% of households with children under eight now own a tablet (Common Sense Media, 2017), this does not mean children are using the latest high-powered devices. We can see within traffic statistics to pbskids.org and the PBS KIDS Games app that a large portion of the PBS KIDS audience is visiting our content using four- and five-year-old devices. To reach as wide an audience as possible, we regularly test our content across an extensive (some might say excessive!) number of devices and operating systems.

We also regularly review how our technical development practices can help us best distribute content across a wide variety of platforms. The Ready To Learn Initiative has supported the team to conduct trials and develop prototypes of content that allows us to consider future distribution platforms. For example, Ready To Learn supported the research and testing that led to the decision in 2013 to develop new games on pbskids.org using HTML5 (a widely accessible programming language) instead of more powerful gaming platforms. Ready To Learn also supported the creation of Springroll, an open-source library of tools for our community of producers to use. Through the use of Springroll tools, PBS KIDS Games can be developed once and easily distributed across all PBS KIDS products, including pbskids.org, the PBS KIDS Games app, the PBS KIDS Plug and Play Streaming Stick, and the PBS KIDS Playtime Pad.

The Learning Ecosystem

While media can have measurable positive effects on a child's learning and development, we know from previous rounds of Ready To Learn research that simple interactions, questions, and activities involving that media can further support a child's learning. Beyond TV series content and games for children, the PBS KIDS team recognizes the critical role parents and early childhood educators can play in supporting the learning goals presented in our series.

Considering a child's full environment—what we refer to as "The Learning Ecosystem"—while creating PBS KIDS content allows us to best identify areas where we can support the early learning and development that is critical to a child's success in school and life. We know that children are learning throughout their home, childcare, and school lives; how can PBS KIDS programs and games best support and extend that learning? How can we best expand a child's access to ideas, concepts, and language through the screens accessible in their homes, community centers, and libraries?

To that end, PBS KIDS and content producers also develop extensive materials for parents and educators related to each program. For parents, content includes hands-on play activities related to the series goals, in-depth articles about different learning areas and how to explore them at home, and tips and suggestions for conversations and play after watching PBS KIDS shows. These resources are distributed through PBS KIDS for Parents, as well as through social media channels, and other digital platforms often used by parents.

Materials for educators are developed with classroom needs in mind: games and activities for larger groups; collections of video clips and game content that are aligned to state and national standards; lesson plan ideas; related resources; and more. We consider ways we can best support teachers' professional development through the use of our content as well—offering articles, videos, and courses about how to effectively incorporate technology and media into an early childhood classroom. PBS KIDS tools for educators are distributed through PBS Learning Media, which also features a Ready To Learn portal that provides easy access to the initiative's past and current multi-platform resources.

Within the Ready To Learn Initiative, many of these individual tools have been curated and developed into more extensive resources such as the Family Community Learning Workshops or week-long *Odd Squad* or *Super Why!* camps that stations can use within their local markets. (See Chapter 13 for a full description of community efforts.)

All of these resources are available to local PBS member stations to take into their communities. The PBS KIDS team provides ongoing awareness and training events for public media colleagues. In turn, stations frequently run informal learning programs, parent events, and activities, or supplement other community initiatives with PBS KIDS content.

Conclusion

The children's media industry has changed dramatically since PBS' inception in 1968, and children now have thousands of choices when they consider what to watch or play. Despite the shifts and fragmentation in the landscape, PBS KIDS has remained relevant, still drawing large audiences and regularly cited as parents' most trusted media source for their children. This continued success is largely thanks to the tone and the formative research approach established by the producers of *Mister Rogers' Neighborhood* and *Sesame Street*. PBS KIDS continues to experiment and innovate within the children's media space, but, most importantly, we focus on the needs of our young audience first. Ready To Learn has supported our process to help develop research-driven educational content that can inspire a lifelong passion for learning.

References

Common Sense Media. (2017). *The Common Sense Census: Media Use by Kids Age Zero to Eight*. San Francisco: Common Sense Media.

McCarthy, B., Tiu, M., & Li, L. (2014). *Learning Math with Curious George: PBS KIDS Transmedia and Digital Learning Games in The Preschool Classroom*. San Francisco: WestEd.

3

USING MEDIA TO FOSTER PARENT ENGAGEMENT

Megan Silander and Elisa Garcia

Introduction

Parents are their children's first teachers. Before entering formal learning environments, children typically spend the majority of their time with their families. Many children thus encounter words, books, and numbers for the first time in the home environment. As a result, parents play a crucial role in the development of children's early cognitive and academic skills.

Starting in 2010, researchers at the Education Development Center (EDC) and SRI International (SRI) began an in-depth exploration of how media *at home* could support children's learning. This chapter describes two studies we conducted that focused particularly on using media to engage parents and children in learning. We describe our findings and how these studies informed our understanding of the role that media can play in fostering parent engagement.

The initial study we describe was the first to examine the impact of Ready To Learn mathematics media resources on parents' engagement and young children's learning. As described in more detail in Chapter 6, the study design built on knowledge gained from prior math work that focused on school-based media interventions by adapting the curricular approach for use in homes. Our findings suggested that providing families with access to media resources that focus on foundational content and provide guidance about how to use these resources can effectively support children's learning. However, we also learned that families did not follow the order of the loose curriculum that organized the educational media.

In our second study, our goal was to build on what parents already think about and do to support learning, particularly informally, with a broader sample of parents (not just the motivated ones who elected to join our intervention study). We explored the ways in which families perceive of and support early science learning—one focus of the Ready To Learn Television Grant Program at that time, but also, a subject about which little is known. We found that many parents lack confidence when it comes to early science, that many parents engage in early science less frequently than other content areas such as literacy and math, and that most parents do not think science-based media help their children learn a lot. Public media has the potential to improve access to the resources families feel would help them do more science with their young children.

Conceptualizing Parent Engagement

Parent engagement in learning activities to promote literacy, math, and social-emotional and behavioral skills can take many forms. Broadly, effective parent engagement is sensitive and responsive to children's needs, and includes both formal and informal teaching and learning experiences (Bardack, Herbers, & Obradović, 2017; Sénéchal & LeFevre, 2002). Formal parent engagement refers to directly teaching children skills that are intended to promote learning, such as teaching and practicing letters, sounds, numbers, and shapes, or interactive storybook reading. Informal parent engagement refers to a broad range of activities wherein children's learning occurs indirectly through exposure to language, numbers, and other concepts (Niklas et al., 2016; Sénéchal & LeFevre, 2002). In this way, informal learning often takes place through every-day social interactions (Lave & Wenger, 1991) and responsive conversations that use rich language and ask *"wh-"* questions (Benjamin, Haden, & Wilkerson, 2010; Haden et al., 2014).

Parent Engagement and Children's Media Use

Providing children with access to high-quality educational media is one way that parents formally and informally engage their children and support learning. Parents can also scaffold children's learning from media by using media with them. A national survey suggests that children under eight years of age are exposed to more than two hours of screen time a day, on average. This rate is higher for low-income children (Rideout, 2017). Parents' use and selection of media can ensure that children devote some of this screen time to media that is designed to support learning, and make certain that children are not exposed to media in ways that disturb sleep patterns and healthy activity. However, even with access to well-designed educational media, young children are unlikely to learn without adult support and scaffolding. Particularly effective strategies parents can use to help their children learn from media include asking open-ended questions, providing feedback, labeling and describing complex content, and modeling responses. Together, these strategies draw children's attention to the most important content so that they are better able to interpret what they see and connect it to their own life (Strouse, O'Doherty, & Troseth, 2013, Strouse, Troseth, O'Doherty, & Saylor, 2018). Parents can also offset the potential negative effects of media by monitoring and curating content children use so that it is developmentally appropriate (Gentile et al., 2012), or by helping children think critically about negative content, such as violent cartoons or ads (Buijzen, 2009; Nathanson, 1999, 2004).

Associations between Parent Engagement and Children's Development

Parent engagement in both informal and formal learning activities at home is associated with children's academic development (see National Academies Press, 2016, for a review). For example, upon kindergarten entry, children whose parents frequently engage them in literacy and math activities have a stronger vocabulary and improved early numeracy skills (Burchinal, Peisner-Feinberg, Pianta, & Howes, 2002; Kainz & Vernon-Fagans, 2007; Skwarchuk, Sownski, & LeFevre, 2014). Parents' informal and formal engagement are differentially related to children's learning. Children whose parents directly teach them literacy and math skills tend to know more letters, sounds, and numbers (Niklas et al., 2016; Sénéchal & LeFevre, 2002; Skwarchuk, Sownski, & LeFevre, 2014). In contrast, children whose parents informally engage them in reading and math activities tend to have better vocabularies, verbal fluency, and non-symbolic arithmetic ability (e.g., counting using objects, as opposed to Arabic numerals) (Niklas et al., 2016; Sénéchal & LeFevre, 2002; Skwarchuk, Sownski, & LeFevre, 2014).

Associations between Parent Engagement and Children's Learning with Media

Parent mediation and parent–child co-viewing of television and other media is one way that parents engage their children during media use. Parent co-viewing with children can increase young children's language-related learning from videos, compared to children viewing videos alone (see Chapter 8 for a deeper discussion of joint mediation) (Krcmar, Grela, & Lin, 2007; Linebarger & Vaala, 2010; Strouse, O'Doherty, & Troseth, 2013). Studies have found that active parental engagement with their children while they watch videos improves children's vocabulary and language skills, compared to the impact of viewing videos alone. Greater parent mediation is also associated with an increased development of social-emotional skills (Rasmussen et al., 2016) Evidence on the impact of parental mediation of *apps* or *digital games* on children's learning is quite limited (most evidence on joint media use relates to co-viewing videos).

One study of an app that was designed to be used by both parents and children together suggests that parental mediation can increase the effect of apps and digital games on children's mathematics learning (e.g., Berkowitz et al., 2015). Meta-analyses of teacher mediation of games also suggest that children gain greater conceptual understanding with cognitive support from adults than from playing games alone (Clark, Tanner-Smith, & Killingsworth, 2016; Wouters, van Nimwegen, van Oostendorp, & van der Spek, 2013). However, more research is needed to understand the extent to which parent support can lead to increased learning from interactive media and digital games, and on parental mediation effects on other kinds of knowledge outside of language learning.

Promoting Parent Engagement—And the Role of Media

Interventions may help promote more frequent, high-quality parent engagement. Parenting interventions typically focus on instructing parents and providing resources or information on how to enhance interactions with children. For example, shared book reading interventions teach parents to actively engage their children when they read together, to ask "*wh-*" questions, and to connect the contents of the books to children's everyday lives. These interventions have been consistently linked to children's emergent literacy skills, including vocabulary and phonological awareness (see Lonigan, Shanahan, & Cunningham, 2008, for a meta-analysis). Parent engagement also can be bolstered by interventions that point out opportunities for deeper learning within everyday activities. Two recent experimental studies with parents of preschoolers found that text messages that suggest ways to embed learning in everyday activities resulted in improvements in children's literacy and math scores in kindergarten (Doss, Fahle, Loeb, & York, 2017; York, Loeb, & Doss, 2018).

Media itself also has the potential to influence how parents engage with their children to support their learning. Media can engage parents in topics that they initially perceive as too complex, scaffolding parents' learning by modeling and simplifying tasks into smaller steps. For example, one recent study of an app designed to support parents' engagement in math learning with their children found that the app not only increased children's mathematics learning, but that it was most effective for children whose parents felt anxious about mathematics (Berkowitz et al., 2015).

Media could help parents do more active co-viewing when their children use media, but the evidence about the extent to which interventions help parents use more effective mediation to help children learn from media is mixed. Studies of media interventions that include a parental mediation component have found both positive effects on child learning (Krcmar, Grela, & Lin, 2007; Linebarger & Vaala, 2010; Strouse, O'Doherty, & Troseth, 2013) and no added effects as a result of the additional mediation (e.g., Rasmussen et al., 2016), suggesting that parents may need particular targeted support (rather than just encouragement to talk more) to effectively engage in using media with their children.

More research is needed on the role media can play in engaging parents to help their children learn generally, learn from media, and to identify effective mechanisms—media-based and otherwise—to help parents provide effective learning support. In the next section, we describe two studies conducted under the CPB-PBS Ready To Learn Initiative that focus on building knowledge about how media can enhance parent support for learning.

Ready to Learn Home Study: Supporting Parent–Child Experiences with PEG + CAT Early Math Concepts

The first study under the Ready To Learn Initiative that examined parent engagement using media was a randomized control trial assessment of Ready To Learn mathematics-focused media. This study followed a strand of research that had been focused on assessing the impact of the mathematics resources in the classroom. We conducted the study at the conclusion of the 2010–2015 Ready To Learn grant cycle, and examined whether using a curated set of public media resources—a collection of content from the PBS KIDS property *PEG + CAT*—influenced children's mathematics knowledge and their approaches to learning. Rosenfeld and Rutstein describe this study in greater detail in Chapter 6; below we focus on the aspects specific to parent engagement. (Also see Chapter 5 for a description of the *PEG + CAT* production process.)

Study Intervention

A particular challenge we faced in assessing the impact of *PEG + CAT* was in reconciling the wish to understand the impact of the resources as they would typically be used by children and the constraints of a study, which included time limitations and exposure or dosage requirements. In real life, children's engagement with media at home is likely parent- and child-directed, in which children can experience a full range of resources, sometimes repeatedly, over an extended period of time such as months or even a year. However, developers and the funder needed a relatively immediate understanding of the effectiveness of their design in order to inform future work. To increase the likelihood of supporting learning, we had to devise a way to expose children to enough content within the study's constrained timeframe, and we needed to expose children to a coherent selection of content that proceeded logically and built upon prior skills. We tried to replicate children's media engagement "at home," while targeting a narrow set of learning goals within a defined timeline. We felt learning would be maximized if children were exposed to skills multiple times and in a certain order, similar to the design of the prior classroom-based studies, which had demonstrated effectiveness on children's math skills. To assess the effects of the media, researchers created an experience for families to interact with, consisting of a set of media resources targeting specific early math skills, that built over time within a defined and limited timeframe.

Researchers organized the *PEG + CAT* family intervention into a loose curriculum for families to follow—similar to what children might experience at preschool. Researchers designed a 12-week experience that incorporated a carefully selected set of Ready To Learn media—videos and digital games— that introduced key early math skills and content. Researchers also focused on gathering resources that focused on math content not typically taught in preschools or by parents—content focused on patterns, geometry, measurable attributes, ordinal numbers, and, to a lesser degree, on the foundational skill of counting, which was present throughout all *PEG + CAT* materials.

The intervention also intended to foster joint media engagement to support learning by encouraging families to:

1. Be present with their children as much as possible during media and technology interactions;
2. Approach these interactions with the goals of helping children learn, sharing what they know, and learning something new together;
3. Talk with children, asking questions and making observations to learn how they are understanding the experience, where their interests are focused, and difficulties or challenges they may be having;
4. Help children make connections between media and other experiences at home, at school, and in the community; and
5. Help children apply and extend their learning and further explore their interests by repeating activities and by engaging in new experiences with and without media and technology.

These encouragements were embedded in four short videos that encompassed these strategies with tips for families, and a printed guide that provided parents with information about the basic math concepts embedded in the *PEG + CAT* digital resources. The videos also promoted math talk and problem-solving skills. To supplement these videos, researchers also sent weekly text message tips to intervention families to encourage parents to incorporate math into their child's daily life and to use the joint engagement tips. Comparison group families were asked to continue with their typical home behaviors with regard to children's technology and media use.

Findings

The study found the intervention had small effects on children's learning that were focused on the foundational skills that children are typically less exposed to in school. We also found a positive effect on parents' reports of their use of joint media engagement strategies. At the end of the study, parents in the intervention were more likely than parents in the comparison condition to report watching videos and playing games along with their children every week or more, and they were more likely to say that they had talked to their children about how media connected to their daily life.

Parents' reports also suggested that the intervention improved their ability to support their children's math learning. Parents in the intervention were more likely to say they were confident about supporting math learning for their children and were more likely to report engaging in problem-solving strategies (such as exploring "what if" scenarios) with their children.

Implications

The positive findings from the study provided us with some initial early evidence of the effectiveness, for both children and parents, of using media to help families engage in learning together. It also provided compelling evidence of the power of media to engage families in important content and skills that they might not otherwise experience in school or at home. Specifically, an effective design to support learning was one that included compiling a set of high-quality media resources that provided children with repeated opportunities to engage with multiple videos and games as they practiced and mastered a focused set of skills, along with support for parents about how to engage with their children in these experiences. We did not, however, test each component of the intervention separately and therefore did not determine whether each was necessary and important for learning. Our findings that parents used the intervention frequently, did not follow the curriculum in order, and that use of the resources declined over the course of the study suggest that the "curriculum" approach to family learning through media might not be the most appropriate design.

In light of these findings, in Ready To Learn 2015–2020, as our research moved on to focus on science, in contrast to the math home study, we chose not to start by designing a specific intervention. Rather, we and our partners at the CPB and PBS felt it was essential to better understand the broader context—parents' attitudes and needs—in which media might support learning more broadly, particularly given the lack of evidence on parents' engagement in science-related activities at home. We also wanted to explore the role of media in fostering more informal learning opportunities. Parents' beliefs, attitudes, and behaviors toward early science learning are likely to be associated with children's early science knowledge, to predict their long-term development in science, and to contribute to closing achievement gaps. Understanding activities related to science that parents already do with their children, and how they perceive their needs for science-related support, would help inform the development of resources and interventions. However, few studies have examined parenting interventions related to science, and a greater understanding of parents' beliefs and practices related to early science learning is required, particularly at a national level. Moreover, while media can model to parents' ways of talking with their children and provide opportunities for parents to actively engage their children in science, little is known about parents' and children's engagement in early media related to science and parents' perceptions of such media.

A Nationally Representative Survey and Qualitative Study

What parents talk about when they talk about learning: A national survey about young children and science (Silander et al., 2018) builds on prior research on parents' engagement in early literacy and math-related activities, as well as on early digital media (see Figure 3.1). The first goal of the study, which was commissioned by the CPB-PBS Ready To Learn Initiative, was to examine parents' beliefs and practices related to early learning in general, and to science learning in particular. Consistent with models of parent engagement advanced by Sénéchal and LeFevre (2002), this study focused on everyday interactions that provided opportunities for learning, and not simply on formal learning experiences. The second goal of this study was to inform the production of high-quality early learning science media by gaining an understanding of how parents engage in science-related early learning media with their children. We examined four research questions:

1. How do parents and caregivers help their young children learn in general?
2. How do parents and caregivers help their young children learn science?
3. How do parents describe their children's use of educational media?
4. How do interactions that support early learning differ among families?

To address these questions, we first conducted a nationally representative telephone survey of parents of three- to six-year-old children. Second, we conducted focus groups and interviews with a smaller sample of low-income parents.

The telephone survey included a nationally representative sample of 1,442 parents with at least one three- to six-year-old child living at home. The survey over-sampled low-income parents and included 909 families with an annual household income of $50,000 or less. The survey asked parents to report on their attitudes, beliefs, and practices related to early learning, science learning, and digital media use. We described parents' responses across all respondents and examined whether each finding differed by parents' family income and educational status.

FIGURE 3.1 Images from the report *What parents talk about when they talk about learning: A national survey about young children and science* (Courtesy of Education Development Center; Photo: Burt Granofsky)

The qualitative study was intended to gather rich, descriptive data about parents' interactions and everyday learning experiences with their children, particularly those related to science and digital media. The focus of the qualitative study was specifically on low-income parents' perspectives, experiences, and needs related to helping their children learn. Researchers recruited parents from a rural location in the Southeast, an urban location in the Central South, and a suburban location in the Midwest. Data collection included eight focus groups with eight to twelve families per group, for a total of 65 parents, and home visits with 11 families. Two focus groups and one home visit were conducted in Spanish. Focus group and home visit questions were broadly focused on the same themes as the survey but delved deeper into parents' perceptions of their attitudes toward early learning and early science learning, the learning activities they engage in with their children, and their use of educational digital media. During the home visit, researchers also conducted a brief observation of families engaging with a researcher-provided video and iPad game. After the first home visits, researchers asked parents to keep "journals" of activities related to science in which they engaged with their children. Qualitative data were summarized and coded using an iterative coding scheme.

Findings

Our survey results showed that parents wanted to be involved in their child's education. Virtually all parents (99%) believed that it was important to help their children learn reading and writing, math, and social skills at home. Accordingly, most parents surveyed (94%) reported engaging their children daily in at least one activity related to learning, including reading or telling stories, working on numbers, singing songs, or playing games and completing puzzles.

Parents saw science as being different than other skills. Although parents frequently engaged in learning activities related to reading, math, and behavioral skills at home—and felt that it was important to do so—the survey suggested that parents viewed science, and to some extent math, in a different way than reading and social-emotional skills. For instance, parents reported feeling less confident about their ability to help their child learn science skills than they did about their ability to help their child learn other skills (see Figure 3.2).

This gap between parents' confidence in science and in other domains was larger for parents with fewer years of formal education (see Figure 3.3).

Findings from our qualitative study helped illuminate why parents lacked confidence in certain subjects. Parents discussed their confidence, or lack thereof, in teaching early skills at home in terms of school-related expectations. Some parents reported that they had difficulty supporting their children's learning because the ways that children learn today differ from how the parents were taught. Others felt that they lacked content knowledge, preventing them

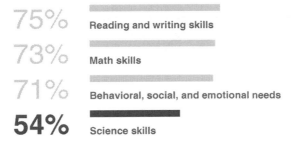

75% Reading and writing skills

73% Math skills

71% Behavioral, social, and emotional needs

54% Science skills

FIGURE 3.2 Percentage of parents who felt "Very Confident" in their ability to help their children learn age-appropriate skills (Courtesy of Education Development Center and SRI International)

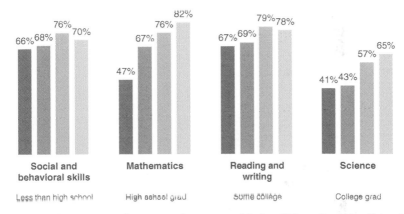

FIGURE 3.3 Percentage of parents who reported being "Very Confident" in their ability to help their child learn various types of age-appropriate skills, by parent education (Courtesy of Education Development Center and SRI International)

from adequately supporting their children. Regarding science, parents felt that they lacked the ability to answer children's spontaneous questions, such as why leaves change colors. They also reported struggling to talk with their children about science in developmentally appropriate ways, and to distill complex ideas into simpler terms.

Parents engaged in science-related learning activities far less frequently than in other activities. In comparison to the 94% of parents who engaged their child in at least one general learning activity daily, 58% of parents engaged their child in at least one science-related activity daily. The most common activities related to science were exploring science in the outdoors (36%) and exploring science in everyday activities (26%).

Surveyed parents responded to an open-ended question about the kinds of science activities their children liked to do. Responses reflected a variety of interests in nature, the planets, and building with Lego. Figure 3.4 displays the most frequently occurring words parents used to describe the science activities their children like to do.

Together, these findings demonstrate that parents are interested and engaged in early learning activities with their young children. Yet several differences emerged between parents' attitudes toward and engagement in science compared to other areas of learning such as literacy and to some extent, math. These differences suggest that parents perceive science as difficult and complex, and that they consequently did science activities less frequently than other learning activities.

Media and Science Learning

Similar to respondents in other recent surveys about media use, the parents in this Ready To Learn study reported frequently watching educational TV shows and videos and playing educational games and apps—94% had done so in the past month.

The low-income parents in our qualitative study reported using educational media primarily to occupy the child while the parent was busy, to help their child learn, and to search for information about how to help their child learn, such as by searching for developmentally appropriate answers to their child's questions. Less frequently, parents mentioned using educational media for mutual entertainment. Parents also said that their children learned from media in and of itself—that shows, games, and apps had taught their child letters, numbers, and colors. Many parents agreed that media was beneficial because children found it more engaging than other activities, and that media was therefore valuable and successful. A few mentioned that they felt the parents' presence increased the child's attention to media.

Aside from educational media in general, parents also reported that their children engaged in media specifically related to science. Most parents (88%) said that their child had watched a TV show or video about science in the past month. Fewer parents (69%) reported that their child had played a video game or app about science in the past month, and fewer than half (45%) reported that their child had engaged with a website about science in the past month.

Our qualitative study sheds light on what types of science-related media parents and their children are using. Parents mentioned PBS KIDS TV shows such as *The Magic School Bus, Sid the Science Kid*, and *Nature Cat*. Fewer parents recalled science-related video games and apps, but a few mentioned *ABCmouse, Minecraft*, and *Scratchjr*. Parents' use of science-related media was similar to their use of other educational media and was primarily for information and

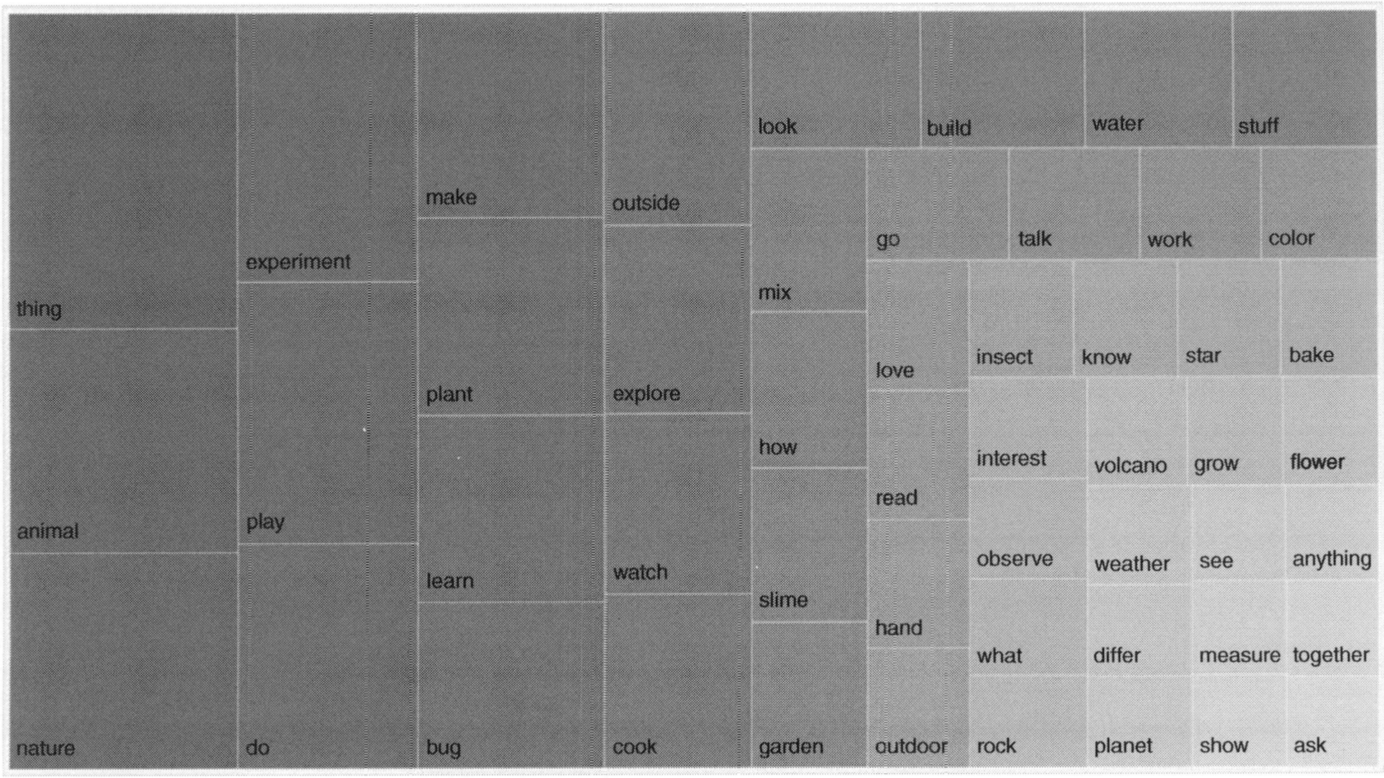

FIGURE 3.4 Frequency of words parents used to describe science activities their children like to do (Courtesy of Education Development Center and SRI International)

entertainment. When parents used science-related media for information, they referred to "Googling" questions their children had. Parents primarily seemed to value science-related media for its ability to engage and entertain their children, rather than to educate them. Some parents reported their belief that their children learned about science from educational videos and shows. At the same time, a few parents worried that their children were not attending to the science parts of the science shows, and instead were simply entertained.

Survey findings also provided insight into how parents mediated their children's engagement with science-related educational media. Parents most frequently reported monitoring their child's viewing and were less likely to talk about making connections between what they are watching or playing and their daily lives (see Figure 3.5)

Findings from our survey and qualitative study thus suggest that parents frequently engage in educational media generally and science-related media specifically. Yet many parents use media simply to engage and occupy their children, and likely do not maximize the learning opportunities that are presented. Moreover, parents are less likely to engage their children in ways that are more likely to promote learning while using science-related media.

Findings from this second study suggest a host of implications for the role that public media can play in fostering greater family involvement in early science.

Conclusions and Implications

The ways in which parents help their young children learn is a key predictor of children's school readiness and development. Media offers an opportunity to

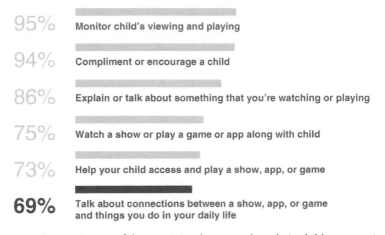

95%   Monitor child's viewing and playing

94%   Compliment or encourage a child

86%   Explain or talk about something that you're watching or playing

75%   Watch a show or play a game or app along with child

73%   Help your child access and play a show, app, or game

69%   Talk about connections between a show, app, or game and things you do in your daily life

FIGURE 3.5   Parent reports of the strategies they use when their children use science-related media (Courtesy of Education Development Center and SRI International)

support and enhance parents' engagement with their young children while capitalizing on activities that children find naturally engaging and that are already ubiquitous in their lives. The results of both our Ready To Learn studies suggest that media developers and organizations that serve parents can do more to ensure parents have resources to help their young children be ready for school. Providing access to high-quality media resources is an important goal but helping children access and make sense of media is equally important—parents may be the best resource for this task. However, while parents feel it is important to help their children learn and be ready for school, many lack time, resources, and confidence about what experiences, beyond literacy and counting, are important for young children. Our *PEG + CAT* home study and parent survey and qualitative study provide some implications for next steps.

Using media that focus on content that are foundational but less likely to be addressed by schools and parents, such as science and math, may be a particularly valuable approach to helping young children learn. Similarly, we should take advantage of the power of media resources to engage families in important content that parents have some anxiety or lack confidence about, such as science and math. Videos and games can engage families in content that some may perceive as complex or not relevant to young children. Moreover, high-quality educational media can model what doing science and math looks like and sounds like, with diverse families and children in a variety of home environments. Providing these models can help families relate to, identify with, and see themselves engaging in the content and activities. Some parents felt that they lacked the math or science knowledge to do these activities with their children; thus, media should model parents engaging in math and science in a way that does not involve having the right answers and that incorporates joint exploration and discovery. Although an instructional curricular approach may be an effective method to engage families in structured weekly activities that build knowledge over time, we also should explore approaches that build on what families are already doing, and that strengthen the relationships that families bring to learning. For example, we can take better advantage of the time children spend with their families during their everyday routines—anytime-anywhere apps that work on mobile phones might be one approach to capitalize on the time children spend with their parents in the car, on the bus, and doing errands. *Daily Vroom*, an app for parents with children from birth through age five is one example, but apps that focus on preschool and school-age children and on math and science are needed.

We found that many parents are not watching shows or playing games along with their children, suggesting that we can better communicate the importance of joint mediation to parents. The effectiveness of the *PEG + CAT* videos and text messages suggests that parents are able to do more. However, because there are many demands on parents, and because many parents use media to occupy children, encouraging parents to watch or use media with their children may not be sufficient. Instead, it may be beneficial to encourage children to engage their parents in media they are using. Prompting children to ask their parents or older siblings about their own thoughts or experiences related to the content of the media also might support learning from media. Additionally, results from our second study suggest that children take an active role in selecting media to watch. Media developers and parent program leaders should consider carefully curating the ways episodes and games are presented to children and parents so that content can build over time.

Finally, while these studies provide ideas and hypotheses about the kinds of resources that can meet families' needs, more research is needed to assess the effectiveness of these suggested approaches for learning and to determine how media can scale up effective approaches to reach more parents from diverse backgrounds. Ready To Learn focuses on low-income children. Parents with lower incomes say they need more support, and parents with less education are less confident about helping their children learn science—we have to ensure media are designed to meet these needs. For example, app developers should be mindful of the potential for families to have low literacy, inconsistent wireless access, and old smartphones with little available space. Therefore, apps should be designed to be readable, to be able to be downloaded and used offline, and to have low memory requirements. Finally, researchers and developers should seek creative approaches to engaging parents in learning-related activities, online and off, that capitalize on everyday opportunities and don't require a large time commitment for low-income parents.

References

Bardack, S., Herbers, J. E., & Obradović, J. (2017). Unique contributions of dynamic versus global measures of parent–child interaction quality in predicting school adjustment. *Journal of Family Psychology, 31*(6), 649.

Benjamin, N., Haden, C. A., & Wilkerson, E. (2010). Enhancing building, conversation, and learning through caregiver-child interactions in a children's museum. *Developmental Psychology, 46*(2), 502–515.

Berkowitz, T., Schaeffer, M. W., Maloney, E. A., Peterson, L., Gregor, C., Levine, S. C., & Beilock, S. L. (2015). Math at home adds up to achievement in school. *Science, 350*(6257), 196–198.

Buijzen, M. (2009). The effectiveness of parental communication in modifying the relation between food advertising and children's consumption behaviour. *British Journal of Developmental Psychology, 27*(1), 105–121.

Burchinal, M., Peisner-Feinberg, E., Pianta, R., & Howes, C. (2002). Development of academic skills from preschool through second grade: Family and classroom predictors of developmental trajectories. *Journal of School Psychology, 40*(5), 415–436.

Clark, D., Tanner-Smith, E., & Killingsworth, S. (2016). Digital games, design, and learning: A systematic review and meta-analysis. *Review of Educational Research, 86*(1), 79–122.

Doss, C., Fahle, E., Loeb, S., & York, B. (2017). Supporting parenting through differentiated and personalized text-messaging: Testing effects on learning during kindergarten. *CEPA Working Paper No. 16–18*. Stanford Center for Education Policy Analysis. Retrieved from http://cepa.stanford.edu/wp16-18.

Gentile, D. A., Nathanson, A. I., Rasmussen, E. E., Reimer, R. A., & Walsh, D. A. (2012). Do you see what I see? Parent and child reports of parental monitoring of media. *Family Relations*, *61*(3), 470–487.

Haden, C. A., Jant, E. A., Hoffman, P. C., Marcus, M., Geddes, J. R., & Gaskins, S. (2014). Supporting family conversations and children's STEM learning in a children's museum. *Early Childhood Research Quarterly*, *29*(3), 333–344.

Kainz, K., & Vernon-Fagans, L. (2007). The ecology of early reading development for children in poverty. *The Elementary School Journal*, *107*(5), 407–427.

Krcmar, M., Grela, B., & Lin, K. (2007). Can toddlers learn vocabulary from television? An experimental approach. *Media Psychology*, *10*(1), 41–63.

Lave, J., & Wenger, E. (1991). *Situated learning: Legitimate peripheral participation*. Cambridge: Cambridge University Press.

Linebarger, D. L., & Vaala, S. E. (2010). Screen media and language development in infants and toddlers: An ecological perspective. *Developmental Review*, *30*(2), 176–202.

Lonigan, C. J., Shanahan, T., & Cunningham, A. (2008). Impact of shared-reading interventions on young children's early literacy skills. In National Early Literacy Panel (Ed.), *Developing early literacy: Report of the National Early Literacy Panel*, Jessup, MD: National Early Literacy Panel, pp. 153–171.

Nathanson, A. I. (1999). Identifying and explaining the relationship between parental mediation and children's aggression. *Communication Research*, *26*(2), 124–143.

Nathanson, A. I. (2004). Factual and evaluative approaches to modifying children's responses to violent television. *Journal of Communication*, *54*(2), 321–336.

National Academies Press. (2016). *Parenting matters: Supporting parents of children ages 0–8*. Washington, DC: National Academies Press.

Niklas, F., Nguyen, C., Cloney, D. S., Taylor, C., & Adams, R. (2016). Self-report measures of the home learning environment in large scale research: Measurement properties and associations with key developmental outcomes. *Learning Environment Research*, *19*(2), 181–202.

Rasmussen, E. E., Shafer, A., Colwell, M. J., White, S., Punyanunt-Carter, N., Densley, R. L., & Wright, H. (2016). Relation between active mediation, exposure to Daniel Tiger's neighborhood, and US preschoolers' social and emotional development. *Journal of Children and Media*, *10*(4), 443–461.

Rideout, V. (2017). *The Common Sense census: Media use by kids age zero to eight*. San Francisco, CA: Common Sense Media.

Sénéchal, M., & LeFevre, J. A. (2002). Parental involvement in the development of children's reading skill: A five-year longitudinal study. *Child Development*, *73*(2), 445–460.

Silander, M., Grindal, T., Hupert, N., Garcia, E., Anderson, K., Vahey, P., & Pasnik, S. (2018). *What parents talk about when they talk about learning: A national survey about young children and science*. New York, NY & Menlo Park, CA: Education Development Center, Inc., & SRI International.

Skwarchuk, S., Sownski, C., & LeFevre, J. (2014). Formal and informal home learning activities in relation to children's early numeracy and literacy skills: The development of a home numeracy model. *Journal of Experimental Child Psychology*, *121*, 63–84.

Strouse, G. A., O'Doherty, K., & Troseth, G. L. (2013). Effective coviewing: Preschoolers' learning from video after a dialogic questioning intervention. *Developmental Psychology*, *49*(12), 2368.

Strouse, G. A., Troseth, G. L., O'Doherty, K. D., & Saylor, M. M. (2018). Co-viewing supports toddlers' word learning from contingent and noncontingent video. *Journal of Experimental Child Psychology*, *166*, 310–326.

Wouters, P., van Nimwegen, C., van Oostendorp, H., & van der Spek, E. D. (2013). A meta-analysis of the cognitive and motivational effects of serious games. *Journal of Educational Psychology*, *105*(2), 249–265.

York, B. N., Loeb, S., & Doss, C. (2018). One step at a time: The effects of an early literacy text messaging program for parents of preschoolers. *Journal of Human Resources*, doi: 10.3368/jhr.54.3.0517-8756R.

4

BUILDING LEARNING PATHWAYS AND COMMUNITY FOR EARLY CHILDHOOD EDUCATORS

Lori Brittain, Jean B. Crawford, Sara Schapiro, Jeanne R. Paratore, Alejandra Salinas, Lisa O'Brien, and Sarah D. Blodgett

Introduction

The proliferation of technology has changed the ways we live and learn. As new technology platforms and related media content have made their way into some classrooms, studies have documented a positive impact on children's cognitive and social skills (Fisch, 2014; Fishman & Dede, 2016). Yet, we know that all educational media are not created equal. Positive outcomes are realized when high-quality digital media that are conceptually accurate, cognitively and linguistically challenging, and developmentally appropriate are closely aligned with the classroom curriculum. But even this is not enough. Achieving optimal outcomes requires expert teachers who understand evidence-based teaching approaches and practices and implement them in response to the needs of the children in their classrooms.

In this aspect of the Ready To Learn Initiative, PBS, and a team from Boston University Wheelock College of Education and Human Development (BU Wheelock) collaboratively sought to extend the likelihood that children in all early childhood learning settings would have access to instruction grounded in both high-quality, developmentally appropriate educational media and highly expert teaching practices. To achieve our goal, we joined PBS KIDS media content developed under the 2015–2020 Ready To Learn Television Grant Program with excellent early childhood teaching practices. We created a classroom curriculum infused with PBS KIDS resources, built a collection of classroom videos that captured teachers' implementation of the curriculum, and designed professional development materials and experiences to support highly effective teaching.

This chapter is organized into two parts. First, we explain why we viewed the introduction of high-quality educational media into early childhood classrooms as an urgent educational imperative; and we provide evidence to support PBS KIDS content as an especially rich and appropriate resource to help us meet this imperative. Second, we describe the resources we developed to meet that imperative by (a) integrating high-quality digital media into mathematics and science instruction and, (b) supporting teachers' development of pedagogical content knowledge – knowing what to teach and how to teach it.

Part 1: The Importance of Technology Integration and Use Right from the Start

For decades, children who are economically poor and culturally different from the American mainstream have been inadequately served by the traditional school curriculum, as evidenced by continued low rates of literacy and mathematics achievement (Hemphill, Vanneman, & Rahman, 2011). Many have argued that in a world that is increasingly dependent on new technologies for daily routines and tasks, early school-based access to technology learning and use is fundamental to achieving equitable and just educational opportunities for all children (Gee, 2008; Jenkins et al., 2006). This argument is supported by solid evidence that, in addition to traditional academic skills, the increased presence of technology demands an additional, complex skill set. The skill set includes not only the ability to analyze and understand the images, sounds, and organizational structures that are common to digital resources but also a set of social skills required to navigate the participatory culture created by new technologies (e.g., Jenkins et al., 2006).

Like other academic abilities, we cannot assume that these new skills will emerge on their own. Rather, studies (e.g., Gutnick et al., 2010) tell us these abilities develop when children have many opportunities to observe, try them out, and refine them with support from knowledgeable others. Leaving the acquisition of such important behaviors to chance – or a "laissez-faire approach" (Jenkins et al., 2006) – ignores three important realities: (1) outside of school, young people have unequal access to new media technologies; (2) we cannot assume children will independently reflect on and learn from their media experiences; and (3) without mentorship, we cannot expect children to develop appropriate "ethical norms to cope with a complex and diverse social environment online" (Jenkins et al., 2006).

To understand what we can expect of educational media use in early childhood classrooms, we reviewed a collection of rigorous studies and literature reviews related to educational media use and early literacy and mathematics achievement and development of cognitive and socio-emotional abilities. Findings generally indicate that when media content is educational and child-oriented, it has consistently significant positive effects on children's learning of early literacy and mathematics content (e.g., Cohen & Hadley, 2009; Hurwitz, 2018; Linebarger, Moses, & McMenamin, 2010; Linebarger & Piotrowski, 2009; Neuman,

Newman, & Dwyer, 2011; Pasnik et al., 2007; Schmitt et al., 2010). In some cases, use of high-quality media in combination with high-quality instruction even erases the early learning gap between low-income children and their higher-income peers (e.g., Neuman, Newman, & Dwyer, 2011). There are also positive correlations with the development of imagination, creativity, and problem solving (e.g., Singer & Singer, 2011). Furthermore, the effects of educational media use in the early school years may be long lasting, as they are linked to academic achievement ten years later (Kirkorian, Wartella, & Anderson, 2008).

How Do We Know PBS KIDS Content is the "Right" Tool for Technology Integration and Use?

Throughout nearly two decades of the Ready To Learn Television Grant Program, numerous studies have confirmed that PBS KIDS online content, including games, is successful at both engaging and instructing students in academic content in and out of school (e.g., Hurwitz, 2018; McCarthy, Liu, & Tiu, 2012; Pasnik & Llorente, 2013; Tiu, McCarthy, & Li, 2015). Of particular note, resources created specifically for informal learning environments are found to make a difference in children's learning in school, effectively crossing home/school boundaries (McCarthy, Liu, & Tiu, 2012). Moreover, when PBS KIDS content is well supported by parents, caregivers, and teachers, it has a substantial and significant impact on academic learning of children from low socioeconomic backgrounds.

FIGURE 4.1   Image of first graders playing a PBS KIDS game about Animal Adaptations that their teacher introduced to them earlier in the day during a whole-group lesson (Courtesy of PBS; Boston University Wheelock College of Education and Human Development; and Kratt Brothers Company Ltd./9 Story Media Group Inc.)

Are Early Childhood Teachers Prepared for Technology Integration and Use?

Findings of positive outcomes from media use with young children stem from studies in which technology was integrated within the context of sound, research-based curricula and implemented by well-prepared teachers (e.g., Thai et al., 2009; Zevenbergen, 2007). Importantly, in every case, the purpose was not to support technology and media use for their own sake, but to support the learning of mathematics or literacy skills, knowledge development, or critical thinking and problem solving (Harris, Mishra, & Koehler, 2009; NAEYC & the Fred Rogers Center, 2012).

Unfortunately, there is little evidence that technology use in most of today's classrooms matches these conditions. Instead, technology practices are often teacher-directed, emphasize lower-level uses of technology rather than student-directed practices focused on transforming learning (Rebora, 2016), and are added to, rather than integrated within, existing curriculum and pedagogy (Biancarosa & Griffiths, 2012). In a study of early childhood lead and assistant teachers, only a third reported that they were knowledgeable about criteria for selecting children's educational software and less than a third reported including software when planning instruction (Chen & Chang, 2006). Notably, educational level (which varied from a high school diploma to a master's degree) did not relate to teachers' ratings of confidence, skills, or classroom practices and there were no differences in ratings of confidence among lead and assistant teachers. Moreover, a number of years teaching had a small but negative effect on teachers' confidence, skills, and classroom practices related to technology use.

Findings such as these have led to a call for in-service professional development to support teachers' knowledge and integration of instructional technologies (e.g., Barron et al., 2011; Biancarosa & Griffiths, 2012; NAEYC and the Fred Rogers Center, 2012). But precisely what do teachers need to know to make digital technologies an integral and productive part of their academic curricula?

Experts suggest that to become skillful technology users, teachers must not only study the effective uses of technology; they must also experience and witness first-hand effective technology integration as a pathway in their own learning (Belland, 2008; Polly et al., 2010); and they must see effective technology uses in action with young students in classrooms.

Summary of Major Findings

The Ready To Learn work we undertook was driven by four major research findings. First, children in low-income schools experience persistent low rates of achievement, and the differences in access to digital resources and experiences in high- and low-income schools are likely to exacerbate the achievement gap.

Second, when media content is educational and child-oriented, it has consistently resulted in significant positive effects on children's learning of early literacy and mathematics content, and these effects are sustained throughout schooling. Third, PBS KIDS content has been validated as a curriculum resource that results in higher levels of motivation, engagement, and achievement in early literacy and mathematics, and these effects have been found in the home and school settings. Fourth, novice and experienced in-service teachers are underprepared to integrate technology and educational media in ways that advance children's academic success. In the next part, we describe how we acted on this evidence.

Part 2: Evidence-Based Design

To respond to the evidence, we developed a collection of learning resources that (a) integrate high-quality, digital media into interdisciplinary (mathematics, science, literacy) instruction; and (b) support teachers' pedagogical content knowledge – knowing what to teach and how to teach it. The learning resources take two forms: a classroom curriculum, titled *Teaching Tips* (accessible on the PBS Learning Media website; see Figure 4.2) and online professional development courses for educators offered through PBS Teacherline.

Classroom Curriculum: Teaching Tips

The *Teaching Tips* (PreK–Grade 2) comprises of units of study about important STEM content. Four evidence-based teaching principles underlie the instructional framework:

First, effective teachers know a lot about general teaching practices (pedagogical knowledge); they have deep disciplinary (content) knowledge (e.g., science, mathematics, literacy); and they also know a lot about content-specific teaching practices (pedagogical content knowledge) (e.g., Shulman, 1986). In today's global world, each of these types of knowledge routinely outpaces what teachers have learned in preservice education programs (two or four years), leaving many underprepared to meet the challenges of today's classrooms.

Second, effective teachers are knowledgeable about inquiry-based teaching and learning and about the importance of building on children's natural curiosities and following their interests as a pathway to knowledge building.

Third, effective teachers use connected learning as an instructional approach, developing the same ideas, concepts, and understandings across different academic disciplines (e.g., science, mathematics, literacy) and through multimodal resources (e.g., digital and traditional texts, images, games) (Ito et al., 2013). They also develop connections between children's in-school and out-of-school experiences (e.g., Fleer, 2011; Jenkins et al., 2006).

FIGURE 4.2   Cover image of *Teaching Tips* lesson plan (Courtesy of PBS; The PBS logos and wordmarks are trademarks of the Public Broadcasting Service and used with permission; Boston University Wheelock College of Education and Human Development; and Kratt Brothers Company Ltd./9 Story Media Group Inc.)

Fourth, effective teachers view and use digital media and technology as a pathway to knowledge development (i.e., learning content or developing critical thinking and problem-solving skills; see Figure 4.3) (as opposed to using technology for its own sake) (Harris, Mishra, & Koehler, 2009; NAEYC & the Fred Rogers Center, 2012).

Framed by these research-based principles, *Teaching Tips* guide teachers to engage children in authentic disciplinary practices – that is, thinking and acting like "real" mathematicians, scientists, and engineers. The units address

FIGURE 4.3 Picture of first-grade teacher, Alicia Poulin, circulating among her students during small-group time to offer help with reports the students are creating using the PBS KIDS *ScratchJr* app on tablets (Courtesy of PBS and Boston University Wheelock College of Education and Human Development)

a range of important STEM topics (e.g., 2D and 3D Shapes; Energy and Motion, Animal Adaptations; see Figure 4.4). Learning objectives are aligned with recommended standards of various professional organizations and commissions, including Next Generation Science Standards and Common Core State Standards.

Important content is conveyed and experienced through high-quality, multimodal resources (i.e., traditional and digital books and games, videos, images) along with classroom realia such as counting manipulatives, measuring tools, or ramps. Media are introduced and experienced through various technologies (e.g., interactive whiteboards, computers, tablets, Apple TV with portable flat-screens for flexible and shared technology use) and within different learning contexts, including teacher-led (whole class or small group) and independent learning. In each *Teaching Tips* unit:

- General *Teaching Routines* specify the implementation of evidence-based practices related to important topics (e.g., pacing, engagement, vocabulary development, digital game place, scientific reasoning).
- PBS KIDS shows and games serve as an essential curriculum resource, providing children classroom-based experiences with well-known and beloved characters (e.g., The Cat in the Hat, Peg + Cat, The Kratt Brothers), heightening motivation and engagement, and bridging in-school and out-of-school experiences.

LESSON 1
Objectives

Lesson SEQUENCE

DAY 1 25 minutes

Watch and Record
Demonstrate
Read and Record

DAY 2 40 minutes

Read and Record
Get Ready to Play
Play and Record
Conduct and Investigation
(Optional-30 Minutes)

DAY 3 25 minutes

Get Ready to Code Using a
Think Sheet

DAY 4 25 minutes

Write Code Using PBS KIDS
ScratchJr
Review, Reflect, Connect

In this lesson, children will:

- Ask questions (science practice).
- Plan and carry out investigations to extend children's understanding of kinetic energy and potential energy (science and engineering practice).
- Analyze and interpret data about kinetic energy and potential energy (science and engineering practice).
- Construct explanations about the movement of objects in relation to kinetic energy and potential energy (science practice).
- Engage in argument from evidence (science and engineering practice)
- Obtain, evaluate, and communicate information (science and engineering practice).
- Acquire and use vocabulary and concepts including **elevated, energy, kinetic energy, motion,** and **potential energy.**
- Read, respond to, and record information from books about potential and kinetic energy.
- View, respond to, and record information from videos about potential and kinetic energy.
- Use technology to learn, working individually and in groups.

FIGURE 4.4 Image of Energy and Motion Lesson Preview (Courtesy of PBS and Boston University Wheelock College of Education and Human Development)

- Specified teaching actions engage children in *authentic mathematics, science, and engineering practices* (e.g., asking questions, gathering evidence, testing hypotheses, producing, and sharing new knowledge with others).
- *Essential vocabulary* is identified along with specific examples of ways to embed the vocabulary within the lesson itself and in activities throughout the day.
- Each lesson guides the teacher to support children's understanding of how the knowledge *connects to their own lives* (e.g., in the study of Animal Adaptations, understanding how humans mimic animal's characteristics to improve performance or get things done).
- At the end of each unit, specific questions guide teachers to *reflect on their practice and children's learning* to support maintenance and growth of teaching expertise.
- *Exemplar videos* show the implementation of *Teaching Tips* lessons by highly effective classroom teachers. In video-recorded interviews, these same teachers explain their thinking and decision-making as they implemented the *Teaching Tips* in their classrooms.
- Family letters support and engage parents and other family members in building on and connecting learning opportunities at home and at school.

What We Observed

We pilot test each *Teaching Tips* unit in an urban school classroom, and we use data gathered to revise the tested unit and to guide the development of subsequent units. In the initial pilot, we found that teachers needed more explicitness about teaching actions than we had specified. As a result, we redesigned lessons to provide substantially more teaching guidance about specific teaching actions, examples of productive teacher talk (e.g., types of questions, repetitive use of key vocabulary, modeling reasoning), and facilitative feedback. We also added guidance about general teaching routines such as pacing, engaging all children, and managing technology. Overall, we learned that:

- The multimodal nature of the resource sets (i.e., informational picture books, digital images, videos, and games) engaged teachers and children.
- Many children immediately connected to the PBS KIDS videos and games, expressing their familiarity with the programs and characters.
- The teacher found the format easy to follow and the activities engaging and appropriate for their youngsters.
- Children acquired and used the targeted (sophisticated) academic vocabulary (e.g., kinetic and potential energy, friction, and inertia). In one illustrative example, during the unit on energy and motion in a first-grade classroom, a child exclaimed: "Oh, I get it! It's like addition and subtraction. Inertia is like adding energy, and friction is like subtracting energy!"
- Family letters provided a foundation for family members to share in children's learning experiences. In one example, as the teacher explained that the family letters would be disseminated at the end of the day, children excitedly commented on how they would use the information. One child said that at the playground, she would demonstrate how higher and longer slides help you go faster and farther. Another said she would teach her younger brother about potential and kinetic energy so that he could be at the "front of his class" when he attends first grade!

What Teachers Tell Us

Experienced teachers tell us that many of the instructional techniques and strategies contained in the *Teaching Tips* are familiar, but they use them more regularly, with greater effectiveness, and with better outcomes since formally implementing the *Teaching Tips* in their classrooms. For example, Alicia Poulin, a first-grade teacher at Edgar F. Hooks Elementary School in Chelsea, MA, said she knew the importance of building vocabulary but was reluctant to introduce big words and did not realize the importance of repetition. Her initial response to the *Teaching Tips* was that her students, predominantly English learners, would find the concepts and vocabulary too complex. She quickly learned she was wrong, as she observed her students become engaged and motivated and eager to use their newly acquired sophisticated language in their interactions with peers outside of the lessons. She no longer shies away from introducing more advanced words and reinforcing them throughout her lessons. "The biggest impact the *Teaching Tips* had on me was making me more ambitious in my vocab usage," she said.

Similarly, teachers found the *Teaching Tips* helped them integrate digital media into their instructional practice. For example, Allison Frometa, a kindergarten teacher at the John Silber Early Learning Center in Chelsea, MA, reported that she was surprised by how much she can teach using digital games. The *Teaching Tips* showed her how to use digital games as a key part of the instruction during whole-group time. "I can do so much with just one game: build background, teach vocabulary, teach math concepts, and the kids are engaged!" Likewise, Alicia Poulin noted that in her preservice education program, using games to teach was not part of the curriculum. "When I became a teacher, I sometimes used games during learning centers. It didn't occur to me to use them as a key part of my instruction. Now I do!" She said she was surprised by just how engaged the kids were by the digital media (see Figure 4.5). At the end of the school year, when the children reflected on what they had learned, the lessons in the *Teaching Tips* were "definitely the highlight of their year." She said she knew the kids would enjoy the lessons, but

FIGURE 4.5 Image of first-grade teacher Alicia Poulin, using a game from the PBS KIDS show *Wild Kratts* to teach a whole-group lesson on Animal Adaptations (Courtesy of PBS; Boston University Wheelock College of Education and Human Development; and Kratt Brothers Company Ltd./ 9 Story Media Group Inc.)

"didn't think they would latch onto them the way they did!" She believes the engagement was due to a combination of the digital media, quality books, the rich vocabulary, and the way the *Teaching Tips* were structured.

Teacher Professional Development

As part of the Ready To Learn project we designed and implemented two key learning experiences to support the development of teacher knowledge related to technology integration in early childhood education: (1) a face-to-face required, preservice teacher education course and (2) online courses designed to connect in-service teacher professional learning with the *Teaching Tips*.

Preservice Teacher Education Course

The course, "Teaching of Reading," is a semester-long (14 weeks) tuition-based course aimed at developing foundational knowledge for teaching reading, grades K–5. It is required of all students enrolled in Boston University Wheelock College of Education and Human Development teacher licensure programs in Elementary Education, Bilingual Education, Early Childhood Education, and Deaf Studies. We began with the existing required course (focused only on the foundations of literacy learning and teaching) and revised it to integrate technology use into course goals and activities. Integral to the redesign was the addition of a technology lab, *PlaySpace*, to provide opportunities to explore various digital media and technologies including PBS KIDS content. Consistent with the research finding that teachers who, themselves, learn through and with technology, the instructor deliberately used technology as a part of her instruction throughout the course.

What We Learned

We examined outcomes across two-course offerings with a total enrollment of 28 preservice teachers. Survey data indicated that the course had moderate to large positive effects on preservice teachers' confidence and comfort in the use of technology for teaching reading. It also had moderate to large positive effects on their intent to integrate technology in teaching literacy. To control for the possibility that an emphasis on technology would diminish the time and attention teachers give to reading instruction, we also examined the quality of literacy instruction in the lesson plans completed as part of course requirements. Analyses verified that preservice teachers integrated technology use within the context of sound and highly effective literacy instruction (Paratore et al., 2016).

Asynchronous Online Learning: Massive Open Online Course

To build on the fundamental design of the preservice teacher education course and provide access beyond preservice teachers enrolled at BU Wheelock, we developed a massive open online course (MOOC), Teaching Literacy with and Through Technology. The course is free and online, facilitated by a literacy expert, presently offered on the Canvas Network. Its purpose is to prepare teachers to make teaching with technology an essential component of their literacy instruction. The course includes five modules, each integrating an essential aspect of sound literacy instruction with the high-quality and highly effective use of technology. Participants have the option to enroll in one or more modules. The course has been offered twice: in the spring of 2016 and 2017, with a total of 277 participants including classroom teachers, media/library specialists, teachers of English learners, IT professionals, reading/literacy teachers, college instructors, and special educators.

What We Learned

On average, 22% of participants who register for a MOOC with the intent to complete it do so (Reich, 2014). Among the 277 participants who enrolled in Teaching Literacy with and Through Technology with the intent to complete, 34% (77 participants) completed at least one module. Among participants who completed all five modules ($N = 45$), 85% rated the overall value of the course as valuable or highly valuable. Although these outcomes suggest that teachers appreciated and learned from the course, we did not collect data that would allow us to ascertain the extent to which participants acted on the information learned in their teaching, supervising, or administrative roles.

Asynchronous Online Learning: Teaching Science in Early Childhood Classrooms

Two online courses, offered through PBS Teacherline, are designed to support teachers' understanding of inquiry-based and connected learning approaches to teaching science in early childhood classrooms. One course focuses on Animal Adaptations; the other, Energy and Motion. Each is offered in two ways: a three-hour, self-paced course and a facilitated, 15-hour course.

As we developed these courses, we were mindful that in order to support young children's learning about science, early childhood teachers need both deep science content knowledge (e.g., Kallery & Psillos, 2001) and also deep understanding of developmentally appropriate and play-based learning (NAEYC, 2018). Accordingly, the self-paced courses guide participants to explore four topics: Science Standards, Explore Digital and Traditional Teaching Resources, Using Inquiry-Based and Connected Learning in Science, and Putting it All Together – Create a Lesson Plan. The facilitated courses include these topics and two others: a session on assembling a multimodal resource set of their own and another on culturally relevant teaching. In both self-paced and facilitated courses, participants are guided to analyze a *Teaching Tips* lesson plan and then to observe and analyze the plan "in action" by viewing a video of a first-grade teacher implementing the plan. Each task is accompanied by a detailed rubric to guide participants' completion and self-evaluation; in the facilitated course, a facilitator's rubric guides the course instructor's assessment and feedback. These courses are in an early stage of implementation with data not yet available to judge effectiveness.

Meeting Teachers Where They Are

The resources, courses, and collaborative learning experiences we have developed are built on the core tenets of effective professional development and research-based principles on teaching and learning. As we reflect on what we have learned across each of these Ready To Learn–supported initiatives, we believe the following guidelines are vital for supporting teachers in providing children with meaningful opportunities to learn with and through digital media and technology:

1) Provide sustained attention to technology integration aimed at children's use of technology to support creativity and co-construction of deep knowledge.
2) Situate multimodal resources and the underlying technology as an essential pathway for children's learning through seamless integration in preservice education and professional development activities.
3) Meet teachers where they are and make content relevant to their experiences, role as educators, and classroom contexts.

Expanding Our Work

Today, the changing landscape of teacher professional learning and credentialing creates an exciting opportunity for us to build on the work we have done under the Ready To Learn Initiative to meet the needs of twenty-first-century educators across all levels. Guided by PBS' professional learning strategy, we are continuing to build resources and supports for teachers, with a focus on those early childhood educators who serve America's youngest citizens. While our work to date has focused on educators in formal learning settings, we believe there is a tremendous need and opportunity to create professional learning experiences that meet the needs of a broader range of adults who care for young children in less formal settings (e.g. family childcare providers). Our future work will largely focus on designing professional development supports for this often overlooked audience of caregivers so that all children enter school excited about learning and equipped with the skills to thrive.

References

Barron, B., Cayton-Hodges, G., Bofferding, L., Darling-Hammond, L., & Levine, M. J. (2011). *Take a giant step: A blueprint for teaching young children in a digital age.* New York: Joan Ganz Cooney Center at Sesame Workshop.

Belland, B. R. (2008). Using the theory of habitus to move beyond the study of barriers to technology integration. *Computers and Education, 52*(2), 353–364.

Biancarosa, G. & Griffiths, G. G. (2012). Technology tools to support reading in the digital age. *The Future of Children, 22*(2), 139–160.

Chen, J.-Q. & Chang, C. (2006). Using computers in early childhood classrooms: Teachers' attitudes, skills, and practices. *Journal of Early Childhood Research, 4*(2), 169–188.

Cohen, M. & Hadley, M. (2009). *The effects of WordWorld viewing on preschool children's acquisition of pre-literacy skills and emergent literacy: A cluster-randomised control trial.* New York: The Michael Cohen Group, LLC.

Fisch, S. M. (2014). *Children's learning from educational television Sesame Street and beyond.* New York: Routledge.

Fishman, B. & Dede, C. (2016). Teaching and technology: New tools for new times. In D. Gitomer & C. Bell (Eds.), *Handbook of research on teaching* (5th ed.). Washington, DC: American Educational Research Association.

Fleer, M. (2011). Technologically constructed childhoods: Moving beyond a reproductive to a productive critical view of curriculum development. *Australasian Journal of Early Childhood, 36*(1), 16–24.

Gee, J. (2008). *Getting over the slump: Innovation strategies to promote children's learning.* New York: The Joan Ganz Cooney Center at Sesame Workshop.

Gutnick, A. L., Robb, M., Takeuchi, L., & Kotler, J. (2010). *Always connected: The new digital media habits of young children.* New York: The Joan Ganz Cooney Center at Sesame Workshop.

Harris, J., Mishra, P., & Koehler, M. (2009). Content knowledge and learning activity types: Curriculum-based technology integration reframed. *Journal of Research on Technology in Education, 41*(4), 393–416.

Hemphill, F. C., Vanneman, A., & Rahman, R. (2011). *Achievement gap: How Hispanic and white students in public schools perform in mathematics and reading on the National Assessment of Educational Progress, (NCES 2009-455).* Washington, DC: National Center for Education Statistics, Institute of Education Sciences, U.S. Department of Education.

Hurwitz, L. (2018). Getting a read on Ready To Learn media: A meta-analytic review of effects on literacy. *Child Development,* https://doi.org/10.1111/cdev.13043.

Ito, M., Gutiérrez, K., Livingstone, S., Penuel, B., Rhodes, J., Salen, K., Schor, J., Sefton-Green, J., & Watkins, S. C. (2013). *Connected learning: An agenda for research and design.* Irvine, CA: Digital Media and Learning Research Hub.

Jenkins, H., Clinton, K., Purushotma, R., Robison, A. J., & Weigel, M. (2006). *Confronting the challenges of participatory culture: Media education for the 21st century.* Cambridge, MA: MIT Press.

Kallery, M. & Psillos, D. (2001). Pre-school teachers' content knowledge in science: Their understanding of elementary science concepts and of issues raised by children's questions. *International Journal of Early Years Education, 9*(3), 165.

Kirkorian, H. L., Wartella, E. A., & Anderson, D. R. (2008). Media and young children's learning. *The Future of Children, 18*(1), 39–61.

Linebarger, D. L., Moses, A. M., & McMenamin, K. (2010). *A summative evaluation of Martha speaks: Learning outcomes. A report prepared for corporation for public broadcasting.* Philadelphia, PA: Annenberg School for Communication, University of Pennsylvania.

Linebarger, D. L. & Piotrowski, J. T. (2009). The impact of TV narratives on the early literacy skills of preschoolers. *British Journal of Developmental Psychology, 27*(1), 47–69.

McCarthy, B., Li, L., & Tiu, M. (2012). PBS KIDS mathematics transmedia suites in preschool homes. Retrieved from www-tc.pbskids.org/lab/media/pdfs/WestEd-HomeStudy-PBSKids-full.pdf

NAEYC. (2018). *NAEYC early learning program accreditation standards and assessment items.* Retrieved from www.naeyc.org/sites/default/files/globally-shared/downloads/PDFs/accreditation/early-learning/standards_and_assessment_web.pdf

NAEYC & The Fred Rogers Center. (2012). *Technology and interactive media as tools in early childhood programs serving children from birth through age 8.* Washington, DC: National Association for the Education of Young Children.

Neuman, S. B., Newman, E., & Dwyer, J. (2011). Educational effects of an embedded multimedia vocabulary intervention for economically disadvantaged pre-K children: A randomized trial. *Reading Research Quarterly, 46*(3), 249–272.

Paratore, J. R., O'Brien, L. M., Jiménez, L., Salinas, A., & Ly, C. (2016). Engaging preservice teachers in integrated study and use of educational media and technology in teaching of reading. *Teaching and Teacher Education, 59*, 247–260.

Pasnik, S. & Llorente, C. (2013). *Preschool teachers can use a PBS KIDS transmedia curriculum supplement to support young children's mathematics learning: Results of a randomized controlled trial.* New York and Menlo Park: Education Development Center & SRI International.

Pasnik, S., Penuel, W. R., Llorente, C., Strother, S., & Schindel, J. (2007). *Review of research on media and young children's literacy: Report to the Ready To Learn Initiative.* New York and Menlo Park, CA: Education Development Center, Inc., and SRI International.

Polly, D., Mims, C., Sheperd, C. E., & Inan, F. (2010). Evidence of impact: Transforming teacher education with preparing tomorrow's teachers to teach with technology (PT3) grants. *Teaching and Teacher Education, 26*(4), 863–870.

Rebora, A. (2016). Teachers still struggling to use technology to transform instruction, survey finds. *Education Week, 35*(35), 4–5.

Reich, J. (2014, December 8). MOOC completion and retention in the context of student intent. *EDUCAUSE Review.* Retrieved from https://er.educause.edu/articles/2014/12/mooc-completion-and-retention-in-the-context-of-student-intent

Schmitt, K. L., Sheridan, L., McMenamin, K., & Linebarger, D. L. (2010). *Summative evaluation of PBS KIDS Island: Usability, outcomes, and appeal.* Philadelphia, PA: University of Pennsylvania.

Shulman, L. S. (1986). Those who understand: A conception of teacher knowledge. *American Educator, 10*(1), 9–15, 43–44.

Singer, D. G. & Singer, J. L. (2011). Make-believe play, imagination, and creativity: Links to children's media exposure. In S. L. Calvert & B. J. Wilson (Eds.), *The handbook of children, media, and development* (pp. 290–308). Malden, MA: Wiley-Blackwell.

Thai, A. M., Lowenstein, D., Ching, D., & Rejeski, D. (2009). *Game changer: Investing in digital play to advance children's learning and health.* New York: Joan Ganz Cooney Center at Sesame Workshop.

Tiu, M., McCarthy, B., & Li, L. (2015). *Odd Squad: Learning math with PBS KIDS transmedia content at school and at home.* San Francisco, CA: WestEd.

Zevenbergen, R. (2007). Digital natives come to preschool: Implications for early childhood practice. *Contemporary Issues in Early Childhood, 8*(1), 19.

5

WHEN CREATIVITY + COLLABORATION = SUCCESS

The Making of *Peg + Cat*

Kim Berglund

Introduction

It was a simple idea with a really big question: What would life be like if you woke up in a math word problem? Such is a typical day for a precocious red-haired girl named Peg and her best feline friend, Cat, who encounter one problem after another in the groundbreaking, Emmy award-winning PBS KIDS series, *Peg + Cat*. Whether it's cleaning up a messy bedroom, serving a horde of ornery pirates their fair share of food, or corralling 100 curious chickens back into their coop, Peg and Cat devise a plan and solve even the thorniest of problems. Does everything always go as planned? No. Does young Peg get stuck and have a moment of panic in every episode? Yes. But with a simple countdown from five, she is able to refocus, see the problem in a new light, and get back on track. When all is done, there's nothing left to do but celebrate with the "Problem Solved" song ... until the next predicament.

Peg + Cat was developed as part of the 2010–2015 CPB-PBS Ready To Learn Initiative with funding from the U.S. Department of Education. From the moment the series premiered in 2013, it left an indelible mark on young children and their parents and caregivers. With its unique design aesthetic, including graph paper backgrounds and simple hand-drawn characters, *Peg + Cat* has a playful, child-like appeal. Beyond the look of the show is the storytelling which is infused with a preschool math curriculum that encourages children to embark on their own math discoveries. From number sense to measurement to geometry and problem-solving strategies, viewers are exposed to foundational mathematics concepts and mathematical practices in relatable and authentic ways.

Behind the series is a tireless team, led by creators Jennifer Oxley and Billy Aronson, whose creativity and passion drive every aspect of the show. But incredibly, neither of them had any experience at all with preschool math or cross-platform storytelling, also known as transmedia, the two hallmarks of the 2010–2015 Ready To Learn Initiative. How were Oxley and Aronson able to create a property that taught early mathematics clearly and comprehensively? What process did the creators employ to ensure success? The story of *Peg + Cat* is one of collaboration, an impressive example of when children's media professionals and early mathematics experts come together with the commitment to educate, captivate, and inspire young children through public media.

Looking Ahead after the 2005–2010 Grant

The origins of *Peg + Cat* actually start a year before the animated pitch was submitted to PBS. In early 2010, PBS was wrapping up the 2005–2010 grant period focusing on early literacy. As we awaited the request for proposals from the U.S. Department of Education on the next five-year grant, speculations began to surface of the new curriculum priority. As PBS's Curriculum Director at the time, I was eager to know what the next five years may look like for PBS and Ready To Learn. The national conversation about the importance of STEM was picking up steam, which led us to guess that the new priority would focus on creating high-quality science content. This notion excited my colleagues at PBS and our Ready To Learn partners at the Corporation for Public Broadcasting (CPB). *Curious George*, the beloved book property with a science and engineering focus, was a top performer among all preschool series across networks. Young viewers were becoming aspiring paleontologists watching *Dinosaur Train. The Cat in the Hat Knows a Lot About That!*, a reinvention of the Dr. Seuss brand with a life science twist, and the new Kratt Brother's creation, *WildKratts*, were newly in production. If the next Ready To Learn curriculum priority was science, we'd be ready to leverage our existing library of successful properties, while using what we learned from those series to develop new properties.

When the 2010–2015 Ready To Learn Guidelines were released in Spring 2010, we learned the priority was not science; it was early mathematics. The news put us on a new path, so we shifted our thinking as we began writing the grant proposal. While PBS's flagship property, *Sesame Street*, had been teaching audiences math basics for decades, math was not the show's sole curriculum. In PBS's 40-year history, there had only been two math-focused properties. The sketch series produced by Sesame Workshop, *Square One Television*, premiered nearly 25 years earlier and had been off the air for years. Adventure comedy *Cyberchase* produced by WNE/Thirteen was still in production but targeted an older school-aged audience. Since the launch of those shows, best practices in math teaching and learning had changed significantly. The release of Common Core State Standards for Mathematics was imminent yet not available to the public at the time of our grant writing. And then there was the public's skepticism about math. We wondered, "Would young audiences engage in a curriculum that is so often feared? How could we illustrate to children that math is not only fun but useful and, yes, cool?"

What we discovered in our early exploration and grant writing was that our perceptions about math fear were skewed, especially when it came to young children. Little kids like and do math all the time. It is woven into the fabric of their day. I saw it in my own preschool-aged son at the time and how much he engaged in math play as he built with blocks, compared the sizes of his stuffed animals, or asked for the "biggest cup of ice cream with 100 sprinkles" at Ben & Jerry's. Preschoolers are not yet tainted by the apprehensions of their parents or older siblings. However, due to a lack of resources and delayed entry into formal learning environments, children from lower socioeconomic backgrounds tend to show deficits in math knowledge, like number sense, as early as kindergarten (e.g., Duncan et al., 2007). My colleagues and I realized it was our job to foster children's enjoyment of math in their formative years, promote early math development, and perhaps even change the attitudes of fearful parents and caregivers. To accomplish all this, we would need creative producers able to develop content that delivered on this promise.

Selecting *Peg + Cat*

Once PBS and CPB received news of Ready To Learn grant funding for the 2010–2015 grant, we began our search for a preschool math series through a competitive solicitation process. In addition to our concerns about finding a property that depicted math as engaging and useful in everyday life, we wondered how narratives for math might work. In our science shows, writers constructed a story around the life cycle of a plant or created suspense about whether an animal could build a shelter before winter. Some of our literacy shows, like *Super Why!*, used actual stories and fairy tales to help teach foundational reading skills. What stories could we build around counting to 10, addition and subtraction, or measuring height? We worried whether math was too abstract to capture the attention of a young audience.

One thing I have learned over the years as an educator and content creator is to constantly put on my "kid goggles." Kid goggles allow you to see that $2-2 = 0$ is more than just an equation—it is the last two cookies in the cookie jar and your big brother just ate them, and now there is none left for you! To a preschooler, this is a palpable story and the stakes are high. When *Peg + Cat* came across our desks, it was clear that creators Jennifer Oxley and Billy Aronson each had an amazing pair of kid goggles. Word problems are, at their essence, little math stories. The pitch for *Peg + Cat* stood out because it constructed stories and context around math, lifting the veil of abstraction to reveal real-life, preschool-relatable situations.

Oxley and Aronson devised a compelling idea and a beautifully designed pitch. Oxley is a seasoned artist and animation director who earned both an Emmy and a Humanitas award for her work on Nickelodeon's *Little Bill*. She was just finishing as the creative director of *Wonder Pets*, a show known for its striking and unique visual style. Aronson, who was the head writer on *Wonder Pets*, was not only accomplished in television writing but a successful playwright who developed the original concept for the Broadway juggernaut, *Rent*. Their budding partnership was intriguing, and naturally, my colleagues and I wondered if they'd be ready for the rigors of Ready To Learn. We soon would find out in pilot production how quickly they could learn to integrate developmentally appropriate math skills into a story.

Lessons from the Pilot

The piloting process is an effective way to assess a show's creative and educational potential and gain insight into the best pedagogical approaches for the screen. Typically, an 11-minute television pilot episode is produced and tested with children in the target audience. Given the 2010–2015 Ready To Learn Television Grant Program's emphasis on developing story-driven content using multiple platforms, we decided to produce not only a television episode but three story-related digital games. This was a first for both PBS and creators Oxley and Aronson. Interactive content is often developed well after the series is in production when most of the creative elements have been settled. The experiment here was to determine whether television and interactive content could be developed in tandem and potentially result in increased child engagement and comprehension of the math concepts when later tested. The pilot process is always a learning experience, but for Oxley and Aronson, it also became a crash course in math curriculum integration in both story and games.

The story from the pilot episode, entitled "The Chicken Problem," centers on Peg and Cat having a "perfect picnic with a pig" on a farm (see Figure 5.1). Woven into the story were two math objectives. The first objective involved relative measurement, specifically matching items of various size to other items of corresponding size. In the story, Peg, Cat, and the pig, who vary in size, each have a slice of pie that's just the right size for them. However, there's one tiny plate with a tiny slice of pie, but no one to eat it. Soon Cat discovers a chicken coop filled with chicks. He opens the coop, scoops up a tiny chicken for the tiny slice of pie. The problem is solved . . . or so they think. Cat forgets to close the coop and soon, 100 chickens are running wild on the farm, which becomes the Really Big Problem of the episode (see Figure 5.2). This problem leads to the second math goal: understanding the concept of the number 100 (see Figure 5.3).

FIGURE 5.1 Screen still from "The Chicken Problem," the *Peg + Cat* pilot episode that explores relative measurement (Courtesy of *Peg + Cat* © 2013 Feline Features, LLC, All Rights Reserved. *Odd Squad* © 2014 The Fred Rogers Company, All Rights Reserved)

FIGURE 5.2 Screen still from "The Chicken Problem" of 100 chickens running wild on the farm (Courtesy of *Peg + Cat* © 2013 Feline Features, LLC, All Rights Reserved. *Odd Squad* © 2014 The Fred Rogers Company, All Rights Reserved)

FIGURE 5.3 Screen still from "The Chicken Problem" illustrating how the relative measurement goal is reinforced as characters use carts of varying sizes to carry the chickens back to the coop (Courtesy of *Peg + Cat* © 2013 Feline Features, LLC, All Rights Reserved. *Odd Squad* © 2014 The Fred Rogers Company, All Rights Reserved)

The narrative, the alluring math-inspired background designs, and the visual of 100 mischievous chickens scurrying around on screen resulted in a charming production. However, the second learning objective involving 100 was quite controversial. Given that the target audience for the show would be 3- to 5-year-olds, the pilot's math advisor at the time highly discouraged Oxley and Aronson from teaching 100. Many preschoolers have difficulty understanding how much 10 or 20 is much less a number as large as 100. Oxley and Aronson understood that math for a young audience needed to be simple and concrete, but they also believed that their show could stretch kids and captivate them with new concepts. Oxley recalls, "We knew preschool math was simple, but we thought we also could teach kids concepts that were outside of the realm of preschool." In the end, this objective remained in the story with the note to compare 100 to a number that preschoolers may already understand; in this case, the number 10. The hope was that this simple introduction to a large and possibly unfamiliar number would be enough to pique children's interest and lead to further exploration off-screen.

The focus group tests, involving 18 children and their parents, mostly from low socioeconomic backgrounds, proved that both parties—Oxley and Aronson and the math experts—were correct. Many preschoolers, especially 3- and 4-year-olds, did not have a clear concept of 100, but it didn't stop them from enthusiastically talking about it. From an engagement standpoint, the risk worked. Aronson recalls, "We saw from our testing that kids want to be fascinated by something. They don't mind things they can't completely grasp right away. Kids loved the concept of *trying* to count to 100." In fact, many of the children in testing were already proficient in counting to ten and comparing relative sizes. Another surprising finding: parents highly encouraged the series creators to tackle even more challenging content.

Overall, the response in testing to both the episode and the accompanying games was very positive and displayed potential that *Peg + Cat* could deliver on the goal of transmedia storytelling. The three online activities, all set on the farm from the episode, explored relative measurement with various farm animals, counting and adding chickens up to 10, and mathematical patterns also using the chickens (see Figure 5.4).

In testing sessions, the games seemed to increase children's understanding of and excitement about the content and characters in the show. And, very importantly, parents expressed the need for high-quality preschool math content and discussed how *Peg + Cat* could fill the gap. With those findings in mind, *Peg + Cat* was selected to break new ground not only as PBS KIDS' first preschool math series, but also the first series to be conceived as a transmedia property. No pressure!

Diving Into Production

"The Chicken Problem" pilot was a relatively lean, independent production involving a small team of artists, animators, and producers led by Oxley and

FIGURE 5.4   Game still of "Scrub-a-Dub," where players are tasked with washing dirty farm animals using relative measurement skills (Courtesy of *Peg + Cat* © 2013 Feline Features, LLC, All Rights Reserved. *Odd Squad* © 2014 The Fred Rogers Company, All Rights Reserved)

Aronson, based in Brooklyn, New York. The 11-minute story is just one of two stories that comprise a full half-hour episode to be aired on television. Producing a season order of 40 half-hour episodes—that's *80* eleven-minute stories—is a monumental leap and requires a great deal of support and infrastructure to ensure production runs smoothly. Oxley and Aronson teamed up with the Fred Rogers Company, forming a creative partnership that fell in step with Fred Roger's legacy of creating high-quality, inspiring media for children. In addition to the Brooklyn studio, the team partnered with Toronto-based 9 Story Media Group to support the massive amounts of design and animation work. Also crucial to the team was the digital producer, Dave Peth, and interactive production house, CloudKid, who led the development of the interactive games and apps. Add a crew of scriptwriters, an in-house formative researcher, the teams at PBS, CPB, and our Ready To Learn research partners at Education Development Center (EDC) and SRI, and the *Peg + Cat* effort quickly became an international endeavor of epic proportions. It was imperative that the multi-layered production process remained coordinated, structured, and efficient.

Integrating Math and Story

Early into production, Oxley and Aronson approached Francis "Skip" Fennell, Professor of Education Emeritus at McDaniel College, to serve as the education advisor for the show. Fennell was already on the Ready To Learn math advisory board and was just finishing his tenure as the President of the National Council of Teachers in Mathematics (NCTM). When becoming familiar with the property materials and pilot, Fennell was struck not only by the creative and visual execution, but also the potential to teach much more than foundational math skills, like counting and shapes. The series' overall premise of tackling real-life word problems lent itself to teaching mathematical practices that are incredibly important for learners.

Each story in *Peg + Cat* is constructed around the mathematical practices of making sense of problems, developing multiple problem-solving strategies, and reasoning. The practice of persevering in solving problems also is baked into every episode when Peg, after multiple attempts to find a solution, becomes overwhelmed by the task at hand, eventually exclaiming "I'm totally freaking out!" She is then prompted by Cat to count backward by five and collect her thoughts. It is an authentic scene that reassures viewers that frustration is a normal part of the problem-solving process. Fennell was surprised that Oxley and Aronson were unaware of the mathematical practices when they developed the original series concept, for they had intuitively incorporated creative elements that NCTM and the Common Core State Standards would consider exemplars of life-long learning behaviors.

Nevertheless, Fennell was also wary of introducing math content that wandered out of the scope of preschool, although he was open to strategies to make math both accessible and aspirational. After some consideration, the team proposed using the two 11-minute stories to scaffold the learning experience for young viewers. The math goals for the first story, or the "A story," would focus on simpler, more basic concepts often taught in preschool and Pre-K classrooms. The second or "B" story would build on the concepts from the A story and teach viewers a related but more challenging goal. For example, "The Chicken Problem" episode, with goals of counting to ten by ones and introducing the number 100, is paired with "The Space Creature Problem," where viewers gain more exposure to numeracy related to 10 and 100—this time counting to 100 by tens. Not only that, Peg and Cat use the same concrete counting manipulatives—the chickens from the farm—in both stories for continuity.

Throughout the series, Fennell reviewed a detailed outline of every episode and provided constructive feedback. His notes were constant reminders of how young minds require time and space to cognitively process information. Fennell was particularly concerned about the pacing of the narrative, which could be too quick for the audience to comprehend. Additionally, sometimes concepts were not concrete or visual enough, and the explanation jumped too quickly to the symbolic form. For example, the numeral "4" may mean nothing to a 3-year-old, therefore it is imperative to show and carefully count four objects.

Fennell was especially emphatic about the importance of the language of mathematics. Numerous research studies have shown that children's mathematical knowledge is positively impacted by the quantity of math language used in homes and school (e.g., Ginsburg, Lee, & Boyd, 2008; Klibanoff et al., 2006). Oxley and Aronson relished the idea of using rich mathematics vocabulary in every story. Words like "big," "small," "greater than," "less than," and even technical terms like "attributes," "symmetry," and "parallel" give kids the tools to articulate their mathematical thinking. In particular, the use of song brought math vocabulary to life in colorful and playful ways. It is no surprise that music played a significant role in the series, given Aronson's background in musical theater. Aside from the recurring songs that bookend each episode, an original song is featured in every story. Each song is designed to be simple enough for young viewers to understand and help reinforce the math goals and vocabulary featured in the episode. Spanning musical genres, songs about magic cylinders, ordinal numbers, and the pig's ode to triangles (three glorious sides and three amazing angles!) put a unique stamp on an already distinctive show.

In addition to the catchy songs, Oxley and Aronson devised other clever story elements to ensure the math was clear and developmentally appropriate. To solidify math concepts, Peg often uses her trusty twig that magically writes and draws on the backgrounds. Oxley and Aronson also created recurring characters that represent specific math concepts. A crew of pirates who constantly want their equal and fair share help teach early division skills. Stories highlighting Ramone, a charming principal character who loves dance and theater, often focuses on pattern. And a comic book character named the Arch Villain is often featured in episodes about shapes and other geometry concepts. Math ostensibly became a character trait. While some writers and producers' first instinct is to disguise educational concepts, Oxley and Aronson placed them front and center. Their willingness to lean into the curriculum is a powerful statement to viewers that math is fun, creative, and oftentimes, a part of who we are.

Storytelling Across Platform

For a transmedia property like *Peg + Cat*, the story doesn't end at the close of an episode. In fact, the story may not even *begin* on television. But at the beginning of the 2010–2015 grant period, everyone involved in Ready To Learn had to wrap their heads around this relatively novel concept of transmedia. Initially, Oxley and Aronson were frustrated by the notion of transmedia. Throughout their careers, they had worked on shows that had an accompanying website and likewise wrote books based on a series. They considered these to be transmedia. Once they began collaborating with teams across disciplines in the early stages of production, this newer form of transmedia clicked for them. Aronson explains, "Transmedia is a mental difference. It's the difference between house and home. They're the same thing, but home has a sort of spirit about it. And in transmedia, we all live in one home." It was that spirit of working together during the formative phase that enabled the teams to change their mindset and think holistically about production.

When considering how to expand the world to the digital screen, Oxley and Aronson worked closely with Dave Peth, their digital producer and principal architect of the property's content-rich website. The integrated production process enabled them to create continuity of story elements across the platform, sometimes leaving loose ends in the broadcast episode that could be resolved or further explored in digital. For example, in "The Space Creature Problem," where Peg and Cat have to gather the chickens and bring them back to Earth, there is a major question left unanswered: How did the chickens get there in the first place? To answer this question, Oxley, Aronson, and Peth served up a prequel to the episode with the interactive game, "Chicken Blast-off," where kids are tasked with building rocket ships out of farm junk of various shapes, thus exploring geometry and spatial sense concepts.

In addition to a consistent creative voice, the team had to consider that both linear and digital platforms have their own set of affordances and limitations. While linear television provides a contextualized introduction to specific concepts, it is a somewhat passive experience for viewers. The digital space, on the other hand, puts children in the driver's seat and brings them in on the action from the episode. Digital games also have the potential to deepen learning and engagement of the math concepts from the episode; however, translating an episode into an interactive experience requires slower pacing to make space for kids to explore and be the star in the world.

One of the strongest examples of this type of transmedia learning opportunity is in the game entitled "Peg's Pizza Place" based on the episode "The Pizza Problem" (see Figure 5.5). The episode explores fractions, specifically the relationship between halves and wholes, as Peg and Cat help make pizzas for hungry customers. The story lent itself to potential interactivity where children customize pizza orders in a digital game; however, developmentally, young children may not be ready to jump into fractions. Thus the activity begins with an exploration of whole numbers and counting, as players place the correct number of toppings on a whole pizza. The game, designed to level up or down based on the player's performance, increases in difficulty, moving on to counting larger numbers of toppings, then customizing orders for two halves of a pizza, and finally exploring the relationship between quarters and halves (see Figure 5.6). The game extends Peg's world, giving children opportunities to delve deeper into the numeracy concepts introduced in the story.

In addition to content for the screen, *Peg + Cat* offers offline, hands-on activities that allow children and their caregivers to make tangible mathematic connections in their real lives. For example, because the characters are designed from simple geometric shapes, children are able to easily construct their own Peg, Cat, and Ramone puppets out of construction paper and popsicle sticks. Similarly, through familiar activities, like playing card games and following recipes, children and their caregivers begin to recognize how math is woven

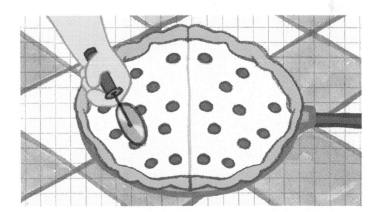

FIGURE 5.5 Screen still from the episode, "The Pizza Problem," where Peg and Cat learn that two halves make one whole (Courtesy of *Peg + Cat* © 2013 Feline Features, LLC, All Rights Reserved. *Odd Squad* © 2014 The Fred Rogers Company, All Rights Reserved)

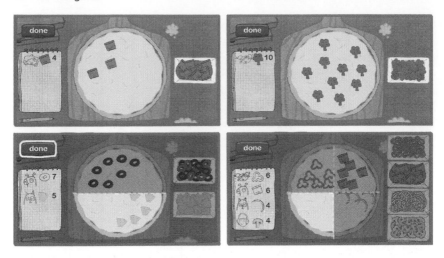

FIGURE 5.6 Game image from "Peg's Pizza Place," designed to get young players practicing counting, one-to-one correspondence and fractions (Courtesy of *Peg + Cat* © 2013 Feline Features, LLC, All Rights Reserved. *Odd Squad* © 2014 The Fred Rogers Company, All Rights Reserved)

into their daily pursuits. This content, along with coloring pages with built-in math activities, DIY animation flipbooks, and board games, provides an immersive experience for kids and allows them a multitude of opportunities to "play the show" when they are not in front of the screen. Eventually, all of the multiplatform content—clips from the television show, the interactive games, and hands-on activities—were curated into "Adventures," where children playfully explore specific early math concepts in a guided experience.

Staying Informed about the Target Audience

Through *Peg + Cat*, Oxley and Aronson set out to redefine math learning and convey to young audiences that *everyone* is a mathematician. Both creators wanted the main character to be female to break the stereotype that girls do not typically excel in math. They also were deeply passionate about creating an ethnically and culturally diverse world where children could see versions of themselves on screen. Throughout the series, Oxley and Aronson employed a diverse staff of writers and voice actors who brought their own experiences to stories. And very importantly, as a Ready To Learn property, the content needed to support math development of children from underserved communities who were most in need of learning resources.

Even with a seasoned crew with the best intentions, it was virtually impossible to know if the content would resonate with the target audience without testing. The production team conducted formative research with children from lower-income backgrounds throughout the run of the series. Many episodes were assessed through either storybook testing, a read-aloud of the script accompanied by still images or animatic testing, a viewing of very rough animation. Led by the veteran researcher, Beth Richman, testing not only evaluated engagement and comprehension but it was the first instance to obtain feedback on math-related visuals. Three-dimensional shapes, for instance, proved to be a particularly thorny issue, given the show's simple, flat design aesthetic. Oxley and the design crew used children's feedback and prior knowledge of real objects to creatively present shapes. Thus, spheres that initially looked like circles to children were effectively redesigned into beach balls.

The PBS KIDS Digital team likewise managed the playtesting of all *Peg + Cat's* interactive games. Like story testing, early indicators of engagement and understanding of the math concepts were critically important, but there also was the added cognitive challenge of the gameplay mechanics. If children have difficulty clicking and dragging objects to count or a character is zooming around too quickly for a player to tap the screen, it could potentially become a distraction to the learning experience. Each game was not only tested for usability and gameplay mechanics but also to ensure that the content resonated with all children, regardless of their background. To this end, formative evaluators noted whether children were familiar with the creative themes that contextualized the games and whether those themes were culturally appropriate. For example, while testing a game that included elements from a circus, evaluators realized that many children had never attended a circus, so they paid particular attention to whether their unfamiliarity interfered with gameplay and math learning. Additionally, the producers used testing data and recommendations to adjust verbal instructions, math vocabulary, and visual cues throughout the game to ensure that children, especially English Language Learners, were supported. Together, the constant vetting and the iterative development process allowed Oxley, Aronson, and the entire production team to remain close to Ready To Learn's target audience and ensure an optimized learning experience for all.

Adding It All Up

It is astounding to think that a series pitch with a simple premise about a girl and her cat would turn into the multimedia force that it is today. Since its premiere, children have helped Peg clean up her room by sorting, searched for buried treasure using maps and measurement, played marbles among the pyramids with Cleopatra, and even eaten bratwursts with Beethoven in 18th-century Vienna. They have explored the connection between math and music theory in the Big Gig app and played interactive games to earn special rocks for a collection that would make Peg, an avid rock enthusiast, proud. The vast assortment of transmedia math content created a home that allowed children to fully immerse themselves in the expansive *Peg + Cat* world through story and become an indispensable member in that world through digital games. Even better, children can apply their newfound knowledge in the real world through hands-on activities and crafts.

At the beginning of the 2010–2015 Ready To Learn grant cycle, there were so many unknowns and questions, but the grand experiment to produce a transmedia property that supported young children's math learning through Ready To Learn worked (See Chapter 6 for a description of the *Peg + Math* studies conducted by EDC and SRI). Oxley and Aronson not only climbed a steep learning curve but embraced and celebrated early mathematics in all of their creations. Their collaboration with teams across departments and disciplines was not just successful but enhanced the production process. Plus, the positive reception from the audience proves that math could indeed be engaging, worthwhile, and yes, cool. When you see a little girl dressed up as Peg for Halloween, or a child holding a DIY version of Peg's twig, or students in Head Start classrooms singing loudly and proudly about magic cylinders, and parents overjoyed that their children are discovering math in all of the little things in everyday life . . . well, it doesn't get much cooler than that.

References

Duncan, G. J., Dowsett, C. J., Claessens, A., Magnuson, K., Huston, A. C., Klebanov, P., Pagani, L. S., Feinstein, L., Engel, M., Brooks-Gunn, J., Sexton, H., Duckworth, K., & Japel, C. (2007). School readiness and later achievement. *Developmental Psychology, 43* (6), 1428–1446.

Ginsburg, H. P., Lee, J. S., & Boyd, J. S. (2008). Mathematics education for young children: What it is and how to promote it. *Society for Research in Child Development Social Policy Report – Giving Child and Youth Development Knowledge Away, 22*(1), 1–24.

Klibanoff, R. S., Levine, S. C., Huttenlocher, J., Vasilyeva, M., & Hedges, L. V. (2006). Preschool children's mathematical knowledge: The effect of teacher "math talk." *Developmental Psychology, 42*(1), 59–69.

6

CHILDREN'S MATHEMATICAL THINKING AND LEARNING

The Importance of Study Design and Aligned Assessments in Promoting and Capturing Learning

Deborah Rosenfeld and Daisy Rutstein

Introduction

As our understanding of early childhood mathematics has expanded, so too have our efforts to promote and assess it. Researchers, teachers, and media developers no longer focus exclusively on counting and shapes but recognize the importance of patterns, spatial relationships, subitizing, and other foundational skills. We have come to see how these ideas develop and build upon each other along a learning trajectory. As a result, the scope, dosage, expectations, and approaches to early childhood mathematics teaching and learning have been transformed for the better.

The Ready To Learn Television Grant Program has capitalized on these advances to inform the development and use of digital resources targeting early math concepts. In our research studies, the goal is to curate from available Ready To Learn media to address developmentally appropriate topics with proper dosage and frequency. We sequence the resources according to a meaningful trajectory and mediate a child's learning from the media-rich resources by engaging teachers, families, and peers as co-viewers and co-players, which in turn support pedagogically sound practices of learning with, and from, media.

In this chapter, we discuss the scope of early childhood mathematics and how Ready To Learn resources are supporting the learning of these skills and concepts. We look at two studies that focused on early mathematics yet had dramatically different approaches. In one, a structured curriculum supplement was implemented by teachers in classrooms with the individualized support of coaches. In the other, families engaged with Ready To Learn resources at home, and support was provided through tip sheets, videos, and text messages aimed at a general audience. These studies highlight Ready To Learn's unique strategies for supporting early math learning through digital resources in various settings and contexts, and in ways that reach even the most vulnerable populations who are the principal targets of Ready To Learn's efforts. We will discuss the learning that resulted from the use of these resources and examine our approach to developing reliable and valid instruments to supplement existing, but imperfectly aligned, assessments.

Early Childhood Mathematics

Early childhood mathematics has received significant attention due to an expanding body of research showing that it strongly affects and predicts future school success (Duncan et al., 2007; National Mathematics Advisory Panel, 2008). This research also confirms that young children enjoy mathematics (Ginsburg, Greenes, & Balfanz, 2006; Ramani & Siegler, 2014) and easily relate it to their everyday lives and free play (Ginsburg, 2006; Seo & Ginsburg, 2004). However, research also tells us that these spontaneous mathematical interactions influence learning more when they are formalized and connected to mathematics concepts by a supportive adult (Ginsburg, 2006). Unfortunately, many low-income children do not experience deep mathematical learning in either preschools or family environments (National Research Council, Committee on Early Childhood Mathematics, 2009), and therefore tend to fall behind their middle-class peers on measures of early mathematical knowledge (National Mathematics Advisory Panel, 2008; Ramani & Siegler, 2014). Fortunately, research has shown that early, developmentally appropriate instruction can engage children in rich mathematics activities and foster math knowledge, particularly for those most at risk for falling behind (Casey et al., 2008; Ginsburg, Lee, & Boyd, 2008; Wolfgang, Stannard, & Jones, 2001).

Many preschools, especially those serving children from low-income families, do not always have comprehensive or coherent approaches to teaching mathematics, and instead mention math in ad hoc or cursory ways within other activities they are already doing (Early et al., 2010; National Research Council, Committee on Early Childhood Mathematics, 2009). Even when a complete math curriculum is used, most focus only on a limited set of math concepts, typically numbers and geometry (Clements & Sarama, 2014). But children's early math explorations include patterns, measurement, investigations of spatial relationships, and even data analysis, and there has recently been national recognition of the need for math teaching to go beyond the limited domains of numbers and shapes (National Governors Association Center for Best Practices & Council of Chief State School Officers, 2010). Fortunately, Clements and Sarama (2014) have done a tremendous job of conducting and consolidating a multitude of early childhood mathematics research to describe learning trajectories for each of these mathematical ideas, all of which begin with the youngest preschoolers, which makes the task of effectively incorporating these topics into instruction and informal early mathematical experiences more feasible.

Learning trajectories are developmental progressions of a concept that describe discrete aspects of the content and how it develops over time. Learning trajectories also include sequences of activities that curriculum research has revealed to be effective in guiding children through these levels of thinking on the way to a learning goal. When learning trajectories form the basis of mathematics instruction, children have a more comprehensive and successful early math experience. Furthermore, an awareness of learning trajectories by a supportive adult allows for more effective instruction, including guided questioning, response, and the provision of activities that further children's learning (Clements & Sarama, 2014). In this way, well-specified learning trajectories for mathematics have led to advances in the scope, dosage, expectations, and approaches to early childhood math education.

Ready To Learn's Resources and Approach

The goal of the U.S. Department of Education's Ready To Learn Television Grant Program is to develop engaging, high-quality educational programming and supports to young children, especially those from low-income households. In 2010, the Corporation for Public Broadcasting and the Public Broadcasting System (PBS) received a five-year grant to develop and distribute television and digital assets focusing on early math learning. The Education Development Center (EDC) and SRI Education (SRI) served as research partners.

Given the scope of early childhood mathematics, and Ready To Learn's mission to reach high-need families, Ready To Learn's resources span the range of early math topics and do so through media that is easily accessed and free. The first PBS KIDS program that was specifically designed to target early mathematics is *Peg + Cat*, an animated series for preschoolers (see Chapter 5 for a description of how *Peg + Cat* was developed). This show features television episodes and digital games that focus on counting, ordinal numbers, addition and subtraction, equal sharing, sorting, patterns, two-dimensional and three-dimensional shapes, spatial relationships, and measurable attributes. But even before this program premiered, other PBS KIDS series included math learning. For example, *The Cat in the Hat Knows a Lot About That!, Sid the Science Kid, Dinosaur Train*, and *Curious George* all included mathematical ideas as content, and it was from these programs that we originally studied math learning from Ready To Learn media.

In evaluating these media resources, the research team sought to uncover best practices regarding their use for learning (McManis & Gunnewig, 2012). We focused on the body of research addressing scope, dosage, expectations, and pedagogy, and how best to organize and present the media so that they were most likely to promote learning, particularly for the most vulnerable populations. This involved mediating the video viewing and game playing experiences. Mediation includes the people, materials, and technologies that support children in making sense of, and extending, an educational experience. It typically involves scaffolding learning by selecting developmentally appropriate and research-based concepts and activities; curating media and materials with specific learning goals in mind; sequencing media and materials into a learning progression; helping children to demonstrate their understanding and to connect prior and current knowledge; and supporting individual and joint engagement of children, peers, teachers, and parents with the learning materials. For our study purposes, this means that resources are first carefully reviewed and selected based on their developmental appropriateness to our target audience, as well as what content is covered, to what extent, and in what manner. These media-rich assets are then sequenced along a learning trajectory and organized so that new concepts or skills are introduced during the first experience, with later exposures offering further practice opportunities. Similarly, digital resources are supported through links with hands-on activities both within and across content areas, as well as to other activities that connect to children's lives. Researcher teams fielding these studies also support teachers and parents and encourage them to jointly engage with their children and the content through sharing, collaboration, and discussion.

In the description of the two studies that follow, we elaborate on these principles to demonstrate how the studies were designed and what children learned about mathematics from engagement with Ready To Learn resources. We also discuss how teachers and parents were supported in promoting learning through media.

PBS KIDS Transmedia Math Study

The first study we describe is called the PBS KIDS Transmedia Math Study (Pasnik & Llorente, 2013). This randomized controlled trial with three conditions explored how technology and educational transmedia resources can enhance math teaching and learning in preschools, especially those serving children who may be at risk for academic difficulties due to economic and social disparities. The study's goal was to understand how the intentional integration of video, computer games, and hands-on activities affects children's mathematics learning. The study also examined whether the experience enhanced teachers' beliefs about their own understanding of math, and consequently their math instruction—changes that would enable the effects to transcend the study period. Study findings confirmed that the thoughtful integration of technology and media, combined with the proper supports for teachers, did indeed positively affect children's math learning and teachers' math instruction.

The study's three conditions were (1) PBS KIDS Transmedia Math Supplement, (2) Technology & Media, and (3) Business as Usual (BAU). In the first condition, teachers received digital tools including an Interactive Whiteboard (IWB) and tablet computers, instructional support through initial training and ongoing coaching, and a structured 10-week curriculum supplement that supported teachers in integrating technology and media into regular classroom instruction and routines. The Technology & Media condition provided teachers with the same digital tools and instructional support, but did not provide them with the structured curriculum guide, and instead pointed teachers to several useful digital resources they could explore and select on their own. The final condition asked teachers to continue with their typical instruction and did not provide any digital tools, instructional support, or curriculum supplement. Table 6.1 summarizes the three conditions.

The PBS KIDS Transmedia Math Supplement (the Supplement) was the centerpiece of the mediation strategy employed in this study (see Figure 6.1); it primarily utilized PBS KIDS videos and online interactive games, but also included non-digital materials, like books and foam shapes. The Supplement was designed to be integrated into existing instructional routines such as circle time and free play centers. The target math skills included counting, subitizing, and recognizing numerals; recognizing, composing, and representing shapes; and patterns. The Supplement was developed by drawing on existing research of early childhood math instruction and learning trajectories (Clements & Sarama, 2014; Ginsburg, Greenes, & Balfanz, 2003), as well as our team's understanding of typical early childhood math instruction from the 2011 Context Study (EDC & SRI, 2011) and 2012 Prekindergarten Transmedia Math Pilot Study (EDC & SRI, 2012). Furthermore, it used existing research on successful technology integration in early childhood classrooms (McManis & Gunnewig, 2012). Thus,

TABLE 6.1 Descriptions of conditions in the PBS KIDS Transmedia Math Study

Condition	PBS KIDS Transmedia Math Supplement	Technology & Media	Business as Usual
MathInstruction	10-week PBS KIDS Math Supplement, integrating digital and hands-on materials	Math as usual	Math as usual
Technology	IWB, laptops, Internet access, tech support	IWB, laptops, Internet access, tech support	Technologyas usual
Media	Curated PBS KIDS videos and games	Teacher-selected	N/A
Professional Development	Math Supplement and technology training and coaching	Math and technology training and coaching	Post hoc PD

Easy Game Play

Fair Shares (Curious George)

George is training dogs. Help him share the dog treats fairly. Sometimes there are two dogs and two treats, other times there are two dogs and four treats. While sharing treats, the children will review how to recognize the amount of treats without having to count them (subitizing) and counting from 1 to 12.

Overview

During **Small Group Time**, demonstrate how to play *Fair Shares* on the **Interactive Whiteboard** (IWB). Use game play as an opportunity to practice **counting** and **one-to-one correspondence** as well as **subitizing** as you call on individual children to try out the game on the IWB. Remind children of **basic game play rules**.

Skills and other important points to cover

- Review counting from 1 to 12
- Review one-to-one correspondence and cardinality from 1 to 12
- Review subitizing from 1 to 10

What you will need

- Interactive Whiteboard (IWB)
- Curious George: *Fair Shares*

FIGURE 6.1 Sample page of the PBS KIDS Math Supplement (From *Curious George* by H.A. Rey. Copyright © 1941, renewed 1969 by Margaret E. Rey and H.A. Rey. Curious George®, including without limitation the character's name and the character's likenesses, are registered trademarks of Houghton Mifflin Harcourt Publishing Company. Reprinted by permission. All rights reserved.; Education Development Center; and SRI International)

enacting the Supplement enabled the teaching of the breadth of early mathematics concepts in a systematic sequence and necessitated joint engagement with the materials between peers, and between teachers and students. Additionally, it allowed for the connection between learning in digital and real-world spaces as part of familiar classroom activities.

The study took place in early childhood education centers primarily serving children from low-income households in New York City and San Francisco. The final sample consisted of 966 children in 85 classrooms (40 in New York City and 45 in San Francisco). While all children in participating classrooms were invited to engage in study activities, researchers randomly selected approximately ten children from each classroom to participate in assessments. A sample of 157 teachers, which included lead teachers, teacher assistants, and aides, comprised an ethnically diverse group. There were no significant differences between the teachers in the three conditions.

Child math outcomes were measured using a Supplement-Based Assessment (SBA) and the Research-Based Early Mathematics Assessment (REMA Short Form, Weiland et al., 2012). (See Table 6.2 for more information on the assessments.) As measured by the SBA, children in the PBS KIDS Transmedia Math Supplement condition learned significantly more mathematics than did children in both the Technology & Media (1.43 points, effect size of 0.22, $p < 0.001$) and BAU (1.51 points, effect size of 0.24, $p < 0.001$) conditions. This means that being in the Math Supplement condition would lead to a 9% increase in percentile rank for an average student in the Technology & Media group and a comparable increase for an average student in the BAU condition. A marginally significant effect was detected in REMA data. Children in the Math Supplement condition exhibited higher REMA scores than did children in the Technology & Media condition (1.09 points, effect size of 0.15 and $p < 0.06$) and in the BAU condition (1.09 points, effect size of 0.15 and $p < 0.07$).

Teacher outcomes were measured through pre- and post-teacher surveys focused on attitudes and beliefs toward teaching preschool mathematics and using technology for instruction with young children. A range of implementation data was collected to evaluate how the Supplement and technology were used in classrooms. Implementation data were gathered through classroom observations, teacher logs, and through coach logs in classrooms where instructional support was provided.

Preschool teachers generally enacted the Supplement with fidelity, and these teachers reported significant changes in their confidence and comfort with both early math concepts and teaching with technology. PBS KIDS Transmedia Math Supplement teachers' beliefs about their own mathematics knowledge and the benefits of technology experiences for preschoolers improved after the study. There was a significantly greater increase in the proportion of teachers who reported teaching shapes, numeracy, and patterns in the PBS KIDS Transmedia Math Supplement condition compared to teachers in the

TABLE 6.2 Summary of the PBS KIDS Transmedia Math Supplement impact estimates

Impact Contrast	Coefficient	Std. Error	Hedge's g (Effect size)	p	Multiple Comparison Test
SBA					
(1) PBS KIDS Transmedia Math Supplement vs. Business as Usual	1.51	0.302	0.24	<0.001	significant
(2) Technology & Media vs. Business as Usual	0.08	0.309	0.01	0.789	—
(3) PBS KIDS Transmedia Math Supplement vs. Technology & Media	1.43	0.288	0.22	<0.001	significant
REMA					
(1) PBS KIDS Transmedia Math Supplement vs. Business as Usual	1.09	0.589	0.15	0.064	—
(2) Technology & Media vs. Business as Usual	0	0.587	0	0.996	—
(3) PBS KIDS Transmedia Math Supplement vs. Technology & Media	1.09	0.571	0.15	0.056	—

Source: Courtesy of Education Development Center.

Technology & Media condition. For more details on the teacher outcomes, see Pasnik and Llorente (2013).

These positive findings—children learning significantly more math and teachers expressing greater comfort with technology and confidence in their math teaching as a result of implementing the Supplement—support the notion that the intentional and careful integration of well-designed digital resources, coupled with adequate teacher supports, can positively influence child and teacher outcomes. The sharp, cohesive curricular focus of the Supplement stands in contrast to a common approach to technology integration, which tends to leave teachers to select resources piecemeal and on their own, without regard to the scope of math skills to be covered, the developmental progression of these concepts, or the dosage needed to promote learning in the target population. Further, this study found that there were no learning gains for children in the Technology & Media condition, and that teachers in this condition reported spending less time on math instruction than teachers in the BAU condition, suggesting that the difficult work of thoughtfully integrating media and technology actually interrupted or interfered with typical instructional routines. Conversely, when teachers are prepared with the content and pedagogical resources needed to mediate children's learning with technology, children are able to make use of the learning opportunities available through engagement with digital media. Finally, the strength of the study's results suggested that transmedia's potential to advance subject-area learning for young children may be the most valuable for those children who are most in need of academic support.

Peg + Cat Home Study

In contrast to the previous study of transmedia use in preschool settings, the next study we describe examined how time spent with similar educational, noncommercial media could benefit young children's mathematics learning at home. It again focused on children from low-income communities who typically have less access and exposure to math-oriented school-readiness skills. The study addressed the central role parents and caregivers play in children's learning lives, their perceptions of transmedia use, and the contexts and ways that families jointly engage with transmedia. Study findings revealed that just as when teachers are supported with the content knowledge and pedagogical experience to mediate children's learning with technology, parents similarly foster children's engagement and learning when exposed to well-designed transmedia resources and helpful information and supports.

The study employed a randomized controlled trial with a two-condition design. Families were randomly assigned to the (1) PBS KIDS treatment group or the (2) Business as Usual comparison group. Families in the treatment group were asked to participate in a 12-week intervention and were provided with a tablet and laptop, a curated set of digital experiences, and supports for joint engagements with media. BAU families were asked to continue their typical home behaviors related to children's technology and media use.

The intervention provided children with repeated opportunities to engage with a set of early math learning experiences comprised of public digital media, and for parents and caregivers to engage with their children before, during, and after experiences with the study resources. The study website provided access to the resources and was organized to guide children and families through weekly, curated learning experiences (see Figure 6.2). Content was presented in a spiraling format where children first explored new math content and skills and returned to it for repeated practice, thereby presenting learning opportunities that built on past successes and provided new challenges. Each week involved approximately 30 minutes of content comprised of videos, games, apps, and non-digital activities organized into an "adventure" (see Figure 6.3). Thirty additional minutes of digital activities enabled families to voluntarily go beyond the weekly materials.

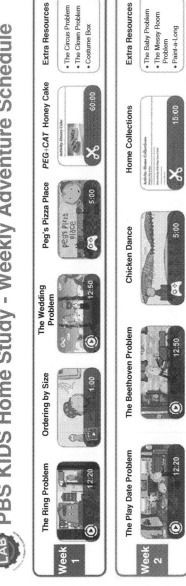

FIGURE 6.2 Sample Weekly Schedule from the study website (Courtesy of Education Development Center; SRI International; and Excerpts from *Peg + Cat* and *Odd Squad* provided courtesy of The Fred Rogers Company)

Full Video: The Play Date Problem

FIGURE 6.3 Screenshot of Week 2's videos and activities (Courtesy of Education Development Center; SRI International; and Excerpts from *Peg + Cat* and *Odd Squad* provided courtesy of The Fred Rogers Company)

As part of the study design process, the research team engaged in a formal review process in which each potential *Peg + Cat* game was played, and each video viewed by several members of the team who then rated them on the quality and quantity of the math content, and the manner in which it was addressed. The resulting intervention resources focused on patterns, geometry (2-D and 3-D shapes, spatial relationships), measurable attributes, ordinal numbers, and the foundational skill of counting. Media assets also focused on approaches to learning skills such as flexible problem-solving, persistence, and productive collaboration. The research team then sequenced the content along a coherent trajectory so that the content built in difficulty and provided repeated exposures for practice opportunities. This process is not very different from what a teacher might do when planning a curriculum unit, but it is time-consuming and requires significant knowledge of the available digital resources as well as how to integrate those resources into instruction in pedagogically effective ways. This is clearly not a realistic expectation of a parent or caregiver and is, therefore, a key piece to our embedded mediation strategy.

Support materials for parents and caregivers provided ongoing guidance for engaging with study experiences. Tip videos focused on co-viewing media with children, supporting their use of math talk, and supporting problem-solving and persistence skills. A printed Experience Guide helped parents navigate the 12-week study experience, and weekly text messages encouraged caregivers to engage with their children in the study experience. Along with the curating and sequencing of the digital content of the study, these supports provided mediation at scale for families in their own homes.

Researchers recruited families from preschools in New York City and San Francisco. Approximately 200 children participated, and families were predominantly Latino, Asian American, and African American. The majority (53%) spoke more than one language at home, and more than half (52%) of families reported an annual household income of less than $25,000.

To assess children's mathematics outcomes, researchers administered a set of items aligned to the skills addressed in the study, but not aligned with the resources themselves. (See below for more information on the assessment.) Before and after the study, parents completed surveys focused on home media and technology use, their informal strategies to support early mathematics learning, and children's problem-solving and persistence behaviors at home. Parents completed weekly media diaries to document media use and interactions.

Researchers visited a subset of families in their homes on two occasions to directly observe when, and for what purposes, children and families accessed media content, the social arrangements in which media are used, and any obstacles or supports encountered during media use. A different subset of caregivers participated in focus groups to share opinions about media's role to support learning, beliefs about supporting learning through media, information on how they jointly engage with media, and opinions of study resources.

As a result of participating in the intervention, children in the treatment group exhibited statistically significant improvements in their understanding of ordinal numbers, spatial relationships, and 3-D shapes compared to children in the BAU condition (see Table 6.3). Parents and caregivers in the treatment condition reported a significantly higher frequency of joint parent-child technology use, more joint gameplay, and more conversation connecting digital media and daily life than did BAU parents and caregivers. They also reported significant increases in their confidence to support their children's math learning, as compared to BAU parents, as well as in their agreement that technology and media are tools for math learning. Furthermore, a higher proportion of intervention parents reported engaging in problem-solving strategies with their children at the close of the study than did BAU parents.

TABLE 6.3 Summary of the *Peg + Cat* findings of the impacts

Impact Contrast	N	Coefficient	Hedge's g (Effect size)	Std. Error	p
Factor 1: Ordinal Numbers, Spatial Relationships, and 3-D shapes	172	5.26	0.51	1.12	0.000
Factor 2: Measurable Attributes and Pattern Creation	180	-1.02	-0.10	1.06	0.336
Factor 3: Counting, 2-D Shapes, and Pattern Continuation	182	-0.40	-0.038	1.00	0.689

Source: Courtesy of Education Development Center.

Finally, patterns of family engagement with the resources indicated that study resources were frequently accessed throughout the 12-week study period and treatment children were typically exposed to all target mathematical skills. However, the majority of families diverged from the suggested sequence, and overall use of the resources steadily declined during the study. Since the sequence was a major component of the mediation strategy, by allowing skills to build over time and be practiced with appropriate frequency, this may have been responsible for the lack of change in some of the math skills assessed. Still, treatment families reported finding the majority of study resources fun and engaging. Some parents expressed appreciation that the resources provided opportunities to practice math skills, while others found the games and videos complemented each other, thus making the content more meaningful.

Assessment

Assessments that capture the changes in children's learning that occur as a result of the use of Ready To Learn resources are critical for showcasing the media's effects. In the area of early mathematics, this can be a particular challenge. First, preschoolers are just beginning to develop the cognitive endurance, attention span, and physical and linguistic skills that enable participation in focused conversations about what they know (Shepard, 1994). Similarly, items that require children to read and write independently are not viable for young students. Even questions requiring verbal responses can be difficult for preschoolers, and differences in children's facility with language may be misinterpreted as differences in knowledge (Hobbs, Williams, & Sherwood, 2012).

Second, there are only a few standardized mathematics assessments designed for preschoolers. For the PBS KIDS Transmedia Math Study, the Research-Based Early Mathematics Assessment (REMA Short Form) (Weiland et al.,

2012) served as a valid and reliable standardized assessment of children's math skills. The 19 items in the REMA short version assess math skills considered essential in preschool and kindergarten—recognition of number and subitizing, shape composition, and patterning (Clements & Sarama, 2014; National Governors Association Center for Best Practices & Council of Chief State School Officers, 2010; Weiland et al., 2012). Each item includes a game-like activity where the assessor reads a verbal prompt and, at times, demonstrates with manipulatives. Children provide a verbal response, point, or engage with manipulatives. Still, despite its validation, scope of math topics, and developmentally appropriate manner of engaging children, the REMA Short Form is designed to assess general math ability and does not allow for assessing only the targeted subskills within the intervention resources. Furthermore, it is intended to measure the change in general math ability following a year of instruction rather than a shorter and supplemental intervention.

When evaluating students' learning, it is important to align the instructional goals, the curricular materials, and the assessments (National Research Council, Committee on the Foundations of Assessment, 2001) to ensure the assessment is measuring knowledge, skills, and abilities that are supported by the curricular materials and the instructional practices. Since the REMA was not completely aligned with the instructional goals or timeline of the intervention, we were concerned that it might not pick up on intervention-specific changes in students' knowledge. Therefore, an additional assessment, the Supplement-Based Assessment (SBA) was developed to align specifically with the instructional goals of the Ready To Learn properties and their associated curricular materials. For the same reasons, the *Peg + Cat* Home Study also used a researcher-developed assessment to measure children's understanding of the math concepts within the resources.

The development of these assessments followed an Evidence-Centered Design (ECD) approach. ECD is a process by which the connections between the skills and understandings that are measured, the evidence needed to demonstrate that understanding, and the tasks used to elicit the evidence are clearly laid out during the development process (Mislevy & Riconscente, 2006). Using a principled approach to assessment development such as ECD helps to ensure that the assessment is targeted at the desired knowledge and skills while minimizing construct-irrelevant variance. This process provides evidence to support the validation of the assessment for its specified purpose (Mislevy, 2007; Mislevy & Haertel, 2006).

The research team began the ECD process by determining the focal knowledge, skills, and abilities (FKSAs) the assessment should target. The video and digital resources, curricular materials, and activities were all reviewed, and the goals of each activity were listed. The *Peg + Cat* review also included a rating of how present the FKSAs were within a resource. The results were used to develop sample items that were piloted and refined. The SBA included items on counting, number recognition and subitizing, shapes, and patterns. The *Peg + Cat* assessment included items on patterns, 2-D and 3-D shapes, ordinal numbers, measurable attributes, spatial relationships, and counting. Both assessments involved game-like activities where assessors read a verbal prompt and children provided a verbal response, pointed, or engaged with manipulatives. For example, in the *Peg + Cat* assessment, the child is presented with a picture of some children at a birthday party, standing beside a table with wrapped presents, cake, juice, and a soccer ball. The child is asked to point to the object that looks like a sphere. (The entire instruments can be found at http://cct.edc.org/rtl/data-collection-tools.) Special attention was given to the language within the prompts to ensure each item contained visual stimuli to orient children to the task and to keep them engaged. Finally, it is important to note that, while the goals of the assessment and the resources overlapped, the assessment was intentionally designed to not be overly aligned with the materials. This minimizes any advantage a student may have from interacting with the target resources in the studies. (For a fuller description of these measures, see Pasnik & Llorente, 2013; Pasnik et al., 2015.)

Conclusion

The National Association for the Education of Young Children (NAEYC) and the National Council of Teachers of Mathematics (NCTM) have drawn attention to the need for challenging and effective early childhood math programs (National Association for the Education of Young Children & National Council of Teachers of Mathematics, 2010). Yet most preschool teachers are not trained in early math content, the development of young children's acquisition of math skills, or teaching strategies to promote math learning (Ginsburg, Lee, & Boyd, 2008), nor do they have access to high-quality, comprehensive curricular content (Clements & Sarama, 2014). At the same time, young children spend more time than any other groups viewing and playing with educational and noncommercial programming (Rideout, 2013), and children with less educated parents spend more time with television and other media than do their peers whose parents attained higher levels of education (Putnam, 2015). Thus, Ready To Learn has tried to reach the most vulnerable children with mediated digital resources for their teachers and families to promote early math learning in the settings where they are most likely to access them. As a result, these children have learned significantly more mathematics, and their teachers and parents feel more confident in supporting this learning in the future.

Critical to this effort has been the development of assessments that are valid and able to capture the learning from the actual Ready To Learn resources in the communities that Ready To Learn targets. This has involved attention to the length, language, and format of the assessment items, as well as the specific content targeted. Furthermore, the development of aligned assessments has helped to document specific changes that typically occur in the shorter time frame of a study as opposed to a general measure that is meant to measure change over a longer period. Finally, the use of ECD to develop these assessments provides an example and tool for the research community, allowing for future research into how and what young children learn about mathematics from digital resources.

References

Casey, B. M., Andrews, N., Schindler, H., Kersh, J. E., Samper, A., & Copley, J. (2008). The development of spatial skills through interventions involving block building activities. *Cognition and Instruction, 26*(3), 269–309.

Clements, D. H. & Sarama, J. H. (2014). *Learning and teaching early math: The learning trajectories approach* (2nd ed.). New York, NY: Routledge.

Duncan, G. J., Dowsett, C. J., Claessens, A., Magnuson, K., Huston, A. C., Klebanov, P., Pagani, L. S., Feinstein, L., Engel, M., Brooks-Gunn, J., Sexton, H., Duckworth, K., & Japel, C. (2007). School readiness and later achievement. *Developmental Psychology, 43*(6), 1428–1446.

Early, D., Iruka, I., Ritchie, S., Barbarin, O., Winn, D-M., Crawford, G., Frome, P. M., Clifford, R. M., Burchinal, M., Howes, C., Bryant, D. M., & Pianta, R. C. (2010). How do pre-kindergarteners spend their time? Gender, ethnicity, and income as predictors of experiences in pre-kindergarten classrooms. *Early Childhood Research Quarterly, 25*(2), 177–193.

EDC & SRI. (2011). *Year one context studies. A report to the Ready To Learn Initiative.* Waltham, MA and Menlo Park, CA: Education Development Center & SRI International.

EDC & SRI. (2012). *2012 Preschool pilot study of PBS KIDS transmedia mathematics content. A report to the CPB-PBS Ready To Learn Initiative.* Waltham, MA and Menlo Park, CA: Education Development Center & SRI International.

Ginsburg, H. P. (2006). Mathematical play and playful mathematics: A guide for early education. In D. Singer, R. M. Golinkoff, & K. Hirsh-Pasek (Eds.), *Play = learning: How play motivates and enhances children's cognitive and social-emotional growth* (pp. 145–165). New York, NY: Oxford University Press.

Ginsburg, H. P., Cannon, J., Eisenband, J. G., & Pappas, S. (2006). Mathematical thinking and learning. In K. McCartney & D. Phillips (Eds.), *Handbook of early child development* (pp. 208–229). Oxford, UK: Blackwell.

Ginsburg, H. P., Greenes, C., & Balfanz, R. (2003). *Big math for little kids: Pre-kindergarten.* Parsippany, NJ: Dale Seymour Publications, Pearson Learning Group.

Ginsburg, H. P., Lee, J. S., & Boyd, J. S. (2008). Mathematics education for young children: What it is and how to promote it. *Social Policy Report, 22*(1), 3–22.

Hobbs, M. E., Williams, R. A., & Sherwood, E. A. (2012). Collaborating with teacher researchers to study what young children know and can do in science. *Voices of Practitioners, 7*(1), 1–11.

McManis, L. D. & Gunnewig, S. B. (2012). Finding the education in educational technology with early learners. *Young Children, 67*(3), 14–24.

Mislevy, R. J. (2007). Validity by design. *Educational Researcher, 36*(8), 463–469.

Mislevy, R. J. & Haertel, G. D. (2006). Implications of evidence centered design for educational testing. *Educational Measurement: Issues and Practice, 25*(4), 6–20.

Mislevy, R. J. & Riconscente, M. M. (2006). Evidence-centered assessment design: Layers, concepts, and terminology. In S. Downing & T. Haladyna (Eds.), *Handbook of test development* (pp. 61–90). Mahwah, NJ: Lawrence Erlbaum.

NAEYC & NCTM. (2010). *Early childhood mathematics: Promoting good beginnings*. Washington, DC and Reston, VA: National Association for the Education of Young Children & National Council of Teachers of Mathematics.

NGA & CCSSO. (2010). *Common core state standards*. Washington, DC: National Governors Association Center for Best Practices & Council of Chief State School Officers.

National Mathematics Advisory Panel. (2008). *Foundations for success: The final report of the national mathematics advisory panel*. Washington, DC: National Research Council.

National Research Council, Committee on Early Childhood Mathematics. (2009). *Mathematics learning in early childhood: Paths toward excellence and equity*. Washington, DC: The National Academies Press.

National Research Council, Committee on the Foundations of Assessment. (2001). *Knowing what students know: The science and design of educational assessment*. Washington, DC: National Academy Press.

Pasnik, S. & Llorente, C. (2013). *Preschool teachers can use a PBS KIDS transmedia curriculum supplement to support young children's mathematics learning: Results of a randomized controlled trial. A report to the CPB-PBS Ready To Learn Initiative*. Waltham, MA and Menlo Park, CA: Education Development Center & SRI International.

Pasnik, S., Moorthy, S., Llorente, C., Hupert, N., Dominguez, X., & Silander, M. (2015) *Supporting parent-child experiences with* Peg + Cat *early math concepts: Report to the CPB-PBS Ready To Learn Initiative*. Waltham, MA and Menlo Park, CA: Education Development Center & SRI International.

Putnam, R. (2015). *Our kids: The American dream in crisis*. New York, NY: Simon & Schuster.

Ramani, G. B. & Siegler, R. S. (2014). How informal learning activities can promote children's numerical knowledge. In R. C. Kadosh & A. Dowker (Eds.), *Oxford handbook of mathematical cognition*. New York, NY: Oxford University Press.

Rideout, V. J. (2013). *Zero to eight: Children's media use in America 2013: A common sense media research study*. San Francisco, CA: Common Sense Media Retrieved from www.common sensemedia.org/research/zero-to-eight-childrens-media-use-in-america-2013.

Seo, K. H. & Ginsburg, H. P. (2004). What is developmentally appropriate in early childhood mathematics education? Lessons from new research. In D. H. Clements, J. Sarama, & A. M. DiBiase (Eds.), *Engaging young children in mathematics: Standards for early childhood mathematics education* (pp. 91–104). Hillsdale, NJ: Erlbaum.

Shepard, L. A. (1994). The challenges of assessing young children appropriately. *The Phi Delta Kappan, 76*(3), 206–212.

Weiland, C., Wolfe, C. B., Hurwitz, M., Clements, D., Sarama, J., & Yoshikawa, H. (2012). Early mathematics assessment: Validation of the short form of a prekindergarten and kindergarten mathematics measure. *Education Psychology, 32*(2), 311–333.

Wolfgang, C. H., Stannard, L. L., & Jones, I. (2001). Block play performance among preschoolers as a predictor of later school achievements in mathematics. *Journal of Research in Childhood Education, 15*(2), 173–180.

7

WHAT EARLY CHILDHOOD EDUCATORS NEED IN ORDER TO USE DIGITAL MEDIA EFFECTIVELY

Phil Vahey, Regan Vidiksis, and Jaime Gutierrez

Introduction

Digital media, particularly those that are transmedia-based, have the potential to transform early childhood classrooms by influencing both what young children learn and how they learn it. This potential is perhaps greatest for those in greatest need, as quality educational multiplatform resources are available from public media to all, regardless of zip code, local educational funding levels, or whether early childhood education is part of the formal school system.

However, the mere availability of transmedia content is not enough to spur the kinds of changes that can result in significant learning gains for traditionally underserved children. This chapter describes how the Corporation for Public Broadcasting (CPB) and Public Broadcasting Service (PBS) have utilized Ready To Learn grants from the U.S. Department of Education's Office of Innovation and Improvement to engage in research on how to support teachers in preschool classrooms as they leverage transmedia-based activities to increase children's learning.

The authors of this chapter are from the Ready To Learn research partner organizations, SRI International and the Education Development Center (EDC). We have been deeply involved in designing studies that curate the existing digital and non-digital Ready To Learn materials, developing curriculum guides that use existing Ready To Learn materials, developing additional hands-on instructional materials as necessary, and developing the teacher professional development activities used in the CPB-PBS Ready To Learn studies. We also have been part of other, related research projects, many of them supported by the National Science Foundation, such as the Next Generation

Preschool Math, Next Generation Preschool Science projects and the PBS children's series Monkeying Around (currently in production).

The objective of this chapter is to describe the support we have provided to teachers as part of Ready To Learn research on effective use of transmedia (see Chapter 4 for a description of CPB-PBS Ready To Learn Initiative efforts to support educators, not just the ones who participated in research studies). The research we describe took place in early childhood programs that serve children from low-income households, e.g., children who were eligible for free and reduced lunch and who rarely have access to the resources needed to support effective use of advanced technologies.

The support we provided was based on, and added to, research that showed that the most productive way to engage young children in the use of transmedia is through an interactive process called joint media engagement (JME), where the use of media is in a social context that may be mediated by a familiar and more capable adult (Media and Learning Group at SRI Education, 2010; Moorthy et al., 2013; Stevens & Penuel, 2010; Takeuchi & Stevens, 2011). In the case of early childhood classrooms, the mediation occurs in what we call a curricular activity system (Roschelle, Knudsen, & Hegedus, 2010; Vahey, Knudsen, Rafanan, & Lara-Meloy, 2013). A curricular activity systems approach acknowledges that school-based educational activities take place within a system that includes not only the teacher, child, and educational materials, but also learning expectations, classroom routines, and teacher professional development resources.

This chapter also describes the current context for most early childhood educators, and how the Ready To Learn Initiative has designed teaching and learning environments that support teachers in engaging in the types of learning activities that are most productive in leveraging transmedia-based resources. Ready To Learn studies have shown learning gains for children, and have shown increased teacher confidence in using technology in their classrooms. We end the chapter with lessons learned in supporting teachers in using transmedia-based resources in preschool classrooms.

The Context: Early Childhood Educators

If you've stepped foot in an early childhood classroom, chances are you've had the experience of witnessing an incredibly wide assortment of exploration and learning activities—from watching two young children learning to take turns and share materials at free choice time, to hearing a young child take pride in counting the number of her peers present at school that day during circle time, to seeing a line messily form while children wait their turn to wash their hands before snack time—all orchestrated by the teacher responsible for that class-room. A well-run early childhood classroom can be an astonishing sight, with many things happening simultaneously, and one cannot help but be impressed by the classroom's conductor—the teacher.

Exactly how impressive this is becomes clearer when one considers that early childhood educators have a large demand placed on them: High-quality programs are expected to meet a multitude of standards criteria (National Association for the Education of Young Children [NAEYC], 2017) that range from keeping children healthy and safe, to frequently communicating with families using a variety of strategies, to ensuring that the curriculum used "addresses all aspects of child development." The planning, preparation, and skill required of early educators to ensure that all the children (approximately 20) in their classroom are provided with individualized and varied opportunities in all of the developmental domains—including social-emotional, physical (both fine and gross motor), language (expressive and receptive communication), and cognitive—can be a considerable challenge.

Unfortunately, many preschool teachers, especially those in underserved neighborhoods, are not adequately resourced or prepared for this wide range of responsibilities (Ullrich, Hamm, & Schochet, 2017). Many experts believe that providing the necessary supports to meaningfully guide young children through this crucial time of their lives requires a college degree as well as subsequent professional development (Interlandi, 2018; NAEYC, 2017), both of which are rare for those who teach preschool in traditionally underserved areas. The lack of preparation is particularly acute in building the confidence and skills early childhood teachers need to use media and digital tools to support the learning of their children through mediation and other means (Ertmer & Ottenbreit-Leftwich, 2010).

Fortunately, high-quality professional development has been found to significantly increase the capacity of preschool educators (Ginsburg, Lee, & Stevenson-Boyd, 2008; Isenberg, 2000). And similarly, there are numerous kinds of pre-service and in-service professional development that can increase teachers' confidence and ability to use technology with their children in consequential and dynamic ways (Ertmer & Ottenbreit-Leftwich, 2010). As discussed below, we leverage this research in the Ready To Learn Initiative.

The Context: Media Use in Early Learning Settings

Potential of Transmedia

Although the use of digital media and technology with young children has been a controversial topic (Swingle, 2016), there is a growing consensus that media and technology can play a positive role in the early childhood classroom. The joint NAEYC and Fred Rogers Center position statement maintains that technology resources should "promote effective learning and development when they are used intentionally by early childhood educators, within the framework of developmentally appropriate practice, to support learning goals established for individual children" (NAEYC & the Fred Rogers Center, 2012). While it is clear that not many early childhood educators are aware of the NAEYC and Fred Rogers Center position statements (Wartella, Blackwell, Lauricella, & Robb, 2013), a survey conducted by Teaching Strategies in 2016 found that 63% of teachers would like to have the ability to use more technology in their classrooms (Teaching Strategies, 2015). Our Ready To Learn research seeks to expand our understanding of how to effectively use transmedia resources and associated technology tools with young children.

While effective uses of digital technologies can include helping children learn to use technology as a goal in itself (Teaching Strategies, 2015), recent research has found that technology can increase learning in many topics and subject areas. In particular, recent research has shown that adult mediation of children's media and technology use can play an important role in improving children's learning outcomes in areas beyond what has been traditionally taught in pre-school. Transmedia-based activities can allow opportunities for teachers and children to have experiences that otherwise might not be available. For example, videos can show distant places or cultures, or can provide a space for abstract phenomena—these are not easily replicated by traditional means. Use of such videos allows teachers and children to have a set of shared experiences and to have discussions (either individual, small-group, or whole-class) that can be used to deepen children's understanding. Digital media can then allow the ability to "replay" experiences—anyone who has ever been around a young child knows how much they enjoy re-watching or replaying certain videos or games. This creates opportunities for young children to iterate their experiences in controlled environments and to receive immediate feedback on their decisions. Media-rich resources and technology can also provide teachers the opportunity to extend that learning and to make connections across multiple contexts. Finally, young children can develop relationships with their preferred characters and can share those positive experiences with their peers and teachers. While digital media increase the ways in which young children can learn, taking advantage of these possibilities requires that the technology and resources be available and that teachers know how to effectively use the resources.

Reality of Media Use in Early Childhood Classrooms

While there has been significant research in the use of digital media in the home, less is known about its use in early childhood classrooms. For instance, a study of home technology use conducted in 2017 by Common Sense Media (Rideout, 2017) found that children under the age of eight spend an average of 2 hours and 19 minutes a day with screen media. This survey found that as mobile devices (i.e., tablets, smartphones, etc.) that can connect to the internet became more accessible, the percentage of time children under eight spent on mobile devices increased from 4% in 2011 to 35% in 2017, even though overall media use stayed about the same (Rideout, 2017).

While we know that home use of technology is increasing, less is known about the use of technologies in early childhood classrooms. This is important, as underserved young children spend a significant amount of time in preschools, with 43% of children up to the age of four enrolled in state preschool or Head Start programs (Barnett et al., 2017). To understand how to meet the needs of young children and their teachers, it is important to learn more about the type of technology and media access children have in out-of-home educational settings.

What we do know is that the use of interactive technologies, including tablet computers, is rising in the early childhood classroom, with tablet computer use increasing from 29% in 2012 (Wartella, Blackwell, Lauricella, & Robb, 2013) to 37% in 2013 (Simon, Nemeth, & McManis, 2013), and it is likely that this trend of increasing use will continue. This is critical to the story of technology use in early childhood settings, as smaller, portable technologies (smartphones, tablets, etc.) have seen the biggest increase in educational content over the past five years, and we can expect the use of such technologies to continue to grow in the near future.

Our own research warns us, though, to be cautious about interpreting such findings too optimistically. We have found that availability and access are two different things. For example, when Ready To Learn researchers have performed technology landscape studies of classrooms, we have often found that, while teachers may report that technology is available, the computer is only for teacher use (not for use by the children), or the classroom has access to a technology cart that they can only use once a week. For this reason, we have supplied early childhood classrooms with the technology required to participate in our studies. As the use of transmedia becomes more accepted and more widely adopted, and as the cost of technology continues to drop, we expect that more early childhood classrooms, even those in underserved and under-resourced communities, will have access to the technology necessary to implement transmedia-based materials. Through our research, we hope to ensure that the use of these materials has benefits for children in these classrooms.

Supporting Early Childhood Teachers

Clearly, research is required for us to take advantage of the potential benefits of transmedia, given the current needs and realities of the preschool classroom and the lack of formal preparation of most early childhood educators. Our curricular activity systems approach acknowledges that instruction takes place in an interdependent system that includes many components. We describe some of these components here.

High-Quality Instructional Materials

For teachers to effectively use transmedia, they must have high-quality instructional materials. While high-quality early childhood classroom-based *instructional* materials share some characteristics with high-quality materials used in other settings (such as used in the home), there are some unique characteristics of classroom-based instructional materials. For instance, "high-quality" generally implies that the materials should be engaging, should have a positive message, and should provide children with developmentally appropriate access to interesting and important ideas. However, early childhood classrooms have an additional set of expectations not found in other situations, such as the expectation to meet a wide variety of standards and to do so in a limited amount of time. Early childhood classrooms have a set of instructional routines—whole-class activities, choice time, snack time, and so on—and any use of materials must fit into those existing practices. Early childhood classrooms also are seen as places where children learn to interact and to collaborate with one another. This contrasts with naturalistic home use, which typically (although not always) involves a child watching a video or playing a game individually, with no explicit learning goal—other than the caregiver's goal that use of the media resource have some educational value.

To meet the needs of the early childhood classroom, we provide curated materials ordered in an instructional, logical, and coherent sequence, building on research on learning trajectories (e.g., Clements & Sarama, 2004). We integrate these digital materials with non-digital, hands-on materials that allow young children to take advantage of the norms and routines of early childhood classrooms, such as working together with blocks or participating in the shared reading of a book at circle time. We design activities that use media resources in a manner consistent with JME, allowing children to learn from their peers and to be guided by a more expert adult. The processes of curation, integration, and design for JME are described in detail by Moorthy and Domínguez in Chapter 8.

Teacher's Guides

Once teachers have high-quality materials, they still must skillfully implement them in their classrooms. While it is tempting to believe that each individual teacher is the one best positioned to make the bridge between the materials and their own classroom implementation, we have found that this is often not the case. Early childhood teachers have busy days, with many responsibilities, and finding the most effective way to integrate new transmedia activities into their routine is not something they typically have the time or training to do. Especially in the context of a study, where teachers are being asked by researchers to use a new set of materials, detailed-but-flexible teacher's guides allow teachers to feel comfortable in the use of transmedia resources while helping them to understand how the materials can fit into their own pre-established routines.

Our teacher's guides include a short introduction to the use of educational media resources generally. Many preschool teachers have not used media in their classrooms before, and providing an understanding of the benefits of media, as well as how media will be integrated with non-media resources, allows the teacher to become comfortable with media as something that can augment, not replace, their existing routines. In cases where we are using media to introduce content that goes beyond what is typically found in preschool (such as math ideas that go beyond traditional counting, or scientific practices and content), we also provide a primer on the content itself, and why it is important. We have found this to be especially valued by early childhood educators because they rarely have accessible content that can be used in their classrooms to address the new, more sophisticated subject matter standards.

The majority of our teacher guides focus on productive uses of the specific media being provided, outlining activities that use media and non-media resources in productive ways (see Figure 7.1) and providing example schedules with guidelines for modification (see Figure 7.2). Due to the novelty of using media, and of integrating media and non-media activities, it is important that teachers have explicit models of effective use. However, it also is important that each teacher is allowed to tailor the experience to their own particular context and needs, and to the needs of their children. By providing specific examples, but allowing teachers the freedom to customize, we have found that teachers can effectively use transmedia resources in their preschool classrooms.

Professional Development

Teachers need more than high-quality materials and a good teacher's guide. As described previously, preschool teachers do not typically receive the kind of formal training that prepares them to teach innovative content using digital materials in their classroom. However, it is not realistic to expect that most preschool teachers, especially those in underserved areas, can engage in long-term professional development, due to time and financial constraints.

While the professional development that we have offered has varied slightly in its exact delivery, it typically consists of formal in-person professional development sessions accompanied by on-site teacher coaching. This professional development consists of a minimum of two days of training time distributed in slightly differing ways: We may deliver more training prior to the start of the study with the limited coaching during implementation, or we may deliver less training at the onset of the study with more frequent coaching throughout.

Weekly Activities

In the following sections, you will find scripts and activity descriptions for each of the 10 weeks of the Math Curriculum Supplement. The activities are designed to be simple and repetitive because children need to practice the same math skills many times and in many different situations to learn them. The content changes from week to week, but many activities remain the same or are similar to previous activities so you and your children will have a familiar routine to follow. Below is an overview of the activities you and your children will do each week.

Activity	Setting	Description
Video Co-Viewing (25 minutes)	Circle Time with the Interactive Whiteboard (IWB)	Each week, videos introduce new math concepts or review key math content preschoolers may already know. Pause points marked within the videos indicate places where you pause to explain the focal or review math concepts, ask questions, and open up discussions about math with children.
Math Detective Journal (20 minutes per small group)	Small Group	Every child will receive a Math Detective Journal to use during the 10 weeks of the Math Curriculum Supplement. Journal activities are written activities that take place in small groups and provide an opportunity to reinforce skills introduced or reviewed in the week's video.
Easy Game Play (10 minutes per small group)	Small group with the Interactive Whiteboard (IWB)	This is the first opportunity children have to interact with the IWB each week. In a small-group setting, model the easy interactive game of the week with a quick demonstration, then allow children an opportunity to play the game, reinforcing the skills covered in the week's video, or sometimes reviewing skills from previous weeks.
Math Circle Routine (10 minutes)	Circle Time	The Math Circle Routine combines traditional preschool activities of circle time learning with new materials and novel activities or games to reinforce math skills covered in the week's videos and games in a hands-on way. These activities are designed to encourage children to ask questions and to participate.
Guided Book Reading (15 minutes)	Circle Time	Keeping with familiar preschool routines, once a week you will read aloud a math storybook related to the focal math skills of the week. The books contain pause points to allow you to explain math concepts, ask questions, and open up discussion.
Challenge Game Play (25 minutes)	Circle Time with the Interactive Whiteboard (IWB)	The last whole-group activity of the week is the Challenge Game Play, where you model playing an interactive game and then provide an opportunity for children to practice their math skills in the more challenging game environment. As the name suggests, the game is meant to challenge children and may require varying degrees of support.
Computer Center (10 minutes)	Pairs of children at laptops	Throughout the week, children will team up to play interactive games on the laptops. The focal easy and challenge games of the weeks will be available, as well as games from previous weeks, to allow children to practice and apply the math knowledge they are gaining.
Hands-On Centers (10 minutes)	Pairs or small groups of children	Also throughout the week, pairs or small groups of children can play the hands-on games and activities introduced during the week or from previous weeks. The games allow children to practice concepts covered in the videos and interactive games in hands-on ways.

FIGURE 7.1   Teacher Guide page listing media and non-media activities (Courtesy of the Education Development Center and SRI International)

During the on-site training, we provide study teachers with an orientation to the study and introduce them to the target instructional content and concepts, as well as to ways to use the transmedia resources to explore that content and concepts. This is not only an efficient use of time, but it is consistent with

Sample Schedule

We realize you have many things to teach and that you'll need to fit the Math Curriculum Supplement into an already busy schedule. Keep in mind that the Supplement will be most effective if you use a consistent schedule from week to week. Your coach will help you figure out how to schedule the Supplement activities into your week, as well as support you when holidays and other school closures occur. We recommend spreading the activities over four days, as in the sample schedule below. Please use this as a guide to help you plan how best to integrate these activities into your classroom schedule.

Sample Schedule

Monday	Tuesday	Wednesday	Thursday
Video Co-Viewing (25 minutes)	Math Detective Jour nal (20 minutes)	Math Circle Routine (10 minutes)	Challenge Game Play (25 minutes)
	Easy Game Play (10 minutes)	Guided Reading (15 minutes)	
Computer Center (~10 minutes per pair of children)	Computer Center (~10 minutes per pair of children)	Computer Center (~10 minutes per pair of children)	Computer Center (~10 minutes per pair of children)
	Hands-on Centers (~10 minutes per pair of children)	Hands-on Centers (~10 minutes per pair of children)	Hands-on Centers (~10 minutes per pair of children)

FIGURE 7.2   Teacher Guide page showing example schedule of activity use (Courtesy of the Education Development Center and SRI International)

research showing that professional development is more effective when embedded in activities that are immediately applicable to the classroom (Darling-Hammond, Hyler, & Gardner, 2017). Additionally, we assign on-site coaches to teachers, and these coaches help to translate into classroom practice what teachers learn in the professional development sessions and what is in the teacher's guide. Study coaches also discuss with teachers their specific contexts and questions, and tailor support specifically to teacher needs.

Findings from Ready To Learn Research

The CPB-PBS Ready To Learn Initiative's first area of focus was on literacy, and in 2009, the EDC and SRI conducted a randomized control trial (RCT) study that examined whether children whose teachers implemented a media-rich literacy curriculum supplement exhibited an increase in early literacy skills. Teachers from underserved communities were recruited and randomly assigned to one of two conditions: the literacy intervention condition or a comparison condition that consisted of a science intervention. Teachers in the literacy condition were given a teacher guide and a curated set of public media resources (video clips and games), book-reading activities, and hands-on activities to use with the children in their class for a period of 10 weeks. As part of their participation in the study, teachers received a two-hour orientation, led by a coach, to familiarize them with the materials and the curriculum. After this, coaches provided as-needed, in-person support that included examples of good teaching practice, observations, and implementation assistance. Coaches made an average of eight visits to each class during the implementation period, with each visit lasting approximately two hours, while also providing ongoing support via telephone and email.

A total of 398 children were recruited for this study from 80 classrooms within 47 different early childhood centers in the New York City and San Francisco Bay areas. The study measured children's early literacy skills using a variety of measures: subtests from the Phonological Awareness Literacy Screening (PALS), which measures children's knowledge of letter names, letter sounds, and common initial sounds; an assessment that measured children's knowledge of story and print concepts, developed by researchers from the University of Pennsylvania and Mississippi State University; and a measure that EDC and SRI developed to assess letter knowledge, particularly children's ability to recognize the letters in their own name. Researchers compared the post-test scores of children in the literacy condition with those in the comparison science condition for each outcome by fitting hierarchical linear models (Penuel et al., 2009).

Children in the literacy condition of the study exhibited statistically significant differences from the comparison group in the areas of uppercase letter recognition (letter naming: $p < 0.001$, $n = 358$, effect size $= 0.34$), letter sounds ($p < 0.001$, $n = 358$, effect size $= 0.53$), story and print concepts ($p < 0.026$, $n = 358$, effect size $= 0.26$), and knowledge of letters in their name ($p < 0.035$, $n = 358$, effect size $= 0.19$).

Teachers in the literacy condition reported being able to utilize the digital non-digital curricular materials as often as intended and used the instructional features introduced in the teacher guide and professional development (Penuel et al., 2012). These findings are significant because the teachers in the study sample were representative of those in many early childhood settings that serve low-income communities, with likely little or no prior training or deep exposure to the type of media-rich literacy curricular instruction featured in the study (Penuel et al., 2009).

While the literacy (treatment) group implemented the materials just described, the science (comparison) group implemented a 10-week science curriculum that also incorporated the use of digital and non-digital media resources during whole- and small-group explorations, and through opportunities for individual exploration. With an equivalent level of professional development as the literacy intervention group, including ongoing coaching support and guidance, teachers in this condition guided children through an exploration of the concepts of change and transformation via a weekly in-class investigation. Activities were based on familiar, everyday preschool experiences, and they provided children with the opportunity to explore the content using their five senses.

Measuring the impact of the science curriculum on children's science learning was beyond the scope of this particular study; however, researchers developed a measure to capture caregivers' reports about their children's science talk in the home. This self-report measure included things like whether their child pretended to be a scientist, talked about an investigation, or expressed an interest in some of the things that were included in the curriculum, including how things work, decay, freeze and melt, and about heat and change. Researchers found that there was a statistically significant treatment effect of the science curriculum on science talk ($p < 0.05$, $n = 200$, effect size $= 0.30$), providing affirmation that, when meaningful supports are in place, early childhood teachers have the ability to implement a science curriculum that uses media and non-media resources effectively and in ways that could result in an increase in children's talk about science in the home (Penuel et al., 2010).

In 2013, the EDC and SRI conducted another RCT study to investigate whether a 10-week math curriculum supplement, which included curated media-rich and non-media activities, could result in an increase in preschoolers' understanding of math skills, including subitizing, counting, recognizing numerals, patterning, and recognizing, composing, and representing shapes. (See Chapter 6 for additional study design details.) This study also featured a detailed teacher guide, as well as a lengthier (approximately six–seven hours) in-person professional development session at the start of the study. The professional development session comprised an introduction to the mathematics concepts included in the intervention, instructional strategies for teaching those concepts, and ways that teachers could thoughtfully incorporate the study media (interactive whiteboards and laptop computers) into whole-group, small-group, and individual activities. Similar to the abovementioned literacy study, ongoing coaching also was an important and defining component of the study.

The pre-K math study participants were recruited from 87 preschool centers that predominantly served children from low-income backgrounds across the New York City and San Francisco Bay areas and included 157 teachers and a total of 966 children. Participating centers were randomly assigned to one of three conditions: the PBS KIDS Transmedia Math Supplement condition (receiving interactive whiteboards and laptop computers, a curricular sequence of curated media-rich and non-media math resources, and associated professional development), the Technology & Media condition (receiving interactive whiteboards and laptop computers, as well as professional development), or the Business-as-Usual condition (receiving the curricular sequence and professional development after the study was over, but instructed to continue their typical math instruction and routines during the study period) (Pasnik & Llorente, 2013).

Three assessments of student learning were administered to approximately ten children from each of the classrooms in the total sample: a short version of the research-based early mathematics assessment (REMA), a researcher-developed supplement-based assessment of mathematics, and a standardized assessment of children's self-regulation, called the Head-Toes-Knees-Shoulders (Ponitz et al., 2008; Weiland et al., 2012). In addition, the majority of participating teachers completed a survey both prior to the study and after study completion; the survey was composed of a pre-established set of questions about their beliefs, attitudes, and practices relating to math, and was developed by The Early Math Collaborative at the Erikson Institute (Chen & McCray, 2012). They also completed a researcher-developed survey component about their use and integration of technology in their classrooms.

This study found that, of the children who took the supplement-based assessment, those in the transmedia condition increased their knowledge of math concepts compared to both the children in the Business-as-Usual condition (effect size = 0.24, p < 0.001) and those in the Technology & Media condition (effect size = 0.22, p < 0.001). This shows that when teachers are provided media materials plus the support discussed in this chapter, children in their classrooms learn more than when teachers are provided access to transmedia without supports, or when classrooms are left to engage in Business-as-Usual instruction.

In addition, teachers in the PBS KIDS Transmedia Math Supplement group experienced an increase in their confidence and beliefs about their math knowledge as well as children's ability to learn from technology, as compared to both the Business-as-Usual and Technology & Media conditions. Finally, the number of teachers who reported using technology to teach math concepts increased significantly more in both the PBS KIDS Transmedia Math Supplement and the Technology & Media conditions, as compared to the Business-as-Usual condition, indicating that, while teachers who received the material and limited support used technology more, it did not increase their children's learning in the target math concepts.

Conclusion

New technologies, and recent advances in understanding how transmedia content and related resources can be used to increase early learning, have created tremendous opportunities for early childhood education. However, we cannot expect early childhood educators alone to engage in the efforts that will allow our youngest learners to take advantage of these opportunities. Instead, it requires that the digital media resources be curated, be augmented with non-digital resources, and be presented in a manner that can be applied to the early education setting. It also requires that teachers be provided with professional development and coaching so that they can learn how to take advantage of the new types of interactions that digital media has to offer.

Public media's Ready To Learn research has shown that, when these conditions are met, not only do they yield positive findings relating to children's learning, but early education teachers have an increase in their beliefs about their own mathematics knowledge, and about the benefits of incorporating technology and media into the learning experiences of preschoolers.

References

Barnett, W. S., Friedman-Krauss, A. H., Weisenfeld, G. G., Horowitz, M., Kasmin, R., & Squires, J. H. (2017). *The state of preschool 2016: State preschool yearbook*. New Brunswick, NJ: National Institute for Early Education Research.

Chen, J. & McCray, J. (2012). A conceptual framework for teacher professional development: The whole teacher approach. *NHSA Dialog, 15*(1), 8–23.

Clements, D. H. & Sarama, J. (2004). Learning trajectories in mathematics education. *Mathematical Thinking and Learning, 6*(2), 81–89.

Darling-Hammond, L., Hyler, M. E., & Gardner, M. (2017). *Effective teacher professional development*. Palo Alto, CA: Learning Policy Institute.

Ertmer, P. A. & Ottenbreit-Leftwich, A. T. (2010). Teacher technology change: How knowledge, confidence, beliefs, and culture intersect. *Journal of Research on Technology in Education, 42*(3), 255–284.

Ginsburg, H. P., Lee, S. W., & Stevenson-Boyd, J. (2008). Mathematics education for young children: What it is and how to promote it. *Social Policy Report: Giving Child and Youth Development Knowledge Away, 22*(1), 1–23.

Interlandi, J. (2018, January 9). Why are our most important teachers paid the least? *The New York Times*. Retrieved from www.nytimes.com/2018/01/09/magazine/why-are-our-most-important-teachers-paid-the-least.html.

Isenberg, J. P. (2000). The state of the art in early childhood. In D. Horm-Wingerd & M. Hyson (Eds.), *New teachers for a new century: The future of early childhood professional preparation*. Washington, DC: National Institute on Early Childhood Development and Education.

Media and Learning Group at SRI. (2010). *Joint media engagement and learning*. Menlo Park, CA: SRI International.

Moorthy, S., Domínguez, X., Llorente, C., Lesk, H., Pinkerton, L., & Christiano, E. (2013, April). Joint engagement with media for preschool science. Paper presented at the Annual Meeting of the American Education Research Association, San Francisco, CA.

National Association for the Education of Young Children. (2017). *The 10 NAEYC program standards*. Washington, DC: NAEYC. Retrieved from www.naeyc.org/our-work/families/10-naeyc-program-standards.

Pasnik, S., & Llorente, C. (2013). *Preschool teachers can use a PBS KIDS transmedia curriculum supplement to support young children's mathematics learning: Results of a randomized controlled trial*. (Report to the CPB-PBS Ready To Learn Initiative). New York, NY and Menlo Park, CA: Education Development Center, Inc., and SRI International.

Penuel, W. R., Bates, L., Gallagher, L. P., Pasnik, S., Llorente, C., Townsend, E., Hupert, N., Domínguez, X., &VanderBorght, M. (2012). Supplementing literacy instruction with a media-rich intervention: Results of a randomized controlled trial. *Early Childhood Research Quarterly, 27*(1), 115–127.

Penuel, W. R., Bates, L., Pasnik, S., Townsend, E., Gallagher, L. P., Llorente, C., & Hupert, N. (2010). The impact of a media-rich science curriculum on low-income preschoolers' science talk at home. Paper presented at the 9th International Conference of the Learning Sciences, Chicago, IL.

Penuel, W. R., Pasnik, S., Bates, L., Townsend, E., Gallagher, L. P., Llorente, C., & Hupert, N. (2009). *Preschool teachers can use a media-rich curriculum to prepare low-income children for school success: Results of a randomized controlled trial.* New York, NY and Menlo Park, CA: Education Development Center, Inc., and SRI International.

Ponitz, C. C., McClelland, M. M., Jewkes, A. M., Connor, C. M., Farris, C. L., & Morrison, F. J. (2008). Touch your toes! Developing a direct measure of behavioral regulation in early childhood. *Early Childhood Research Quarterly, 23*(2), 141–158.

Rideout, V. (2017). *The common sense census: Media use by kids age zero to eight.* San Francisco, CA: Common Sense Media.

Roschelle, J., Knudsen, J., & Hegedus, S. (2010). From new technological infrastructures to curricular activity systems: Advanced designs for teaching and learning. In M. J. Jacobson & P. Reimann (Eds.), *Designs for learning environments of the future: International perspectives from the learning sciences* (pp. 233–262). New York, NY: Springer.

Simon, F., Nemeth, K., & McManis, D. (2013). Technology in ECE classrooms: Results of a new survey and implications for the field. *Child Care Exchange Magazine,* pp. 68–75. Retrieved from http://echd430-f13-love.wikispaces.umb.edu/file/view/Technolo gyECEclassrooms.pdf/45107/8632/TechnologyECEclassrooms.pdf.

Stevens, R. & Penuel, W. R. (2010). Studying and fostering learning through joint media engagement. Paper presented at the Principal Investigators Meeting of the National Science Foundation's Science of Learning Centers, Arlington, VA.

Swingle, M. (2016). *i-Minds: How cell phones, computers, gaming, and social media are changing our brains, our behavior, and the evolution of our species.* British Columbia, Canada. New Society Publishers.

Takeuchi, L. & Stevens, R. (2011). *The new coviewing: Designing for learning through joint media engagement.* New York, NY: The Joan Ganz Cooney Center at Sesame Workshop.

Teaching Strategies. (2015). *Early childhood technology survey.* Bethesda, MD: Teaching Strategies. Retrieved from https://teachingstrategies.com/wp-content/uploads/2017/03/Tech-Survey-Findings-Summary-FINAL-002.pdf.

NAEYC & the Fred Rogers Center. (2012). *Technology and interactive media as tools in early childhood programs serving children from birth through age 8.* National Association for the Education of Young Children & the Fred Rogers Center for Early Learning and Children's Media at Saint Vincent College, Joint Position Statement.

Ullrich, R., Hamm, K., & Schochet, L. (2017). 6 policies to support the early childhood workforce. Washington, DC: Center for American Progress. Retrieved from www.americanprogress.org/issues/early-childhood/reports/2017/02/06/298085/6-poli cies-to-support-the-early-childhood-workforce/.

Vahey, P., Knudsen, J., Rafanan, K., & Lara-Meloy, T. (2013). Curricular activity systems supporting the use of dynamic representations to foster students' deep understanding of mathematics. In C. Mouza & N. Lavigne (Eds.), *Emerging technologies for the classroom: A learning sciences perspective* (pp. 15–30). New York, NY: Springer.

Wartella, E., Blackwell, C. K., Lauricella, A. R., & Robb, M. B. (2013). *Technology in the lives of educators and early childhood programs: 2012 survey of early childhood educators.* Latrobe, PA: Saint Vincent College.

Weiland, C., Wolfe, C., Hurwitz, M., Clements, D. H., Sarama, J., & Yoshikawa, H. (2012). Early mathematics assessment: Validation of the short form of a prekindergarten and kindergarten mathematics measure. *Educational Psychology: An International Journal of Experimental Educational Psychology, 32*(3), 311–333.

8

CURATION AND MEDIATION

Essential Ingredients When Supporting Children's Learning

Savitha Moorthy and Ximena Domínguez

Introduction

Ms. C is a preschool teacher in a publicly funded early childhood education program. Her classroom is large and well-lit, with a colorful rug in the middle of the room. On one side of the room are two computers, each containing an assortment of games and apps that can be downloaded for free. During center time, children take turns, usually in pairs or groups of three, to play interactive games. When the children are at the computers, Ms. C stops by often to provide some sort of technical assistance, ask or answer a question, or take advantage of a "teachable moment" to explain something. The games focus on specific skills— like letters and sound recognition, vocabulary, and counting—that connect to what children are learning in the classroom and give children a chance to practice those skills. However, except for the rare occasions when Ms. C is able to find games or videos that line up with what she's teaching, the connections are spontaneous and opportunistic rather than part of planned instruction.

Sonia is the mother of four-year-old Ana, one of the children in Ms. C's classroom. Like many parents, Sonia considers it part of her role as a parent to help Ana learn and she works hard to find activities that are fun and educational. She often guides Ana toward shows on the local PBS channel and educational games that Ana plays on a hand-me-down tablet. When she's watching a show or playing a game, Sonia observes Ana sing along with the theme songs, talk about what she's watching, and do new things she couldn't do before—and she's happy to see her daughter engaged and learning. When Sonia chooses shows and apps and games for Ana, she follows the recommendations of other parents, especially the parents of Ana's peers. Although it is not as often as she would like, Sonia sits with Ana when she watches television or uses the iPad.

It's not because Ana needs help with the technology but because Sonia wants to "do more learning" with Ana and see what areas she needs more help in.

The Changing Conversation about Media and Early Learning

Ms. C and Sonia are examples from real life.[1] As their stories highlight, the conversation about the use of digital media and technology with young children is changing. A number of studies illustrate that media- and technology-supported curricula and instruction can promote early learning and yield positive outcomes for young children in a variety of subject areas, especially for educationally disadvantaged populations. Coupled with advances in touchscreen technology and the increasing availability of digital media resources, these findings are encouraging us to reconsider previous assumptions about technology. Parents, educators, researchers, and policymakers are moving away from the black-and-white binary of *whether* media can help children learn toward the more nuanced question of *how* it can do so—and are grappling with and beginning to understand where media can shine as a resource for promoting children's learning.

Both Ms. C and Sonia believe in the potential of technology to support children's learning but for many educators and parents, concrete strategies for using media at school and home remain elusive. When it comes to identifying and selecting media content for children, teachers and parents are typically on their own. Similarly, while evidence is emerging that media can be productively integrated into early learning experiences, there is little research that has described guidelines or models that teachers and parents could use to structure their interactions with children. This is particularly true in domains like mathematics and science that are gaining greater emphasis in early learning.

As early learning researchers who study how media can be leveraged for children's learning, we are intimately familiar with the shifting narrative around media use with young children. We engage actively in this conversation, and our work, which wrestles with the challenge of designing robust learning experiences for children that integrate media in developmentally appropriate ways, speaks directly to it. In the almost ten-year period that we were part of the CPB-PBS Ready To Learn research team, we've worked on context studies that involved early conversations with parents and teachers, pilots of media-rich interventions for homes and schools, and experimental studies that explored the promise of media for promoting children's learning. Our involvement in this line of research has given us an opportunity to observe firsthand how the organization of digital learning resources is a key design element that structures children's experiences with the media and influences how children and adults interact with one another when using the media.

The questions and concerns that Ms. C and Sonia raise are central to our work and are at the heart of this chapter—and we tackle them here by elaborating on some of the conditions under which young children can learn from media. In particular, we discuss two strategies for using media to advance children's learning: *curation* of content (the grouping of videos, games, apps, and non-digital activities into meaningful units addressing target learning objectives) and *mediation* (how adults can intentionally use media to engage children in learning interactions). A deep dive into two studies, one from preschool and one from home, brings these ideas to life.

Curation

With technology devices such as smartphones and tablets becoming more ubiquitous, there has been a boom of "apps" developed for young children. As of 2018, over 70,000 of the apps in the Apple Store, for example, were categorized as "educational" (Apple, 2018). This designation is not derived based on specific criteria, and furthermore, very few of these apps have been empirically tested (Hirsh-Pasek et al., 2015). Identifying which of these apps is truly educational, or how they promote learning, is, therefore, most often left to the discretion of educators and parents looking to integrate technology to support young children's learning.

Curating, or selecting, apps that align with learning goals is, therefore, a crucial and important step when integrating media to support young children's learning. This selection process not only involves determining *what* content or skill a given app promotes (Does it target mathematics, and if so, which concepts or skills does it intend to support?) but also *how* it does so (Are the skills targeted by the app developmentally appropriate? Does it create opportunities for scaffolded exploration by providing feedback and leveling children's experience? Does it connect with children's everyday experiences or does it provide opportunities that children would otherwise not be able to experience in their environment?).

While a few efforts—several instances from the Ready To Learn Initiative, for example—have articulated design principles and generated tables of content specification that identify concepts, skills, practices, and habits of mind to guide the design and development of apps, most app developers do not articulate the expected learning process or how specific learning goals are expected to be met. To curate digital resources, educators and parents need guidance to determine which resources promote content they are interested in addressing with their children and which involve learning processes that align with their needs and constraints and that approach learning in ways that fit the ecology of their classrooms and homes (Papadakis, Kalogiannakis, & Zaranis, 2017). The Ready To Learn examples in this chapter are intended to help educators and parents develop a list of guiding questions to help during the curating process.

It is important to note that curation often extends beyond the selection process we have described above. Curating, for instance, may involve not only selecting which digital resources could help address certain learning goals, but also determine how to *integrate the digital resources with other non-digital, hands-on learning experiences* to create a suite of activities that complement each other, and together, strengthen children's learning (Domínguez et al., under review). Curation at times also involves determining how best to *sequence* activities. For instance, are some apps or activities more suited and more powerful for introducing concepts or practices? Are other apps or activities more appropriate to use after others have been completed? How focused or comprehensive learning goals are, and the length of time educators and parents will use to address these goals, can influence how such sequencing is determined.

Mediation

An emerging school of thought suggests that media, rather than inhibiting all social interaction as we once assumed, can offer a context and starting point for productive conversations between young children and adults. The latest guide-lines from the American Association of Pediatrics (AAP; Council on Commu-nications and Media, 2016) acknowledge that "screen time" is becoming simply "time" and that "media aren't necessarily so different from other environments in which children hang out." Similarly, the National Association for the Education of Young Children (NAEYC) and the Fred Rogers Center (2012) take the position that "when used wisely, technology and media can support learning and relationships." One approach to using media wisely with young children is to treat screens like books (Dreiske, 2018). This involves the adult sitting next to the child during media use, pointing to, repeating, and reinforcing what is said on the screen—and using shared media experiences as a catalyst for "conversational duets" (Hirsh-Pasek, Alper, & Golinkoff, 2018) that build children's conceptual understanding and communication skills. Experts refer to such shared, interactive media experiences variously as "co-viewing," "co-participation," or "joint media engagement" (Takeuchi & Stevens, 2011). Viewed in this way, videos, games, and apps can introduce and illustrate concepts, generate discussions, and help children formulate questions and share ideas (Mihalca & Miclea, 2007).

Our definition of joint engagement with media (JEM) places the joint nature of engagement front and center, positioning media as the object of such joint engagement. Included under the umbrella of JEM are several specific strategies adults can employ to capitalize on the affordances of media for learning. One, for example, is the intentional use of media to guide conversations with children—or "conversational anchoring" (Barron & Levinson, 2017). By pausing videos to talk about what is happening on the screen, adults can introduce new ideas to children, ask and answer children's questions, and expand upon and reinforce children's ideas. (See Chapter 11 for a detailed discussion of using media to extend conversations.) Similarly, when playing digital games with children, adults can model strategies like thinking out loud, reasoning about ideas, and problem-solving (e.g., Tenenbaum & Callanan, 2008). For children, the joint video viewing and joint gameplay can offer a concrete context for their questions and curiosities that they can then discuss with teachers or parents.

A related strategy for JEM is the use of media for creative purposes. Adults can help children capture photos and videos to document an experience (e.g., record the growth of a plant), or combine photos and videos with text, images, or music to create new artifacts (e.g., a photo book or a slideshow). Such user-generated content can, in turn, serve as a conversational context for adults and children, and adults can draw on media as a resource for exploring topics that are of interest to children. Learning together from media can help adults position themselves as children's partners in learning, rather than experts who are (or have to be) more knowledgeable than children. This can be especially helpful when adults lack expertise in a particular topic or feel less confident about their own ability to scaffold children's learning (Silander et al., 2018).

The Equity Dimension of Using Media for Learning

While JEM can expand our understanding of how media can be used for learning, it also has the potential to exacerbate gaps of educational opportunity. In more privileged communities, parents and teachers are likely to be better positioned to help children select, use, and sustain engagement in appropriate media-enriched learning experiences (Neuman & Celano, 2006), and to scaffold "tech-assisted, human-powered" learning experiences for children. Additionally, JEM experiences are likely to happen casually and informally in these communities, engaging children in learning "that happens without any express intention to teach" (Seiter, 2008) and socializing them into ways of thinking and talking that are valued in school (e.g., Ochs & Shohet, 2006). In communities with fewer economic resources, parents are likely to face systematic barriers that keep them from interacting with their children more often (Enchautegui, Johnson, & Gelatt, 2015), and in the ways that are valued by school; teachers in these communities are likely to be less prepared to engage children in rich learning experiences (Peske & Haycock, 2006), and to use them as contexts for sustained learning conversations. Consequently, children are likely to have less opportunity to develop the discursive prowess and social skills that translate into educational benefits and economic advantages.

Harnessing the potential of educational media and JEM to support learning for *all* children, therefore, calls for a no-nonsense commitment to support educators and parents in low-income communities—and it is one that has been taken up by the CPB-PBS Ready To Learn Initiative. Supported by the U.S. Department of Education, Ready To Learn seeks to develop engaging, high-quality educational programming and support for two- to eight-year-old children living in families and neighborhoods with fewer economic resources. In the 2010–2015 grant cycle, Ready To Learn's emphasis was on mathematics, with the overarching goals of (a) exploring how media resources can be organized to support children's early mathematics learning and (b) substantively addressing the central role that educators and parents play in children's learning.

In the remainder of this chapter, we take a close look at the curation and mediation in two Ready To Learn studies, focusing on children's mathematics learning at home (n = 200) and in preschools (n = 900). Both studies take up the question of how time spent viewing and playing with public media resources can benefit young children's learning, especially those growing up in low-income communities, who typically have limited exposure to experiences that are oriented toward school-readiness. In both studies, the organization of digital learning resources was a key design element that structured children's experiences with the media and influenced how children and adults interacted with one another when using the media.

Curation and Mediation in Action: Classrooms

The context for our first example is a study (Pasnik & Llorente, 2013) that investigated whether the experience of implementing a 10-week curriculum supplement that curates media-rich as well as non-media activities in a set learning sequence would support children's growth on target mathematics skills, including counting; subitizing; recognizing numerals; recognizing, composing, and representing shapes; and patterns; additional details on the study are included in Chapter 6. For our purposes, the salient piece is the 10-week math curriculum supplement. It was implemented by teachers in the treatment condition and was a coherent sequence of curricular activities, comprising media and non-media learning experiences, centered on early childhood mathematics practices. The media experiences included in the curriculum supplement were drawn from a variety of Ready To Learn properties, including *Curious George, Dinosaur Train, Sid the Science Kid,* and *The Cat in the Hat Knows a Lot About That!*

Selecting, Sequencing, and Organizing Math Learning Experiences for the Classroom

The first step in the process of compiling and sequencing the learning experiences comprising the 10-week curriculum supplement involved identifying the target mathematical skills, including counting; subitizing; recognizing numerals; recognizing, composing, and representing shapes; and patterns. Chosen deliberately to deepen children's capacity for complex, abstract mathematical thinking, the target skills include a combination of mathematical content that preschool teachers are familiar with and are comfortable addressing (e.g., counting) and those with which they tend to be less experienced (e.g., subitizing, patterns).

Once the target mathematical skills had been identified, the next step involved a systematic review of Ready To Learn resources (mathematics-focused videos and interactive games) to identify the media content that aligned with the target mathematics skills. Aside from alignment to the target mathematics skills, another key selection criterion emphasized suitability for use in familiar preschool activity formats (e.g., circle time and centers) and the potential for facilitating JEM (i.e., providing opportunity and points of entry for mathematical conversations). The selected media content was organized into an appropriate sequence, informed by research-based understandings of children's mathematical learning trajectories. (For example, subitizing, or the ability to know how many objects there are without counting, is predicated on children's understanding of counting and cardinality, and therefore followed it.)

The research team then took on the task of developing the "educational wrapper" of the curriculum supplement. This involved designing learning activities around each video and game aimed at accomplishing specific learning objectives. For example, each two-week unit involved a circle-time video viewing activity that introduced new concepts to children, whole-group inter-active gameplay that provided an opportunity for children to practice the target math skills with guidance and feedback from the teacher, and small-group gameplay at computer centers where pairs of children practiced the target math skills on their own. It also involved developing non-media activities to comple-ment the media-rich activities such as book reading, math-focused circle-time routines, and hands-on centers emphasizing math manipulatives. Importantly, the activities themselves were designed to be simple and repetitive; although the math skills and media content varied from week to week, the activities themselves remained the same or similar across weeks so as to help teachers and children establish and maintain familiar routines in the classroom. Together, the media and non-media activities came together to offer children a cohesive learning experience that capitalized on the affordances of media for learning.

Designing for JEM between Teachers and Children

Teachers implementing the 10-week supplement received a teacher's guide that described how to use the video viewing and interactive gameplay to promote math talk and math-focused interactions. For example, the introductory material in the teacher's guide pointed out the pause points in each video, where teachers could pause the video and engage children in a short conversation to review the math content onscreen, ask questions, or explain challenging concepts. During gameplay, teachers were encouraged to ask children math questions related to what they are playing (e.g., "How many are there?" and "What shapes do you see?") to help reinforce children's learning. Aside from the pre-set pause points, teachers were also invited to pause the video at other points if, for example, a child raised a discussion-worthy question or if teachers wanted to explain something in more detail.

The activities themselves incorporated prompts for initiating discussions with children and facilitation notes for warm-up and wrap-up conversations at the beginning and end of activities respectively. The warm-up conversations provided children with key contextual information, connected the target math concept with children's everyday experiences, and surfaced children's background knowledge. The wrap-up discussions summarized the key concepts to which children were introduced during the activity, opening up opportunities for reflection, application, and asking questions.

During the 10-week study period, teachers received on-site support from an instructional coach. The purpose of the coaching was to help teachers translate into classroom practice the principles and strategies presented in the professional development sessions and outlined in the guide. The coaching component, which supported teachers in planning and implementing lessons, allowed the coach to provide targeted guidance tailored to the teachers' needs. Coaches also assisted teachers with math knowledge and skills, by modeling and co-leading activities, by observing instruction and providing feedback, and by assisting with materials for media-rich as well as hands-on activities.

Uptake of the Resources by Teachers

Classroom observation data indicated that teachers typically implemented the distinctive features of the curriculum supplement: the warm-up and wrap-up, pause points, and the JEM strategies emphasized in the curriculum supplement. Teachers used pause points as specified in the teacher's guide 95% of the time during video viewing, often adding additional pause points of their own to reiterate ideas, check children's comprehension, and ask questions to spark discussion. Observers noted that discussion during shared media experiences centered on the mathematics knowledge and skills that were highlighted in the teacher's guide. As Chapter 6 describes, children who participated in the Media-Rich Math Supplement condition, which incorporated media from Ready To Learn properties, learned significantly more mathematics than children in the Business-as-Usual condition did.

Curation and Mediation in Action: Homes

Another CPB-PBS Ready To Learn study carried out during the 2010–2015 grant cycle focused on families in low-income neighborhoods and centered on the PBS KIDS program, *Peg + Cat* (Pasnik et al., 2015). The goals of the study were to identify and describe how use of the *Peg + Cat* videos, online games, and other supplemental activities influenced children's knowledge of target mathematics skills; how complementary supports for parents influenced parent/caregiver attitudes, beliefs, and behaviors; and how children and families engaged with selected *Peg + Cat* resources in their homes. As above, we focus this section on the 12-week learning experience, and on the JEM supports that were provided to parents; additional details are available in Chapter 6.

Selecting, Sequencing, and Organizing Math Learning Experiences for the Home

The target mathematical skills at the center of the *Peg + Cat* home study included patterns, geometry (e.g., 3-D and 2-D shapes), measurable attributes and spatial relations, ordinal numbers, and to a lesser degree on the foundational skill of counting which is present throughout all *Peg + Cat* materials. While all children are capable of learning skills and concepts in these four domains, these topics are typically less present in preschool curricula and are not as commonly supported by parents.

After a detailed review of the available *Peg + Cat* episodes, interstitials, and games, we identified assets that were most aligned with the target mathematical skills. In addition to video and game content, the research team also identified a range of PBS KIDS online and hands-on activities that complemented the digital activities to encourage families to extend *Peg + Cat* into their real-world lives. Each of these opportunities represented a chance for children to engage with mathematics, further explore and deepen existing understandings of target math skills, and/or refine emerging skills through application and practice, as often as possible in collaboration with a supportive adult.

Each week of the 12-week supplement included 30 minutes of curated content, organized into a recommended sequence of activities, and 30 minutes of suggested additional material. The first four weeks each focused on one mathematical skill: ordinal numbers, patterns, shapes, and measurable attributes and spatial relations. The activities were selected to capitalize on the excitement and energy of the start of the study with the aim of establishing strong early exposure to target math content. The remaining eight weeks spiraled through the four target skills, within and across weeks. Each week was designed to be an "adventure," including one or more full episodes, short video clips, one or more games, interstitials and/or a hands-on activity. Each adventure was designed to cover two to three skills, with these skills rotating throughout the remaining eight weeks.

Designing for JEM in Families

We asked parents using the *Peg + Cat* resources with their children to (1) be present with their children during media and technology interactions, as much as possible; (2) approach these interactions with the goal of helping children learn, sharing what they know, and learning something new together; (3) talk with children, asking questions and making observations to learn how they are understanding the experience, where their interests are focused, and difficulties or challenges they may be having; (4) help children make connections between media and other experiences at home, at school, and in the community; and (5) help children apply and extend their learning and further explore their interests by repeating activities and by engaging in new experiences with and without media and technology.

At the start of the study, researchers oriented families to study materials (the videos, games, and offline activities, all organized in an adventure guide) and the learning objectives (focal skills). Support materials for parents/caregivers were designed to provide modest guidance and support for engaging with study experiences on an ongoing basis through print and/or online video resources. Specifically, the research team produced four short "tip" videos for parents, available in English, Spanish, and Chinese, that focused on co-viewing media with their child, engaging in and supporting their child's use of math talk, and developing and supporting their child's problem-solving and persistence skills. Parents also received a printed *Experience Guide* aimed at helping them navigate the study experience. This *Experience Guide* provided parents with information about the basic math concepts their children encountered when engaging with *Peg + Cat* resources and included information about the digital resources and the weekly adventure schedule.

Families' Uptake of the Resources

Most families progressed through the *Peg + Cat* intervention experience over the 12-week study period, accessing all the resources that exposed them to the target mathematical skills. Children used the *Peg + Cat* intervention media resources most often with their parents, and parents in engaged in more joint media use with their children when compared to parents in a Business-as-Usual comparison group. Families reported finding the majority of the *Peg + Cat* resources to be fun and engaging, and some parents noted how the games and videos complemented each other in a beneficial way, making the content more meaningful through opportunities for practice.

Parents and caregivers in the *Peg + Cat* group reported a higher frequency of joint parent-child technology use, more joint gameplay, and more conversation connecting digital media and daily life than did Business-as-Usual parents. Parents who engaged with the *Peg + Cat* materials also reported significant increases in their confidence to support math learning for their children, as compared to parents in Business-as-Usual families.

Looking Ahead

Maximizing the educational potential of media resources calls for two critical components: curation and mediation or joint engagement with media (JEM). Curation was one key element of the two studies we describe in this chapter, supporting teachers and parents in crafting cohesive, developmentally appropriate learning experiences for children. Resources that enabled educators and parents to jointly engage with children when using media were another key element. With these resources, teachers and parents were better positioned to offer conversational guidance, direction, and encouragement, thereby fostering children's learning of target mathematical skills well beyond what may have been possible through children's solo or unmediated experiences.

Even with high-quality media resources, the presence of adults—teachers like Ms. C and parents like Sonia—whose explicit goal is to foster the child's learning is vital. The findings we present in this chapter call attention to the importance of supporting such teachers and parents in the process of facilitating children's learning with media, and that in doing so it is ultimately beneficial for children's learning. More importantly, the insights from the two Ready To Learn studies we highlight here open the door to future studies that continue to push the boundaries of how and when such learning can take place for all children, and particularly for children in families and neighborhoods with limited financial resources, who might also be underserved by public preschools.

Note

1 Ms. C and Sonia (both pseudonyms) are composites drawn from the early context studies we conducted as part of the 2010–2015 cycle of Ready To Learn research that involved conversations with teachers (EDC & SRI, 2011) and parents (EDC & SRI, 2012) in low-income communities.

References

AAP Council on Communications and Media. (2016). Media and young minds. *Pediatrics*, *138*(5), 1–5.

Apple. (2018). *iPad in Education*. Retrieved from www.apple.com/ca/education/ipad/apps-books-and-more/, May 15, 2018.

Barron, B. & Levinson, A. (2017). Media as a catalyst for children's engagement in learning at home and across settings. In E. Wartella, L. Takeuchi, & E. Gee (Eds.), *Children and families in the digital age*. New York, NY: Routledge, pp. 31–50.

Domínguez, X., Goldstein, M., Lewis Presser, A., Kamdar, D., Vidiksis, R., & Orr, J. (under review). Next generation preschool science: Findings from design-based research to inform iterative development of an innovative curricular program and an evaluation of its efficacy.

Dreiske, N. (2018). *The upside of digital devices: How to make your child more screen smart, literate, and emotionally intelligent*. Deerfield, FL: Health Communications Inc.

EDC & SRI. (2011). *Year 1 context studies: A report to the Ready To Learn Initiative*. New York, NY and Menlo Park, CA: Education Development Center & SRI International.

EDC & SRI. (2012). *Context study of the use of technology and PBS KIDS transmedia in the home environment*. New York, NY and Menlo Park, CA: Education Development Center & SRI International.

Enchautegui, M. E., Johnson, M., & Gelatt, J. (2015). *Who minds the kids when mom works a nonstandard schedule?* Washington, DC: Urban Institute.

Hirsh-Pasek, K., Alper, R. M., & Golinkoff, R. M. (2018). Living in Pasteur's quadrant: How conversational duets spark language at home and in the community. *Discourse Processes*, *55*(4), 338–345.

Hirsh-Pasek, K., Zosh, J. M., Golinkoff, R. M., Gray, J. H., Robb, M. B., & Kaufman, J. (2015). Putting education in "Educational" apps: Lessons from the science of learning. *Psychological Science in the Public Interest, 16*(1), 3–34.

Mihalca, L., & Miclea, M. (2007). Current trends in educational technology research. *Cognition, Brain and Behavior, XI*(1), 115–129.

NAEYC & Fred Rogers Center for Early Learning and Children's Media. (2012). *Technology and interactive media as tools in early childhood programs serving children from birth through age 8.* Joint position statement. Washington, DC: NAEYC; Latrobe, PA: Fred Rogers Center at St. Vincent College.

Neuman, S. & Celano, D. (2006). The knowledge gap: Implications of leveling the playing field for low-income and middle-income children. *Reading Research Quarterly, 41*(2), 176–201.

Ochs, E. & Shohet, M. (2006). The cultural structuring of mealtime socialization. *New Directions for Child and Adolescent Development, 111*, 35–49.

Papadakis, S., Kalogiannakis, M., & Zaranis, N. (2017). Designing and creating an educational app rubric for preschool teachers. *Education and Information Technologies, 22*(6), 3147–3165.

Pasnik, S. & Llorente, C. (2013). *Preschool teachers can use a PBS KIDS transmedia curriculum supplement to support young children's mathematics learning: Results of a randomized controlled trial.* New York, NY: Education Development Center.

Pasnik, S., Moorthy, S., Llorente, C., Hupert, N., Domínguez, X., & Silander, M. (2015). *Supporting parent-child experiences with Peg + Cat early math concepts.* New York, NY and Menlo Park, CA: Education Development Center & SRI International.

Peske, H. & Haycock, K. (2006). *Teaching inequality: How poor and minority students are shortchanged on teacher quality.* Washington, DC: The Education Trust.

Seiter, E. (2008). Practicing at home: Computers, pianos, and cultural capital. In T. McPherson (Ed.), *Digital youth, innovation, and the unexpected.* Cambridge, MA: The John D. and Catherine T. MacArthur Foundation Series on Digital Media and Learning.

Silander, M., Grindal, T., Hupert, N., Garcia, E., Anderson, K., Vahey, P., & Pasnik, S. (2018). *What parents talk about when they talk about learning: A national survey about young children and science.* New York, NY and Menlo Park, CA: Education Development Center, Inc., & SRI International.

Takeuchi, L., & Stevens, R. (2011). *The new co-viewing: Designing for learning through joint media engagement.* Paper presented at the Sesame Workshop at The Joan Ganz Cooney Center, New York, NY.

Tenenbaum, H., & Callanan, M. (2008). Parents' science talk to their children in Mexican-descent families residing in the USA. *International Journal of Behavioral Development, 32*(1), 1–12.

9

PRESCHOOLERS LEARN TO THINK AND ACT LIKE SCIENTISTS WITH *THE CAT IN THE HAT*

Sara S. Sweetman, Lawrence S. Mirkin, Anne E. Lund, and Shannon K. Bishop

Introduction

The Cat in the Hat Knows a Lot About That! is a PBS KIDS multi-platform media property based on the acclaimed Dr. Seuss's "The Cat in the Hat's Learning Library" book series by Random House and Dr. Seuss Enterprises. The popular television series, produced by Portfolio Entertainment, along with the digital games and offline activities produced by Random House, appeal to preschoolers' natural curiosity about the world around them. Dr. Seuss's *The Cat in the Hat*, voiced by Martin Short, guides friends Sally and Nick—with a little help from Fish, Thing 1, and Thing 2—on fun-filled adventures where they playfully explore and make discoveries through science inquiry and engineering design in fantastical worlds and their own backyard.

In 2015, the Corporation for Public Broadcasting (CPB) and Public Broadcasting Service (PBS) were awarded a five-year grant as part of the Ready To Learn Initiative. When writing the proposal for the Ready To Learn Television Grant Program, it was important to find a then-current PBS KIDS property that aligned with the grant's science focus and met its rigor and mission. *The Cat in the Hat Knows a Lot About That!* (*The Cat*) was an ideal candidate given its successful two seasons on-air, its high-quality digital content, and its curriculum already grounded in science. Furthermore, because the producer would need to hire a new writing team, production team, and cast (besides Martin Short) for the new season, there was an opportunity to reimagine and reinvent elements of the series. The CPB-PBS Ready To Learn Initiative would provide a new level of educational rigor to *The Cat*, making it one of the first media properties to provide preschoolers with a social, emotional, and academic foundation for the Next Generation Science Standards (NGSS). A team with diverse experience and expertise in both education and media came together to develop a suite of experiences, including TV episodes, digital experiences, and hands-on activities to educate children and their families in new and innovative ways.

The PBS KIDS Science Learning Framework

To guide the creation of science-focused content, including *The Cat*, the CPB-PBS Ready To Learn team first developed the PBS KIDS Science Learning Framework (see Figure 9.1). The Framework outlines the age-appropriate, foundational understandings and learning progressions for science and engineering concepts and practices for the PBS KIDS target audience of two- to eight-year-olds. This evidence-based document is a key resource for producers, advisors, and the CPB-PBS Ready To Learn team, ensuring consistent integration of the curriculum. Created with invaluable input from a team of early childhood science advisors, some with experience in educational media, the Framework aligns with National and State standards including the NGSS (NGSS Lead States, 2013) and the Head Start Early Learning Outcomes Framework (U.S. Department of Health and Human Services, 2015). It also takes into account position statements and guidelines from early childhood and educational foundations such as the National Association for the Education of Young Children (NAEYC) and the National Science Teachers Association (NSTA). Universal Design for Learning (UDL) advisors and partners also provided input to ensure that all children would have opportunities to learn (CAST, 2011), while early childhood classroom educators shared insights for practical applications and connections. (See Chapter 14 for a detailed description of UDL considerations within the CPB-PBS Ready To Learn Initiative.)

The PBS KIDS team founded the Science Learning Framework on young children's propensity to engage in and learn science and an awareness that conceptual understanding begins with concrete observations that become more sophisticated and abstract over time and with experience. Further, we were cognizant that effective teaching connects to students' interests and experiences and that science education plays an important role in promoting equity (NRC, 2012). Like the NGSS, the Science Learning Framework outlines the disciplinary core ideas within the domains of life science, earth and space science, and physical science, while also integrating engineering and technology across these domains. It emphasizes the importance of science and engineering practices, providing key ways that children of different ages might engage in inquiry-based learning, helping them learn to think, act, and talk like scientists. Infographics were designed to help content producers understand the dynamic nature of science inquiry and the engineering design process, and to illustrate the interconnectedness of the science and engineering practices (see Figure 9.2). Crosscutting concepts were also included to reflect the focus of NGSS on three-dimensional learning and to help children understand and connect disciplinary core ideas and practices across domains. The concepts also provide a framing device by which

PBS **Ready To Learn**

PBS KIDS Science Learning Framework

Science

The study of the natural world, both living and nonliving, through a process of inquiry that includes observation, prediction, and experimentation leading to understanding/explanation.

Science and Engineering Practices

The practices that develop the skills, thinking, and language of Scientific Inquiry and Engineering Design.

1. Asking questions (for science) and defining problems (for engineering)
2. Developing and using models
3. Planning and carrying out investigations
4. Analyzing and interpreting data
5. Using mathematics and computational thinking
6. Constructing explanations (for science) and designing solutions (for engineering)
7. Engaging in argument from evidence
8. Obtaining, evaluating, and communicating information

Life Science			Earth & Space Science			Physical Science			
The study of the structure, behaviors, and relationships of living organisms.			*The study of processes that operate on Earth and of Earth's place in the solar system and the galaxy.*			*The study of the characteristics and properties of energy and nonliving matter.*			
From Molecules to Organisms: Structures and Processes	Ecosystems: Interactions, Energy, and Dynamics	Heredity: Inheritance and Variation of Traits	Biological Evolution: Unity and Diversity	Earth's Place in the Universe	Earth's Systems	Earth and Human Activity	Matter and Its Interactions	Motion and Stability: Forces and Interactions	Energy	Waves and Their Applications in Technologies for Information Transfer

Engineering & Technology

The practice of design to find solutions to particular human problems (engineering) and the human-made tools, systems, and processes created to fulfill human needs and wants (technology).

FIGURE 9.1 PBS KIDS Science Learning Framework cover page

(Courtesy of PBS; The PBS logos and wordmarks are trademarks of the Public Broadcasting Service and used with permission)

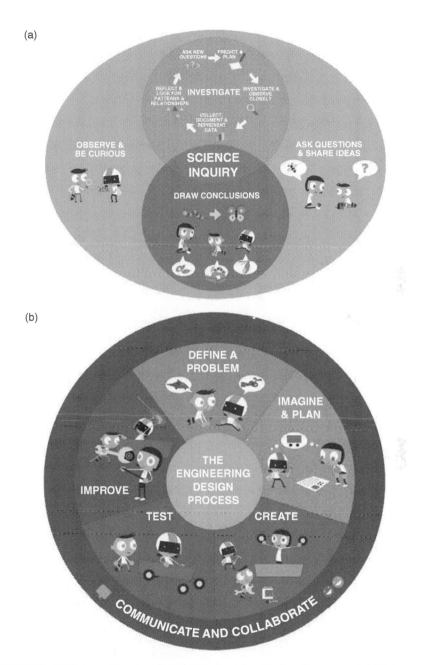

FIGURE 9.2   (a) Science Inquiry, (b) The Engineering Design Process, and (c) Science and Engineering Practices infographics

(Courtesy of PBS)

(c)

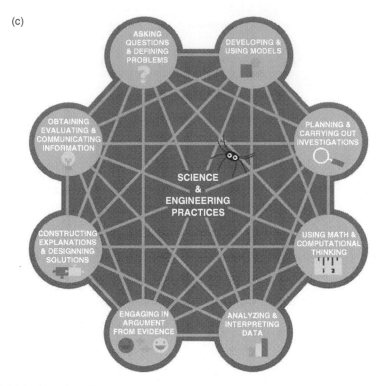

FIGURE 9.2 (continued)

children can think about and apply something they have learned to a novel curiosity (Bradley, 2016; NGSS Lead States, 2013).

The Science Learning Framework was an influential resource when developing content for *The Cat*, providing a basis not only for the show's Curriculum Plan but also for many of the creative and editorial decisions made later.

Reimagining *The Cat* for the Ready To Learn Initiative

Season three of *The Cat in the Hat Knows a Lot About That!* required the production team to reimagine the series creatively, taking into account the experience of the previous two seasons, the aesthetic of Dr. Seuss and his characters, and the educational rigor of the PBS KIDS Science Learning Framework. We shifted the scientific focus from natural and life science to physical science and engineering, recognizing that physical science and engineering topics lend themselves well to visual storytelling and provide opportunities for active, playful learning. Prior to writing the first script, we wrote a Content Plan and Curriculum Plan, followed by a Creative Manual so writers and other creative talent could transform the ideas of the Science Learning Framework into an engaging Ready To Learn television series. The team worked closely with Dr. Seuss Enterprises to ensure that the development of the TV series was consistent with Dr. Seuss's principles and with *The Cat in the Hat* characters.

The following guiding principles led our creative process:

- **Teach pre-conceptions, not misconceptions.** We focused our approach to the science and the story through the lens of young children. Since the target audience is three- to five-year-old children from diverse locations and having diverse background knowledge and experiences, we wanted to provide content with which young children could make connections to their life experiences. We aimed to build foundational and developmentally appropriate conceptual understandings of the complex core ideas while avoiding and correcting common misconceptions in science. During the writing and storyboarding processes of each 11-minute episode, most of the revisions involved stripping away interesting but extraneous ideas to focus on depth of one concept, and model specific science or engineering practices. The science and engineering practices, such as asking questions, planning and conducting investigations, and developing and using models, were easy to dramatize with the TV series characters and formed a kind of "hidden" science architecture congruent with the story structure.

- **Young children learn science through play.** With a desire to model playful learning in the show, the producers spent time observing children in a play-based kindergarten classroom. They saw how children's natural tendencies for play mirror the practices of scientists and cross the boundaries between science, art, and humanities.

- **Story, science, and Seuss need to work together.** Cinematic fiction conveys meaning in complex ways, and in ways different from how it is conveyed in non-fiction, the digital realm, or a classroom setting. In creating a television story that delivers "content" to the audience in a continuous flow of images and words, a number of factors define the specific relationship of a viewer to the story. Narrative strength, character identification, setting, composition, color, music, and comedy all combine to convey the overall "meaning" (idea/subject/theme) in an aesthetic experience. We committed to delivering the intentions of the Science Learning Framework in a way that uses all aspects of that experience for the young viewer. Furthermore, we did not want the science content "added" onto the story but embedded in it. The science practices helped achieve this by fitting easily within the narrative demand for character-driven dramatic action. Fortunately, we had the great gift of Dr. Seuss's work to engage the audience playfully. The purposeful interaction of the science, the story, and the fantastical world of Dr. Seuss became identified as "The Three S's"—Story, Science, and Seuss—which became a kind of lodestar throughout the writing and production processes.

Empowering Characters

Our considerable production experience in creating visual drama for young children, dramatic theory, and research (James, 1884; Rubie, 1996) strongly asserts that a compelling story needs empowered characters who actively drive the story, distinct in personality and identifiable to the audience in terms of their own experience or imaginative life. Constructivist educational theorists claim authentic learning occurs when the learner is actively and socially involved in the process (Piaget, 1964; Vygotsky, 1967). Consequently, the first major change we made was to empower Sally and Nick by making them the protagonists of the stories. In previous seasons, Nick and Sally were passive characters, behaving like tourists, accompanying The Cat (the protagonist) to natural environments where The Cat or guest experts conveyed information verbally to Nick, Sally, and the audience. In the third season, Nick and Sally propel the story and the learning forward, engaging naturally in scientific practices, e.g., asking questions and planning investigations. They use the inquiry or engineering design process to discover new ideas and find solutions without getting direct answers from any other characters.

In addition, Nick and Sally now possess differences in personality and learning styles. Sally is kinetic and spontaneous in how she learns by doing. Nick is more cerebral and a bit more cautious, learning through careful observation before he gets hands-on. Together, Nick and Sally play in everyday and fantastical environments just as children would, while at the same time modeling the practices and behaviors of scientists and engineers.

The Cat *as Ideal Teacher*

The Cat was transformed from an imparter of information into an ideal teacher who engages, guides, protects, and encourages Nick and Sally in their own investigations. Always entertaining and energetic, The Cat is a bit mysterious, both in the writing and in Martin Short's performance. He never answers a key question directly; rather, he takes cues from Nick and Sally's curiosity and transports them to fantasy worlds where they can discover for themselves while having an adventure that is fun for them and the audience alike.

Dramatizing Science Practices and Exploring Core Ideas

Each story begins in the backyard or in one of the houses with Nick and Sally playing. One or both of the kids have a problem, a question, or are wondering about something. For example, Nick and Sally can't get a heavy costume trunk up to the Treehouse ("Pulling Together") or Sally can't make a vase for her mom that does not fall over ("Design Time"). When they play their musical instruments, they are curious about why they can hear each other when the windows are open but not when they are closed ("Making Waves"). They are puzzled as to why a tall glass of juice looks to have more juice than a shorter one, even though Nick's mother poured the juice from identical boxes ("Mind Changing Fun").

The Cat appears in each situation and takes them to a fantasy world where Sally and Nick discover and explore the core idea of the episode while engaging in natural, playful behaviors that are, in fact, scientific practices. In "Pulling Together," The Cat takes the kids to Machine-A-Ma-Zoo, where they have fun with simple machines and learn that a pulley can change the direction of a force. In "Design Time," The Cat whisks them off to Blueprintia where the kids draw 2-D designs that immediately become 3-D objects, so they use the engineering design process to discover how shape affects stability. In "Making Waves," they go to the Soundy Sea where they experience firsthand that sound is a wave. In "Mind Changing Fun" The Cat takes them to Point O'View, a land filled with optical illusions. They find the need to gather accurate evidence through measurement and learn to argue from that evidence (see Figure 9.3).

The adventure in each episode builds with humor and drama and so does the development of the scientific ideas. Nick and Sally never reach the solution, dramatic or scientific, on the first or second try, and they model resilience and perseverance as their curiosity persists. The stories celebrate failure and mistakes as part of learning, and those experiences spur the characters to try new ideas. The Seussian aesthetic gives us unique opportunities for embedding the learning into the entertainment. While the viewer easily suspends disbelief about a talking Cat, a flying "Thinga-Ma-Jigger," or the fantasy worlds, the science content identified in each episode's learning goal remains accurate. The fantasy worlds can also provide flexibility to show some core ideas that would be hard to show in reality. For example, in "Gravity Drop," the kids use a "gravitometer" to change the amount of gravity. They experience the differences, and the viewer sees them, rather than being told about them.

Armed with new information and ideas, Nick and Sally return home to solve their problem or answer their question. The solution is scientifically valid and relatable to the target audience for the show. Nick and Sally find they only need their brains, teamwork, scientific practices, creativity, and of course a little bit of fun to find answers and real-world solutions using everyday materials.

Extending the Learning

Our primary intention for the TV series is to engage the young viewer with fun stories while exploring core ideas by modeling the processes associated with science inquiry and engineering design. We also produced each episode in ways that allowed the initial engagement to be further developed by teachers, parents, other children, or caregivers in formal or informal learning situations. A parent or teacher can use any episode as a starting point to deepen a child's understanding

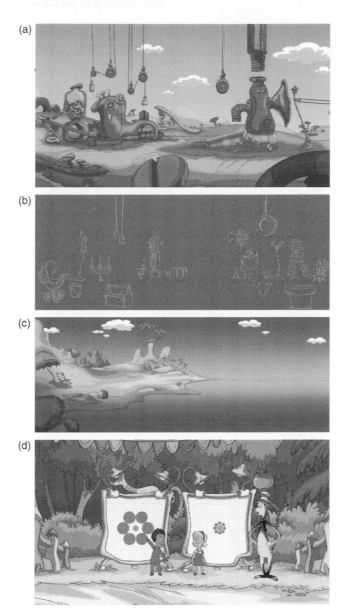

FIGURE 9.3 (a) Image of bridge scene from television series *The Cat in the Hat Knows a Lot About That!* (b) Image of Blueprintia Landing from television series *The Cat in the Hat Knows a Lot About That!* (c) Image of beach scene from television series *The Cat in the Hat Knows a Lot About That!* (d) Image of mind changing fun scene from television series *The Cat in the Hat Knows a Lot About That!*

of a core idea, with real-world investigations, using the practices that are similar to those Sally and Nick model in the story. Related digital games and hands-on activities developed for parents and teachers can enrich the learning in ways that are not subject to the inexorable 11-minute movement of a cinematic story.

A Playful Learning Experience with *The Cat*

As with season three of the TV series, *The Cat in the Hat* digital team was given a unique challenge to engage preschoolers in science inquiry and engineering design through games based on *The Cat* stories and characters. These games were to extend and support children's play and learning from the TV series, promoting positive mindsets and attitudes in science and engineering while teaching core science concepts and practices. The digital team was tasked to use intuitive, accessible, and playful game mechanics to keep preschoolers with varied background knowledge and abilities active, engaged and having fun. Also, these digital experiences needed to be accessible wherever the target audience was, across a variety of mobile devices and on desktop computers. The result was *The Cat in the Hat Builds That* app, a Playful Learning Experience that is a collection of media, games, and hands-on activities developed with an adaptive, multi-platform approach featuring the stories from the series, and Nick and Sally behaving like real scientists. It engages children in science inquiry and engineering design practices and supports guided play, curiosity, and real-world discovery. Personalization features are integrated throughout the content, providing multiple ways for a user to play the games, and empowering preschoolers to learn in the way that best fits their needs. Lastly, *The Cat* Playful Learning Experience features play patterns that reflect the user's preferences through customization.

Early Prototyping

In the first year of development, the team imagined and prototyped simple but innovative game mechanics and digital experiences that were used to shape *The Cat* Playful Learning Experience. These prototypes focused on engaging children in science practices, like planning and conducting investigations, while remaining grounded in core science concepts. We tested the prototypes in local Head Start schools, and our findings influenced the final feature set and engagement strategy. We learned how best to utilize the digital platform capabilities, such as designing experiences around inquiry tools, e.g., a hand lens, and the players' ability to use that tool to help them see a challenge differently, e.g., by taking a closer look at textures of materials. The testing showed the importance of offering both goal-oriented and exploration-oriented play, as well as offering multiple ways for players to show what they know and interact with its features in order to reach our broad audience (Rockman et al, 2016).

A Plan for Playful Learning

With its distinct episode structure, beloved characters, and engaging stories, *The Cat's* third season seamlessly transitioned to a digital play experience, satisfying kids' desire to do just what Nick and Sally do in the show: go on adventures *with* The Cat. With Nick and Sally in the role as scientist or engineer, the player is prompted to ask questions, define problems, make observations, plan and conduct investigations, and reflect on what they have learned. And, just as he does in the TV series, The Cat is the ultimate guide throughout the digital experience, asking questions, providing inspirational prompts and sharing inquisitive thinking to help guide children in making their own discoveries.

Offering a real-world context at the beginning of their science and engineering adventures, players, along with Nick and Sally, start and end in the backyard. The goal is to promote the transfer of digital play to a child's own world and to put learning into action (see Figure 9.4). The backyard play lets children tinker, play at their own pace, and practice what they learned from each guided game experience. Beyond the familiarity of the backyard, children experience the fun of finding answers to their questions and solutions to their problems in the fantasy worlds they visit with The Cat. These imagined lands encourage children to use science and engineering practices by diving deeply into a single game experience, like building, testing, and improving bridges in Spansylvania, or planning and carrying out investigations with slides in the Frictionarium. Gameplay is child-directed and non-linear, and a player's progress is saved within and across games, so they can apply the knowledge and practices learned in one game to other games.

Putting the Plan into Action

Bridge-a-rama was one of the three core games launched in the app and was the first adaptive and personalized game we play-tested and launched specifically for the preschool audience. Bridge-a-rama is based on an episode in which The Cat takes Nick and Sally to Spansylvania where they discover bridges are made of different materials that all need to be long and strong enough to cross the gap. In the game, players build bridges for a friendly dragon, so he can bring presents to the birthday castle. Players learn about the engineering design process, including building, testing, and redesigning. They also develop foundational physical science concepts associated with material properties of length and strength. Players are empowered to build their own bridges with Nick and Sally, who guide them through science practices like making predictions and reflect on their learning with The Cat, who offers contextual feedback.

We learned from play-testing that children had strong background knowledge in identifying appropriate-length bridge parts, but struggled when they were required to use material strength and support designs and/or apply

(a)

(b)

FIGURE 9.4   (a) Image of a backyard tree house scene from television series *The Cat in the Hat Knows a Lot About That!* (b) Image of a backyard tree house scene from *The Cat in the Hat Builds That* app

(Top image courtesy of © Portfolio Entertainment Inc. 2017–2018.; Dr. Seuss Books and Characters TM & © 1957–58 Dr. Seuss Enterprises, L.P. All Rights Reserved.; Bottom image (derived and adapted from the series *The Cat in the Hat Knows a Lot About That!*) courtesy of © Penguin Random House and Dr. Seuss Enterprises, LP. 2018. Used with Permission.; Dr. Seuss Books and Characters TM & © 1957–58 Dr. Seuss Enterprises, L.P. All Rights Reserved)

knowledge of multiple variables to build a successful bridge. Through the application of an adaptive learning system, the player's demonstrated learning proficiency is analyzed based on how he or she played previous levels, and the game identifies variables on which to build the next level that will best serve that individual child. For example, if a player is struggling with the strength of the materials, the level will provide bridge pieces of similar strength, so the player can identify multiple strength solutions to solve the problem. Once the player can solve that challenge, the next level will provide a greater degree of variation in the strength of the materials to continue to appropriately challenge the player.

All the games empower children to succeed by offering inquiry tools to take a closer look or have another opportunity to see the solution. In early game concept stages, it was very clear from the show's science advisors that we needed to give children an opportunity to *do* the science in the games. By having players actually build the bridges, they are actively engaging in the engineering design process. With Seussian tools, like the Measuring Snail, players can measure the gap and individual bridge pieces, and solve the problem through multiple pathways. Some tools encourage creativity and open-ended thinking. For example, the "Doodle-ma-boodle" is a sketch pad and pen that provides black and white line art scenes from the three individual games (see Figure 9.5). Play-testing revealed that children used it as a planning tool before gameplay, as a reflecting tool after gameplay, and as a sharing and collaboration tool, with children drawing their own bridges and asking caregivers if they think the dragon could cross or not.

Engineering The Cat

Throughout the development process, we grappled with how to engage preschoolers in the engineering design process. What does that mechanic look like in a game? What understanding did we want children to come away with regarding the design process? Do we want them to explicitly identify the stages of the process? Or is it more important to get them engaged in the process and using the engineering practices? Maybe a little of both? Play-testing helped answer these questions.

Using a *Cat in the Hat*–branded version of the PBS KIDS Engineering Design Process graphic (see Figure 9.6), we investigated how the graphic could be used in gameplay. Early game versions included an animated engineering design "wheel" that indicated the player's current engineering design stage in the game. Results from testing this mechanic showed that some players were getting distracted by the wheel rather than playing the game, while others completely ignored it. Instead of using the wheel during the games, the development team added a universally known play icon called the "TEST" button, which encourages players to work through the design process without explicitly naming the stages. We also added voice supports like, "Let's test this bridge; it looks strong!" and "Select the arrow to test your prediction."

The more children played the game, the more excited they became about building their bridge. The play-testers heard children repeating The Cat's voiceover lines, using design process language, such as, "We are going to test it now!" and "I'll test my bridge now." When asked what they were doing in the game, players often responded: "I'm testing a bridge." Tying the main game mechanic to the

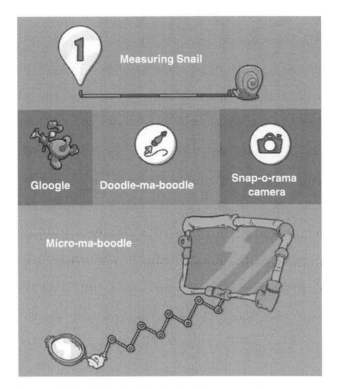

FIGURE 9.5　Image of *The Cat in the Hat Builds That* app tools
(Derived and adapted from the series *The Cat in the Hat Knows A Lot About That!* Courtesy of © Penguin Random House and Dr. Seuss Enterprises, LP. 2018. Used with Permission.; Dr. Seuss Books and Characters TM & © 1957–1958 Dr. Seuss Enterprises, L.P. All Rights Reserved)

specific engineering design process made it an intuitive and fun way for children to engage in multiple engineering practices, while also learning key vocabulary.

Making Choices for Optimal Performance

It was a challenge to engage children in the engineering and science practices and associated mindsets, while also creating a universally designed digital product playable across multiple devices. The multifaceted Playful Learning Experience had limited device capabilities in terms of memory, usage, and support. Research shows that lower-income families rely more on smartphones without broadband internet (Anderson, 2017), so voiceover and animation decisions were made to maximize performance for all devices. Making *The Cat in the Hat Builds That* Playful Learning Experience widely available—through

(a)

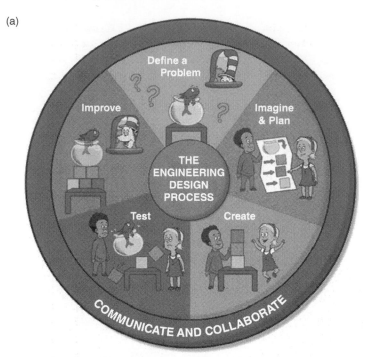

(b)

FIGURE 9.6 (a) Image of *The Cat in the Hat* Engineering Design Process Wheel (b) Image of Bridge-a-rama from *The Cat in the Hat Builds That* app

(Derived and adapted from the series *The Cat in the Hat Knows a Lot About That!* Courtesy of © Penguin Random House and Dr. Seuss Enterprises, LP. 2018. Used with Permission.; Dr. Seuss Books and Characters TM & © 1957–1958 Dr. Seuss Enterprises, L.P. All Rights Reserved)

the Apple, Amazon, and Google Play app stores, PBS KIDS Games app, and PBSKIDS.org—was an important technical strategy for providing a more equitable learning opportunity for children served by the Ready To Learn Initiative. It was configured to be playable offline via mobile apps, making it possible for families to play without worrying about Wi-Fi or data fees. We also had to optimize our production process and be a more flexible, iterative team throughout development in response to the evolving preschool audience, innovative inquiry approach, and multi-media product. This Playful Learning Experience app product and its playful approach to engaging children in science is a core goal of the Ready To Learn Initiative and will be used not just by our audience but also by station communities, educators, and parents as part of a larger learning ecosystem.

Learning Anytime, Anywhere with *The Cat*

As with all PBS KIDS properties, especially those created with funding from the Ready To Learn Initiative, there is a focus on all aspects of a child's learning ecosystem. The goal is to reach children anytime, anywhere, by providing a variety of rich educational media resources that can be accessed by the child at home on their own, with a sibling or parent, at a local PBS station event, or with a teacher in school. These resources should also inspire children to explore the world around them and apply the knowledge of science concepts and practices to learn more at home and with those who support them.

To meet this goal, the team produced complementary offline and supplemental materials for parents, families, and educators to further extend playful learning with *The Cat*. The materials are thoughtfully connected through story and curriculum and include parent-child hands-on activities for learning at home, and teacher lesson plans that use the video and digital media for learning in the classroom. Activities were created for all children and families to participate in no matter what their economic situation. For example, materials for activities were either included in a printable form or were household or natural materials that parents and children could easily obtain at low or no cost.

It Takes a Village ... and *The Cat*

A genuine collaborative development process involving Dr. Seuss Enterprises, PBS, CPB, advisors, producers, developers, and researchers, the 2015–2020 CPB-PBS Ready To Learn Initiative made it possible to adapt and enhance a successful media property, ultimately bringing more science learning experiences to preschoolers with the help of *The Cat*. Each piece of content—videos, digital games and apps, hands-on activities, family engagement workshops, teacher-focused lessons—was created with the goal of providing children, especially those in under-resourced communities, with fun, playful, and robust ways to engage in science and make discoveries about the world around them.

Copyrights and Disclosures

References

Anderson, M. (2017). *Digital divide persists even as lower-income Americans make gains in tech adoption.* Washington, DC: Pew Research Center. Retrieved from www.pewresearch. org/fact-tank/2017/03/22/digital-divide-persists-even-as-lower-income-americans-make-gains-in-tech-adoption/.

Bradley, B. A. (2016). Integrating the curriculum to engage and challenge children. *Young Children, 71*(3), 8–16.

CAST. (2011). *Universal design for learning guidelines (Version 2.0).* Wakefield, MA: CAST. Retrieved from wwwudlcenter.org/aboutudl/udlguidelines.

James, H. (1884). The art of fiction. *Longman's Magazine, 1882–1905, 4*(23), 502–521.

National Research Council. (2012). *A framework for K–12 science education: Practices, cross-cutting concepts, and core ideas.* Washington, DC: National Academies Press.

NGSS Lead States. (2013). *Next generation science standards: For states, by states.* Washington, DC: National Academies Press.

Piaget, J. (1964). Part I: Cognitive development in children: Piaget development and learning. *Journal of Research in Science Teaching, 2*(3), 176–186.

Rockman et al, Inc. (2016). *Findings for Cat in the Hat story and digital prototype testing.* San Francisco, CA: Rockman et al.

Rubie, P. (1996). *The elements of storytelling: How to write compelling fiction.* New York, NY: John Wiley & Sons Inc.

U.S. Department of Health and Human Services (USDHHS), Administration for Children and Families, Office of Head Start. (2015). *Head start early learning outcomes framework: Ages birth to five.* Washington, DC: USDHHS.

Vygotsky, L. S. (1967). Play and its role in the mental development of the child. *Soviet Psychology, 5*(3), 6–18.

10

SCIENCE TAKES CENTER STAGE

Design Principles to Support Young Children's Science Learning with Media

Marion Goldstein, Claire Christensen, Sarah Nixon Gerard, and Megan Silander

Introduction

Young children are natural scientific thinkers. When they ask questions (again and again), describe what will happen next, observe something closely, and offer ideas about why, they are acting like scientists. Through these activities, and with the right support from adults, they are developing foundational knowledge about how the physical, biological, and social worlds work.

Although children are inclined to explore science-related ideas and questions on their own, they need help to develop the important science knowledge and skills that can come from those explorations. Providing children with these supports from an early age sets them up for success later in life; children who have high-science-related knowledge at the start of kindergarten are likely to be high-science achievers at the end of middle school (Curran, 2017). Unfortunately, many children do not have frequent, robust opportunities to learn science and their exposure to science is limited in preschool (Piasta, Pelatti, & Miller, 2014). This lack of opportunity is particularly pronounced for children from low-income families, and gaps in science achievement between children from high- and low-income families are evident as early as kindergarten (Curran, 2017). Starting in 2015, the Education Development Center (EDC)/ SRI International (SRI) research team, working in collaboration with the CPB-PBS Ready To Learn Initiative, has aimed to address these gaps by examining ways to use media to increase and enhance opportunities for children, especially those from low-income families, to engage with science. This work builds on research we have been conducting for the past several years, described below, which has generated knowledge and resources for incorporating science in preschools.

Leveraging the affordances of technology and media for learning has been central to our science-oriented work. For science, digital media can allow children to manipulate time and space (e.g., by speeding things up or zooming in) to "see" scientific phenomena that are usually not observable, experiment like a scientist by trying out solutions quickly and without real-world consequences, and deepen children's understanding of cause-and-effect relationships by providing instant feedback. In these and countless other ways, digital media have the potential to engage children with important concepts and practices of science.

However, certain conditions must be met for digital media to fulfill their potential and support early science teaching and learning. Evidence for the design and use of media more broadly suggests it can improve children's attitudes, behavior, and learning, but these impacts depend on the quality of the resources, as well as the contexts and adults scaffolding children's use. Little research has examined connections between science media and young children's learning, in particular. Because of this lack of evidence, our CPB-PBS Ready To Learn research and development efforts rest initially on a set of guiding principles we feel have the potential to create the conditions necessary to support learning. These principles draw from research about the role that technology and media can broadly play in improving children's learning and behaviors, and the kinds of design and use that research suggests are effective. We rely particularly on lessons learned from a recent National Science Foundation–funded initiative, involving a team of researchers at SRI and the EDC and media producers at WGBH, to develop and test a curricular program (Early Science with *Nico & Nor*) for use in preschool classrooms. The program, which uses media in conjunction with hands-on activities and includes professional development supports for teachers, led to significant improvements in children's science learning and generated evidence about the effective design and use of media to support preschool science instruction and learning (Domínguez et al., 2018). We believe this work provides a foundation for looking beyond classrooms to support children's science learning at home and in community programming.

Our work under the 2015–2020 CPB-PBS Ready To Learn Initiative provides opportunities for us to embed, examine, and refine the following guiding principles, as well as test the efficacy of the emerging science resources. Our first principle focuses on developing high-quality, accessible media resources.

Guiding Principle 1. Develop resources accessible to all children that leverage the affordances of technology and media, and align with what we know about how to support developmentally appropriate science teaching and learning.

We know that resources alone are not sufficient to promote science learning: Parents and educators are essential, and resources must support adults in fulfilling their roles.

Guiding Principle 2. Use technology and media to empower the people who can play a critical role in supporting children's science learning.

Quality media and supports are meaningless if they are not used. Resources must be designed with an eye toward feasible implementation.

Guiding Principle 3. Use technology and media to enable the integration of science into children's everyday lives and across contexts.

In the following sections, we describe how each guiding principle is informing our current line of research. We also offer suggestions for designers who wish to create and leverage media in ways that foster young children's science learning. We draw from our work involving multiple CPB-PBS Ready To Learn properties, but at the time of this writing, many resources are still in development or available only to PBS member stations. Ultimately, most resources from the CPB-PBS Ready To Learn Initiative will be available for free via the PBS KIDS website, PBS KIDS Video and Games apps, PBS KIDS Parents' website, and PBS Learning Media website.

Addressing Resource Needs

To achieve the first goal—*develop resources accessible to all children that leverage the affordances of technology and media, and align with what we know about how to support developmentally appropriate science teaching and learning*—digital resources must address issues of equity, align with how children learn and what they can do, and take advantage of the affordances of different types of digital tools.

Equity: Reaching Low-Income Families

At its core, the CPB-PBS Ready To Learn Initiative is focused on equity: supporting the millions of children who otherwise would lack access to early learning experiences that prepare them for school and beyond. Television was once the primary means of conveying educational content to low-income children, but in the past decade, the device landscape has expanded significantly to include a wide range of computing and mobile devices that create exciting avenues to promote young children's learning. Despite prevalent device access, many low-income families cannot access digital resources because they lack consistent or high-speed internet access or have older devices whose operating systems were not designed for apps. Monthly data plans also often limit families' ability to make use of data-hungry resources, such as videos and games. This means merely offering digital resources for free is insufficient to ensure access.

What Media Producers Can Do

- Develop resources to be downloadable to ensure access when the internet is unavailable.
- Make resources available on phones or tablets; low-income families are more likely to have mobile devices than laptops and larger computers.
- Ensure apps can work on older versions of technology and accommodate typical space limitations on those devices.
- Provide printed versions of resources or related supports when possible.

Helping to ensure equity of access also entails designing resources for families with less education and lower levels of literacy. Additionally, to be truly equitable, resources must be available for the 21% of families in the U.S. for whom English is not a primary language. Although Spanish is just one language of many spoken by families, it is the second-most common language (16% of children in the U.S. speak Spanish at home; U.S. Census Bureau, 2016).

What Media Producers Can Do

- Use clear and simple language throughout media resources.
- Make use of audio narration and video to relay text-based information.
- Provide media in Spanish and other widely used languages. Ready To Learn resources, for example, include Spanish versions of *The Cat in the Hat Knows a Lot About That!*, and *Sid the Science Kid* digital games, and *PEG+CAT* hands-on activities.
- Provide diverse science role models, such as parents and children who represent the racial, ethnic, cultural, linguistic, and geographic diversity of the target audience. This may include characters who speak languages other than English, live in low-income areas, and have a variety of skin colors.

Targeting Developmentally Appropriate Concepts and Practices

Science resources must be designed and used in accordance with what is known about how children learn and what they can do. We posit that developmentally appropriate resources focus on engaging children with science concepts, or core ideas, rather than discrete facts. The PBS KIDS Science Learning Framework provides a blueprint for developing the resources emerging from the CPB-PBS Ready To Learn Initiative. The Framework names four content domains aligned with the Next Generation Science Standards (NGSS, 2013), including Physical Science, Life Science, Earth and Space Sciences, and Engineering and Technology, and identifies appropriate core science ideas and topics within each domain. Resources are grounded in children's likely background knowledge and understanding of concepts, as well as what is relevant to children's lives, observable, and can be explored over time through a range of engaging and challenging activities. For example, Ready To Learn science resources provide opportunities to explore topics such as plants, animals, weather, and how objects move.

Design elements can support engagement with science concepts. Videos and other media can pose questions that direct children's attention to focal concepts, and motivate them to continue exploring them through digital or hands-on investigations. Designers also can minimize extraneous elements in digital resources, such as unrelated movements or sounds, to orient children's attention to central concepts. Additionally, children are more likely to maintain their focus on concepts when those concepts are central to the narrative driving the media experience. In CPB-PBS Ready To Learn narratives, questions and challenges relating to science concepts are what motivates characters to travel to outer space (*Ready Jet Go!*) or hop in a "Thinga-ma-jigger" to further the adventure (*The Cat in the Hat Knows a Lot About That!*). An ongoing challenge is to ensure that fantastical elements of such narratives support children's engagement with concepts and motivate learning, without planting misconceptions or leading children to overlook the real science underlying the media experience.

Children learn science concepts by participating in science practices. They engage in these practices when they observe and describe phenomena; engage in scientific talk; compare and categorize observable phenomena; ask questions, gather information, and make predictions; plan and conduct investigations and experiments; and analyze results, draw conclusions, and communicate results. Digital resources can heighten children's focus on the practices involved in an investigation, such as by modeling scientific thinking, scaffolding an investigation, limiting the variables that children can manipulate at once, and controlling environmental conditions (in digital activities, investigations are never foiled by uneven floors that affect how objects move or a drought that inhibits plant growth).

The ways in which media foster real-world interactions with science content and practices are also important. Our research is consistent with other leading early science experts' findings (Chalufour & Worth, 2006) that children's science engagement must involve hands-on activities, which help children learn concepts and make sense of complex information. When digital tools are integrated into hands-on experiences, they can enhance and provide additional opportunities for children to engage with science concepts using a range of science practices (Goldstein et al., 2015).

What Media Producers Can Do

- Emphasize science concepts rather than facts. For example, focus on the broader idea of habitats and how animal characteristics fit into them, rather than emphasizing specific animals living in the Alaskan tundra or Kenyan savannah.
- Integrate science concepts and practices into the central narrative, rather than saving it for interstitials. Each episode of *The Cat in the Hat Knows a Lot About That!* introduces a question or challenge relating to a focal concept that characters go on to explore, so the concept is central to every aspect of the narrative.
- Organize properties around certain topics so children can explore topics in different contexts. Science resources associated with *The Ruff Ruffman Show* are organized around four NGSS-aligned themes, including material properties (wearable science), force and motion (sports science), mixtures (kitchen chemistry), and stability (structures).
- Use media to model and encourage children to engage in scientific practices. "Fish Force," a *Ruff Ruffman* personalized and adaptive game, helps children conduct investigations by prompting them to predict where they think an object will land given a particular force, test predictions, and revise predictions.
- Use media in conjunction with, to enhance, and to motivate hands-on investigations, as is exemplified in CPB-PBS Ready To Learn child and family events, such as the PBS KIDS *ScratchJr* Family Creative Learning Workshops, *Ruff Ruffman* Sensational Science Camps, and *Odd Squad* "Be the Agent" Science Camps (See Chapter 13 for more detailed descriptions of these events).

Affordances of Different Types of Digital Tools

Our classroom-based work identified the advantages that different digital tools offer for promoting science learning (Domínguez et al., under review), and we are working to ensure that the emerging CPB-PBS Ready To Learn resources leverage those and other affordances. Videos, for example, can allow children to observe and discuss phenomena that are normally unobservable, such as by magnifying or slowing down or speeding up a phenomenon. Moreover, short video clips can provide a quick and easy way to generate excitement about a topic that may otherwise seem complex or uninteresting, support parents and educators who may lack experience explaining science content, provide questions to explore, and model how to explore questions together. Goal-oriented games and simulations often are highly engaging to children and can extend hands-on investigations by allowing children to practice what they learned and receive instant feedback.

What Media Producers Can Do

- Use videos to introduce or explain concepts, or observe what's normally unobservable, such as by showing the growth of a plant in a matter of seconds or slowing the motion of two objects rolling down a ramp.
- Foster reflection by encouraging children to take videos or photos of observations or experiments for later review and discussion.
- Use simulations or games to extend hands-on investigations, deepen understandings of concepts, and offer new ways to practice skills. In the *Ruff Ruffman* Sensational Science Camps and Family Creative Learning Workshops, participants watch a video segment from "Eye of the Hamster," in which children build a maze for a hamster. Then they experiment by making a digital path for a hamster using the app "Hamster Run." Finally, they transfer these skills to the real world by designing and building a playground for a hamster-sized Ruff stuffed animal.

Supporting People

Digital media can be well-designed in many ways and still miss the mark in supporting children's learning if resources do not properly support the people involved. For this reason, the second principle guiding our R&D work has been to use technology and media to empower the people who can play a critical role in supporting children's science learning. In the context of the CPB-PBS Ready To Learn Initiative, this most often includes children, educators, and parents. In this section, we describe what we're learning about how to help them fulfill the roles they play.

Children

Several support strategies can help children learn from media-rich science experiences. The first involves modeling scientific thinking. Video segments can be means to model activities and the thinking and vocabulary involved, such as when characters ask testable questions, investigate to find answers, or revise ideas in response to new information. Seeing these science behaviors, particularly when they care about and relate to the characters, can encourage children to mimic those behaviors later, and provide a good segue for activities similar to those featured in the media resources.

Media-rich science experiences are best for learning when they take place in a social context and spur social interactions and discourse. Media may encourage children to interact with characters featured in videos or other resources, and also can motivate real-world interactions with peers or adults around important science concepts.

Finally, play is critical for fostering children's learning and, therefore, is also a characteristic of high-quality media-rich learning experiences. For science, guided play supports the development of productive mindsets to foster learning, provides a supporting context for trial and error, and enables children to practice skills used in scientific investigations.

What Media Producers Can Do

- Model scientific thinking. Children featured in live-action *Ruff Ruffman* video segments demonstrate how to conduct investigations systematically to solve real problems; they ask, test, and draw conclusions about which ball is best for knocking things down, which material is best for a leash, and which structure will withstand the wind.
- Use scientific language, such as "predict" instead of "guess," or "habitat" instead of "home."
- Communicate concepts in multiple ways, such as through visuals, sound, spoken language, text, and other symbols. An episode about the weather might include images of weather patterns, language to describe the weather, symbols to illustrate weather processes, and print text to reinforce key vocabulary.
- Minimize extraneous elements such as noises, movements, or disconnected narratives that can distract children from focal science concepts.
- Use audio narrations to make testable questions explicit and help children focus on the purpose of experiments. Audio instructions also can guide them through multi-step investigations.
- Use mobile devices as data-collection tools. "Photo Stuff with Ruff," a *Ruff Ruffman* app, engages children in observations of material properties by encouraging them to photograph materials with different characteristics (e.g., something shiny).

- Design media in ways that invite children to interact with characters during media use, such as by following audio instructions, making choices in response to questions, and responding to feedback.
- Encourage children to interact with peers, educators, parents, or others by providing questions to support learning during and after media use. Families using the *Play and Learn* app to explore shadows during a Family Creative Learning Workshop use Center Support Cards that offer prompts to spark thinking and discourse ("Predict what will happen to the shadows on the screen if you change the sun's position in the sky"; "Why are some shadows big and some are small?").

Informal Educators

Much of our past research has focused on supporting preschool teachers, many of whom lack training, experience, resources, and confidence to teach science or integrate technology into instruction (Davidson, Fields, & Yang, 2009; Greenfield et al., 2009; Kallery, 2004). At the time of writing, we are testing and examining the best types of supports for informal educators in positions to implement CPB-PBS Ready To Learn science camps, family workshops, or other media-rich events. Our preliminary research suggests informal educators face similar challenges to educators working in formal settings—such as a lack of comfort with science, and lack of science content knowledge—so we are drawing on our knowledge about supports that help classroom teachers use media for science. The facilitator guides developed for CPB-PBS Ready To Learn family workshops and science camps are designed to prepare educators for media-rich science programming and support them throughout implementation. Those guides share characteristics with the SRI-EDC-WGBH-developed "Early Science with *Nico & Nor* Teacher Guide," which positively influenced teachers' instructional practices and their use of digital tools to engage children with science (Domínguez et al., under review). Both supports provide information about developmentally appropriate science concepts and practices, specifications and facilitation guidance for digital and hands-on activities, and context-specific questions and strategies for engaging children in practices and discourse. There remains a great deal to learn about how best to support informal educators. Encouragingly, educators we have worked with recently reported that the supports emerging from the CPB-PBS Ready To Learn Initiative helped them implement digital science activities effectively and increased their confidence in leading similar activities in the future.

Designers looking to help informal educators use media to support children's science learning might consider the following:

What Media Producers Can Do

- Think beyond developing individual resources and consider how media might be used in the context of connected experiences, such as in a sequence of activities or multi-session experiences.
- Develop guides to prepare educators for leading science activities and support them throughout implementation.
- Specify activities' learning objectives, media resources, supplies involved, and prompts in educator materials to stimulate discussion among children and families and ensure focus on the science practices and content.
- Use media to model for educators what effective, inquiry-focused science activities look like, such as through photo slideshows or videos of activities being implemented.
- Offer in-person or video-based training in which educators practice activities and exchange ideas. Pair training with a message board or listserv so educators can share experiences.

Parents

Many parents lack confidence when it comes to helping their children learn science (Silander et al., 2018). Digital media can play a large role in supporting parents and boosting their confidence. For those intimidated by science, videos and digital games can serve as appealing jumping-off points for engaging children with science or doing it together. Moreover, some parents hold a narrow, formal view of science as experiments and chemical reactions. Videos that model science activities can help these parents see that science is about asking questions about the world and exploring answers, which can happen in everyday settings, involve household materials, and require little preparation. Some parents feel anxious because they lack the specialized knowledge they think is needed to answer children's science questions, or simply don't know what sorts of science activities are age-appropriate. Media can model what science exploration looks like as adults and children work together to explore questions by observing, collecting data, and sharing their ideas about the how and why of things.

What Media Producers Can Do

- Use media to establish inviting contexts for parents to do science with their children.
- Give parents activity ideas they can do right away and without special materials.
- Use diverse characters to show that anyone can be a scientist if they approach questions with an attitude of curiosity, persistence, and flexibility.
- Use videos or other media to model parents exploring science questions along with their children. Emphasize that helping young children learn science is not about providing answers; it's about discovering together.
- Offer an organizer for parents to preview key science ideas and communicate those to children. For example, "Today we're learning about mixtures. We'll see that liquids can't be unmixed, but solids can." A summary of expected takeaways can also be helpful.
- Provide prompts to help parents and children talk about science media. For example, "That episode was about how to build a tower. What happened to Ruff's first tower? What can we use to build a tower?"
- Make use of printed activity sheets that provide ways for parents to extend digital activities.

Addressing Implementation Feasibility

Widespread, sustained use of media to promote children's science learning can happen only if those resources can be implemented easily in early childhood settings. For this reason, a third design principle guiding our work has been to *use technology and media to enable the integration of science into children's everyday lives and across contexts.* In this section, we describe what we've learned so far about designing for feasible implementation in community programs and homes.

Community Settings

Many community-serving organizations have long histories of success offering fun, active, social learning experiences for children and families. However, the idea of offering science programming is often new, as is the idea of using technology and media. New initiatives become more feasible when organizations can integrate them into existing programming, so designers are wise to consider how resources they create can coexist or align with common organizational priorities. A number of local PBS stations were able to partner with diverse community organizations to embed The *Ruff Ruffman* Sensational Science Camp into existing afterschool programs, such as the local YMCA. Existing programs typically have their own schedule and set-up, so organizations appreciate the ability to make use of media-based science activities they can adapt as needed (See Chapter 13 for more details about our community work).

Although digital public media resources are freely available, organizations wishing to use them need basic technology infrastructure and materials for hands-on science activities. Choosing, preparing for, and implementing science events for children is difficult when resource expectations are unclear. Specifying resource expectations helps organizations assess whether a particular event is feasible for them, allocate resources appropriately, and set the stage for smooth implementation. Suggestions for adapting activities can help organizations address capacity constraints.

Online social networks also can be an effective means for community-serving organizations to learn how to make programming achievable and better. Within and across PBS member stations, Basecamp serves as a valuable online social network for making the implementation of science and technology programming more feasible. It provides a useful way for education and engagement staff at stations to support each other by sharing modifications they made to better serve children and families. With regard to family workshops, station staff shared adaptations that helped them maximize educator capacity, explain the science goals of the program to parents, involve siblings outside of the target age range, and accommodate families with low literacy or English proficiency.

Here are suggestions based on what we are learning about how to make media-rich science programming accessible, flexible, and adaptable for use by a wide range of community-serving organizations:

What Media Producers Can Do

- Embed guidance for organizations looking to integrate science into existing programming, such as specifying potential stopping points in activities to leave time for other priorities.
- Specify resources that organizations will need in order to take advantage of the media-based science programming, and identify potential alternatives when possible to offer more flexibility. CPB-PBS Ready To Learn Facilitator Guides specify the ideal materials and technology, duration of activities, and educator and participant ratios. They also include information about how to prepare the setting.
- Design activities that make use of materials that are common in community settings, affordable, and easily stored.

- Provide or suggest online social networks that community-serving organizations can use to share ideas for executing and improving programming.

Homes

At home, parents of young children juggle a long list of responsibilities, including household chores, meal planning, helping older children with homework, bedtime routines, and more. To fit into families' busy lives, science activities must be short, modular, involve common household materials, and require little preparation or cleanup. Science activities also become more realistic when they integrate well into what families are doing already. In our national survey of families, which is described in greater detail in Chapter 3, parents we spoke with described cooking as a regular activity they do with their child at home. Cooking provides a rich context for practicing science-oriented skills (e.g., by inspiring children to closely observe and experiment with ingredients), and for engaging with a range of science concepts (like those relating to states of matter or change and transformation). In these ways, cooking is one of many potential entry points for science in family life. Integration into homes becomes all the more feasible when activities make use of common formats of family time, such as by involving one-on-one time among a parent and child, or among parents and siblings.

Children spend a significant amount of time using media, and almost half of the parents in our national survey reported using these media with their child daily. Digital media, therefore, provide a way to integrate science into activities that children and families are doing already. CPB-PBS Ready To Learn digital games have natural breakpoints (such as when a child completes a level), and videos come in clips (typically 11 minutes or less), so many parents can find time to watch or play with their child while dinner is in the oven or laundry is running. Digital media also provide ways for school-based and informal science programs to connect the experiences they offer to home activities, so children can explore concepts in more depth and in different contexts.

What Media Producers Can Do

- Develop modular media experiences, such as short video clips that can stand alone and games with distinct levels, easing the way for families who are short on time.

- Design science activities for integration into what families are doing already.
- Design activities to align with common formats of family time (one-on-one; parent and siblings) and make use of common household materials. The *Ruff Ruffman* "Grab It and Run" activity, for example, involves a relay race in which children and parents can test the strength of common materials at home, such as rope, toilet paper, or plastic bags.
- Suggest digital resources or provide activity sheets to encourage families to extend the learning that happens in other settings. For example, families who do a series of ramp activities during a *Ruff Ruffman* Family Creative Learning Workshop receive resources to continue experimenting with digital and real-world ramps at home.
- Use videos to model ways for parents to weave science into daily life, such as by showing parents talking about liquids and solids while making breakfast, stopping to observe insects during a morning walk, or rolling toy cars down a hill.

Conclusion

Engaging young children with science is a critical part of preparing them for the academic expectations of elementary school. It is also a developmentally appropriate endeavor, given what young children do naturally and the foundational knowledge and skills they are ready to develop. The growing awareness that science is important has inspired calls to action among child-serving organizations and development groups (National Research Council, 2012; National Science Teachers Association, 2014; U.S. Department of Health and Human Services, 2015), which stress the need to engage children with science early, often, and well.

But such calls to promote science are unlikely to lead to action unless certain conditions are met. Specifically, science resources to be developed must align with what is known about how to promote early science teaching and learning, support the people best positioned to foster that learning, and be feasible for use. When developed with these conditions in mind, technology and media can play a key role in bringing science learning opportunities into children's everyday experiences and across the contexts of their lives. We still have more to do; in our ongoing research with the CPB-PBS Ready To Learn Initiative, we will continue to refine these early design principles, learning more about how media-based science opportunities are brought to life for children across all economic backgrounds.

References

Chalufour, I. & Worth, K. (2006). Science in kindergarten. In Dominic F. Gullo (Ed.), *K today: Teaching and learning in the kindergarten year* (pp. 85–94). Washington, DC: National Association for the Education of Young Children.

Curran, F. C. (2017). Income-based disparities in early elementary school science achievement. *The Elementary School Journal*, 11(2), 207–231.

Davidson, M. R., Fields, M. K., & Yang, J. (2009). A randomized trial study of a preschool literacy curriculum: The importance of implementation. *Journal of Research on Educational Effectiveness*, 2(3), 177–208.

Domínguez, X., Goldstein, M., Lewis-Presser, A., Kamdar, D., & Vidiksis, R. (Under Review). Next generation preschool science: Findings from design-based research to inform iterative development of an innovative curricular program and an evaluation of its efficacy. Submitted to *Early Childhood Research Quarterly*.

Domínguez, X., Goldstein, M., Lewis-Presser, A. E., Kamdar, D., Vidiksis, R., & Sharifnia, E. (2018, April). *Findings from iterative development and a randomized controlled trial to examine preschool science learning*. Paper presented at the annual conference of the American Educational Research Association, New York.

Goldstein, M., Domínguez, X., Vidiksis, R., Lewis-Presser, A., Kamdar, D., Zanchi, C., & Blackwell, C. (2015). *New content, strategies, and tools, oh my! Preschool teachers navigate innovations to promote science learning*. Paper presented at the National Association for Research in Science Teaching, Chicago, IL.

Greenfield, D. B., Jirout, J., Domínguez, X., Greenberg, A., Maier, M., & Fuccillo, J. (2009). Science in the preschool classroom: A programmatic research agenda to improve science readiness. *Early Education and Development*, 20(2), 238–264.

Kallery, M. (2004). Early years teachers' late concerns and perceived needs in science: An exploratory study. *European Journal of Teacher Education*, 27(2), 147–165.

National Research Council. (2012). *A framework for K–12 science education: Practices, crosscutting concepts, and core ideas*. Washington, DC: National Academies Press.

National Science Teachers Association (NSTA). (2014). *NSTA position statement: Early childhood science education*. Washington, DC: NSTA. Retrieved from www.nsta.org/about/positions/earlychildhood.aspx; www.magnetmail.net/actions/email_web_version.cfm?recipient_id=1454170149&message_id=4423972&user_id=NAEYC&group_id=1269573&jobid=18739698.

NGSS Lead States. (2013). *Next generation science standards: For states, by states*. Washington, DC: The National Academies Press. Retrieved from www.nextgenscience.org.

Piasta, S. B., Pelatti, C. Y., & Miller, H. L. (2014). Mathematics and science learning opportunities in preschool classrooms. *Early Education and Development*, 25(4), 445–468.

Silander, M., Grindal, T., Hupert, N., Garcia, E., Anderson, K., Vahey, P., & Pasnik, S. (2018). *What parents talk about when they talk about learning: A national survey about young children and science*. New York, NY and Menlo Park, CA: Education Development Center, Inc., & SRI International.

U.S. Census Bureau. (2016). *Characteristics of people by language spoken at home, 2016 American Community Survey 1-year estimates*. Washington, DC: U.S. Census Bureau. Retrieved from https://factfinder.census.gov/faces/tableservices/jsf/pages/productview.xhtml?pid=ACS_16_1YR_S1603&prodType=table.

U.S. Department of Health and Human Services. (2015). *Head start early learning outcomes framework*. Washington, DC: U.S. Department of Health and Human Services. Retrieved from https://eclkc.ohs.acf.hhs.gov/hslc/hs/sr/approach/pdf/ohs-framework.pdf.

11

PERMISSION TO SPEAK

How Educational Media Can Start and Extend Dialogue for Kids and Adults

Naomi Hupert and Alexandra Adair

Introduction

Effective learning environments for young children are social, physical, sometimes loud, and often active as they support the different ways in which young children learn. Step into the early learning classroom of any veteran teacher and you'll likely see children busy at the work of play. In these environments, children encounter challenges that might require mediation by an adult or another child ("I was using that hat first!"), they develop questions about their environment ("Why don't frog eggs float?"), and they engage in discourse throughout their daily interactions that include making statements, asking and responding to questions, restating other's thoughts, clarifying information, and verbalizing their own thinking. While all this is going on, they are taking in information about the human-made and natural world around them, and part of this process includes exposure to new vocabulary and concepts about things and actions that children may learn intentionally (through a teacher's or parent's intentional introduction), or incidentally (through listening to and talking with others). What happens to conversations among children and between children and adults when digital media are woven into early learning experiences?

In this chapter, we draw on 11 years of thinking through and designing Ready To Learn research studies, in order to explore questions about children's learning and the role of oral language and discourse, especially within communities with limited financial resources. As researchers involved in this sustained line of inquiry about digital media, our many interactions with educators, parents of young children, and the kids themselves who were often the focus of our work have us asking:

- How can we leverage digital media in ways that take advantage of their unique abilities to reach children from every economic and social sector, and their potential to use visual and audio information to model and make accessible complex language, vocabulary, concepts, ideas, and examples of discourse among children and adults?
- How do we help adults, especially those with limited formal education, see their own role within the context of children's digital media use?
- How do we help the decision-makers, creators, designers, and producers of digital media amplify the central importance of language in their work? For example, how can they promote vocabulary and dialogue among children and adults by modeling meaningful discourse among characters?

The Importance of Language Development When Using Media

Early learning is intertwined with language development. Any opportunities for a child to hear language used in a range of ways will contribute to a child's understanding of how words can be used, what they mean, and how they convey important information. Children learn by hearing others speak and by communicating with others, including their family members, other adults, and other children. The primary sources of language exposure for young children are home and school, yet research examining teacher language in early childhood programs suggests that teachers rarely introduce, model, or use strategies such as questioning to support advanced vocabulary development during their interactions with young children (Justice et al., 2008; National Institute for Literacy, 2005). An examination of commercially available pre-K curricula suggests that most do not systematically attend to vocabulary development and that they provide teachers with little guidance regarding instructional strategies to support vocabulary development (Neuman & Dwyer, 2009). At the same time, ongoing research exploring the role of home environments on vocabulary learning among children from various socioeconomic backgrounds (Fernald, Marchman, & Weisleder, 2013) has explored the persistent "word gap" that exists between children at different ends of the economic spectrum, and there are a growing number of organizations, such as the Campaign for Grade Level Reading, Too Small to Fail, and Zero to Three, seeking to address this at earlier and earlier stages in children's lives.

Where does children's media use fit into this context, and is there a role for digital media in addressing this issue, particularly for children without access to high-quality early learning experiences to build and expand language exposure and practice? There is a substantial body of work addressing children's media and its impact on child language (Barr et al., 2010; Kirkorian et al., 2009; Nathanson & Rasmussen, 2011; Pempek, Kirkorian, & Anderson, 2014; Pempek & Lauricella, 2018). Many of these studies suggest that media—and television in particular—can have a negative effect on aspects of children's development, specifically with regards to language and parent-child interaction.

Studies have documented television viewing as an activity that lowers and lessens the level of discourse taking place between parent and child, negatively affecting children's language development. Research has also shown that parents are less engaged and interactive with their child during media experiences. However, other studies have examined how digital media can alter interactions between children and adults, with some identifying positive learning outcomes for children. One approach that has demonstrated a positive impact is joint media engagement: A child and adult engage together with digital media and, as part of that engagement, an adult asks and responds to questions about the media and provides some guidance and support for the child's media experience (Lavigne, Hanson, & Anderson, 2015; Takeuchi & Stevens, 2011), and our ongoing research through the Ready To Learn Initiative has drawn on this work and provided evidence that digital media can provide models of engagement between children and adults that carry over into non-digital activities. (See Chapter 8 for a detailed description of joint media engagement.)

For nearly 25 years, the CPB-PBS Ready To Learn Initiative has addressed the ways in which television, and in more recent years, digital media, can support economically disadvantaged children's early learning so that they will be *Ready To Learn* on arrival in kindergarten. Research conducted through this initiative has expanded insights into the ways in which digital media can support learning and also can be a catalyst for adult-child conversation. Studies of Ready To Learn resources have demonstrated positive impacts broadly in terms of children's readiness for school (Kearney & Levine, 2015), and more specifically in terms of early literacy and math skill development (Hurwitz, 2018; McCarthy, Li, & Tiu, 2012; Pasnik & Llorente, 2013; Pasnik et al., 2015; Penuel et al., 2009).

Some studies suggest adults are less engaged and vocal when using digital media because they do not know *how* to engage and interact with children when viewing videos or playing digital games. Related to this is adults' sense of self-efficacy. Many parents and teachers, particularly those with less education and fewer resources to support their children's learning, assume that educational media programs are developed for children by "experts," so believe these shows can teach, explain, and talk to children in a better and more appropriate manner than they can; as a result, they allow the television to have the dominant voice in the room.

An example of this is evident in a recent national survey of parents of young children where many parents described a lack of confidence with regard to helping their children learn, particularly in science, though in other academic areas as well (Silander et al., 2018; see Chapter 3 for more information about this study). Parents described not knowing the answers to challenging questions children asked and noted that digital resources could provide children with more accurate information than a parent could, leading to less interaction between child and parent. Despite this, there is evidence that digital media can model and support interactions for children and adults. Studies have identified digital media as effective in modeling behavior such as ways of talking and cooperating (Gola et al., 2013; Troseth, Saylor, & Archer, 2006), and also supporting learning through providing feedback or inviting active responses (Anderson et al., 2000; Crawley et al., 2002).

Embedding Supports for Oral Language Engagement

In 2009, Ready To Learn researchers were charged with conducting a study to examine the role of digital media in supporting early literacy learning for young children (Penuel et al., 2009; see Chapter 7 for more information about this study). The study targeted four-year-old children in low-income communities and specifically focused on resources from *Super Why!*, *Between the Lions*, and *Sesame Street*. The challenge faced by the research team was this: How could we design a study that 1) accomplished the task of measuring digital media impact on children's learning, 2) limited the amount of passive viewing of digital media that was a concern to nearly every early childhood educator we encountered at the time, and 3) engaged best practices for supporting early literacy development, which included an emphasis on oral language development? We knew the potential for learning from digital media, particularly in the area of early literacy, had been documented in numerous studies (Pasnik et al., 2007), yet we also knew that many early childhood educators had a healthy distrust of television and computer games as learning tools, and few had any experience or professional guidance in how to use these resources to support the learning goals they targeted in their classrooms. After considerable discussion and research, we settled on what we described as an "active viewing" experience for children that would engage them verbally in the content of videos and games in ways that mirror educators' practices for reading books in a group setting. Our intention was that this would encourage teachers and children to talk about what they were seeing, and to make connections between video content and other resources such as games (digital and non-digital), books, and drawing, writing or other hands-on activities through question-asking and answering, through using the language presented in the video, and through connecting that language to children's daily experiences.

We encouraged teachers to treat video viewing in the same way they might treat reading with a group during circle time: as an opportunity for introducing characters, telling a story, and integrating the learning of a specific skill or reinforcing information about words or concepts. Book reading, by parents or teachers, is an activity that results in some of the strongest oral language development outcomes among young children (Justice et al., 2008); by introducing video viewing accompanied by some characteristics associated with book reading, we were exploring how to move teachers toward behaviors that have been shown in research to support child language learning. Teachers were encouraged to pause the video at various points, so they could ask questions, point out interesting developments in the narrative, new vocabulary or new concepts, and draw connections to children's prior experiences.

These "pause points" became a key feature of the Media-Rich Literacy Study experience (see Figure 11.1). Teachers were provided with videos that included numbers embedded in the videos to indicate where teachers should pause and then ask a question about what children were seeing. The numbers in the videos aligned with numbers in the *Teacher's Guide* that language teachers could use while watching and pausing the video. Inserting this approach to video viewing was an experiment and something that we had not encountered in our reviews of prior studies. Part of our theory of change was that it would give teachers permission to stop the video whenever they saw something worth talking about and that this would encourage more active video viewing including more conversation about what children and adults were seeing.

Findings for this study were positive, with significant learning outcomes for children in the literacy condition when compared to those in the comparison condition on four key early literacy skills: letter naming, letter sounds, concepts of print, and recognizing letters in a child's own name (Penuel et al., 2009). However, the research team discovered that the study led to additional

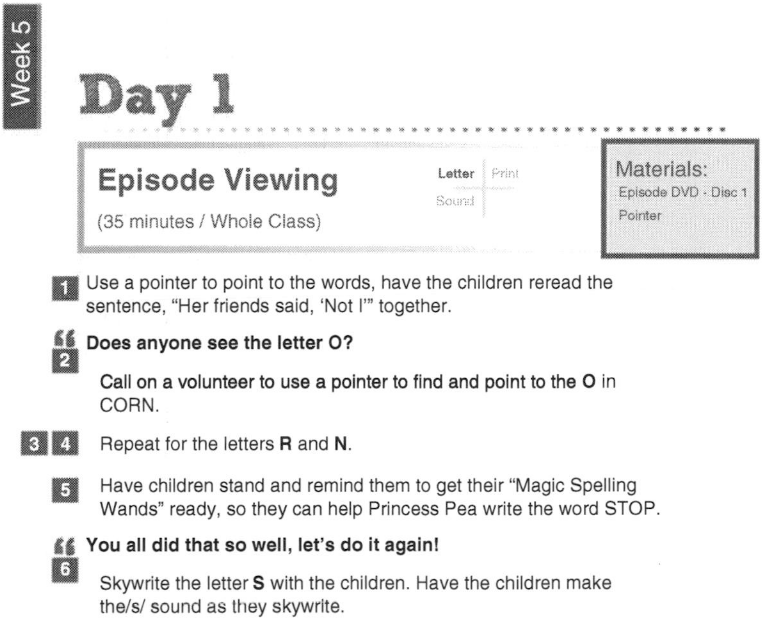

Week 5

Day 1

Episode Viewing	Letter	Print	Materials:
(35 minutes / Whole Class)	Sound		Episode DVD - Disc 1 Pointer

1 Use a pointer to point to the words, have the children reread the sentence, "Her friends said, 'Not I'" together.

2 Does anyone see the letter O?

Call on a volunteer to use a pointer to find and point to the O in CORN.

3 **4** Repeat for the letters R and N.

5 Have children stand and remind them to get their "Magic Spelling Wands" ready, so they can help Princess Pea write the word STOP.

6 You all did that so well, let's do it again!

Skywrite the letter S with the children. Have the children make the /s/ sound as they skywrite.

FIGURE 11.1 Example of Literacy Study *Teacher's Guide*: Numbered "pause points" indicate what teachers might say when pausing the video

(Courtesy of Education Development Center and SRI International)

interesting outcomes. We designed the study to include two conditions: our intervention, which focused on early literacy, and our comparison, or countervention, which focused on early science. First, we learned that our science countervention seemed to result in shifts in child language and behavior at home, as reported by parents who noted their children using new words that were present in the science content (*decay*, for example), and pretending to be a scientist when playing at home. Second, we heard from teachers, and then found months later when re-contacting these same teachers, that the videos and games from the study provided opportunities for a different kind of engagement between teachers and children, and among children, than we had anticipated.

What We Learned from Teachers

During semi-structured exit interviews with study participants, teachers described using the study video segments with their children as jumping-off points for extended explorations, discussions about new vocabulary, and activities that were offline, such as planting seeds after watching an episode about how young children planted seeds in a garden or allowing a banana to decay over time. These educators also talked about how watching the videos with their children helped extend the types of question-asking and exploration of materials that children did during various kinds of activities, such as feeling what ice is like or tasting pieces of frozen fruit. During these interviews, we were surprised to hear how teachers were continuing to use study resources as models for their own activities and interactions with children after the study period was over, and so we captured some of these conversations and instructional moments on video (view videos at cct.edc.org/rtl/videos). We created ten video clips in different locations that integrated interviews and classroom activities, with educators describing how they use digital media to support the learning goals they have for their children in early literacy and science development.

The conversations we had with these educators, and the topics they discussed during the video-filming process, sparked a new round of thinking and questioning within our research team. If teachers were using videos to model how they might interact with children, then could we build on this as a way to target and support teacher engagement with digital media? Would this approach carry over to using digital games, or would it only be effective with video? What might we learn from other educators about how to support child engagement with digital media in ways that support and extend learning?

Examining the Contexts Where Digital Media Are Used

In 2011, our Ready To Learn research team had another chance to extend our data gathering and thinking about the role that digital media could play in early learning and language experiences for young children in low-income communities. During this period researchers conducted several studies that sought to document the different ways in which digital media were used in different contexts. These studies marked the start of a new five-year funding cycle, included a shift toward mathematics in addition to literacy, and also addressed the changing landscape of media platforms as increasingly mobile devices, like tablets, and applications appeared and targeted users of all ages. The studies sought to gather information about how teachers of young children in formal and informal settings made use of the digital media they had; what kinds of media (devices and content) they had access to; how these related to the math and science instructional goals teachers had; what kinds of strategies teachers employed in their classrooms to support media use as a learning tool; and what kinds of media experiences took place in the homes of young children.

Because our prior experiences in early learning settings had tuned our thinking into the possibilities of language engagement as part of a digital media experience, and because we continued to see oral language support and modeling as a key role that media could play in young children's lives, we gathered information about this issue in the context of our other research questions.

How Social Arrangements Shape Children's Media Experiences

An advantage of an initiative like Ready To Learn is that it provides opportunities to study a particular issue in ways that are not possible with smaller or shorter initiatives. Through this program, we were able to spend time observing and documenting how digital media is used in a range of settings, with a range of adult supports and for a range of purposes. We conducted many observations and interviews over a two-year period in classrooms, structured yet informal learning environments like homework clubs or Boys & Girls Club locations, and at unstructured events where children could "drop-in" to use a computer or tablet for a time, as well as with parents who documented use of digital media at home, and all contributed to a picture of varied use, varied resources, and varied understandings of how digital media can support learning (Pasnik & Llorente, 2013). While these activities led to a wealth of information about children, adults, and digital media use, we identified two central issues that continue to inform how we think about digital media and learning: 1) the ways in which children use media, and 2) the ways in which adults support children's use of media. Each of these has an impact on how the media can support language development through promoting discourse, and each sheds light onto how adults (those who are creating content, and those using it) view the role of digital media—and where change is possible.

What we saw in every environment where children and digital media were present was a breakdown of use into three categories: Solo use by an individual child with an individual device; paired or group use with one or more devices and a group of children; whole group use with a teacher leading a digital media activity that children follow (see Table 11.1).

We also recognized a pattern in adult behavior with regard to digital media that we identified as having four components: basic technical support, one-on-one trouble-shooting, comprehensive guiding role, and a curatorial role that could include integrating digital media across the curriculum (see Table 11.2; Pasnik & Llorente, 2013).

With these patterns of use in mind, we came to see the assumptions that adults, including teachers, parents, digital media content designers, researchers, and game and app developers all make with regard to how digital media is used. Much of digital media engagement is intended for solo use, with the assumption

TABLE 11.1 Three common ways children experience media (Courtesy of Education Development Center and SRI International)

SOLO	WITH CLASSMATES	TEACHER-LED
Independent media experiences rely on a child's prior knowledge, individual mastery, and technological fluency; the child controls the experience, using her own hands and judgment to navigate the activity	Using media in pairs or small groups creates the chance for turn-taking, cooperative learning, and social development, in addition to learning academic skills and content knowledge	Whether as a whole class, in small groups, or with an individual child, the technology tool is controlled by a teacher; typically part of an activity intended to focus children's attention rather than to provide a hands-on media experience

TABLE 11.2 Four common roles teachers take in supporting children's media use (Courtesy of Education Development Center and SRI International)

TECH SUPPORT	POP-UP GUIDE	SHERPA	CREATIVE DIRECTOR
The teacher jump-starts children's media use, keeps them from getting stuck when a technical problem arises, and helps them move to another activity when it is time to transition	The teacher makes welcome, surprise visits to children's media play, turning an otherwise stand-alone technology experience into a stand-beside engagement	Teacher sticks with a media experience a child is having, nimbly making use of the tool's format and functions to draw the child into a rich exchange and guide them through it	Teacher helps children use media tools to generate content and express themselves, often over a longer period of engagement

that technical support from an adult will be available as-needed. Yet these two options within the use patterns of children and adults lead to the most limited opportunities for discourse or any kind of verbal engagement with the content (Solo engagement for the child; Tech Support for the adult), and this goes against what we know from research about the best practices to support learning in general, and with digital media specifically. Interestingly, we also saw evidence that children and teachers wanted to change this scenario: Nearly every observation of children engaged in gameplay documented the ways in which children overcame the Solo-engagement expectation and created their own social co-play experience either by sharing devices (which required well-orchestrated turn-taking and sharing of controls) or through group gameplay where every child had a device and maintained a continuous stream of commentary and question-asking during gameplay.

Additionally, most teachers were not able to break out of the Tech Support role for a variety of reasons (ranging from challenging technical issues, to lack of technical knowledge); however, one teacher stood out as a model for how to engage whole groups of children in a guided gameplay experience that made explicit learning goals, supported a wide range of gameplay experiences, and engaged children verbally in discourse about the game, aspects that were challenging, and ways to share information for game progress. This approach also did something we had not directly addressed in our own thinking and planning for technology use in our studies: It helped to level the playing field for all students, regardless of their prior access to technology, ability to read instructions on a screen, or process audio directions delivered too quickly for a child to follow. In this way, the teacher ensured that the resources introduced to children were set within a universally designed for learning context: broadly accessible and more likely to be engaged with by children regardless of their reading level, their language processing speed, the resources or experiences they had access to at home, or their general grasp of gameplay mechanics.

Building on What We Learned: Rethinking Dialogue and Discourse in Digital Media Integration

In 2013, the Ready To Learn research team designed and implemented another study, this time focusing on early mathematics learning for prekindergarten children engaging with *Peg + Cat* resources (Pasnik & Llorente, 2013; see Chapter 6 for more information on this study).

Building on what we learned from the 2009 Preschool Literacy Study, the context studies and from teachers, researchers created a Teacher Guide that used "pause points" in videos, and also asked teachers to use a "Think-Aloud" approach to talk through gameplay as they played on an interactive whiteboard during a whole class activity. In this way, they verbally and physically modeled the goals of the game, its mechanics, and the adjustments to play that they made to achieve the desired outcome, including how to manage failure at a game task and how to ask questions when something is not clear. They also modeled any relevant vocabulary (measurement, rectangle, etc.) and demonstrated how new words could be used in different ways (e.g., by characters in the game, by a teacher pointing out a rectangle in the room); and the core learning goal was made explicit through this visual and auditory modeling process so that children would understand why they were playing a game.

Researchers also provided headphone splitters with each laptop, so that any game modeled on the interactive whiteboard could later be played on a computer by two children, with two sets of headphones and a single split headphone cable. This was a practical solution to counteracting the assumption of solo child use of digital media. It was also a physical reminder that we did not want children to be playing games in isolation, and that joint play (and therefore joint communication) was both allowed and even planned for. As a result, we observed a great deal of talking among children despite the headphones, with children sometimes taking them off to talk, sometimes talking with them on, sometimes gesticulating as they worked together to play the game.

Again, our study found positive effects on children's mathematics learning (Pasnik & Llorente, 2013) for those in the mathematics intervention condition; it also shed light on some of the new approaches to using technology that we integrated into the experience. We found teachers calling out and using specific math vocabulary that was modeled in the videos and games, we noted teachers encouraging children to verbalize what they were doing when playing a game, mirroring the ways in which the teacher had modeled gameplay for the whole class, and we noticed teachers increasing use of pausing both videos and games to engage in dialogue with young children. Many teachers began the study by taking a somewhat formal and stilted approach to interrupting video segments at identified pause points; however, as the study progressed, teachers reported that sometimes they stopped the video at other moments to point out something they noted, but that was not called out in the Teacher Guide. In these ways, we found that encouraging teachers to pause, or talk over, a game or video at specified moments gave them permission to do so when they saw something relevant to their teaching, and this, in turn, encouraged increased dialogue between teachers and children, and among children in relation to digital media.

From Early Learning Classrooms to Home Settings

In 2014, we designed and implemented a different kind of Ready To Learn study. Though it also focused on resources from *Peg + Cat*, it was located in children's homes and examined whether digital media could support early mathematics learning among four-year-olds. The challenge we saw in designing this study was how to translate what we had learned about teachers' effective use of digital media in a fairly structured learning environment, into an unstructured home environment. If engagement in dialogue between adult and child was a central goal of the media activities in classrooms, was there a way to translate this into homes? The Family Math Study included the use of video, games, and an app in young children's homes.

As part of the study design, we chose to build in and support joint media engagement between parent and child (Pasnik et al., 2015) as a way to help families engage with the digital resources we were providing. Parents in the study had access to short "parent tip" videos about how to help children engage with digital media and math concepts. Videos were available in English, Spanish, and Mandarin and were between one and five minutes long. We created these tip videos because, as had been the case for teachers, we knew that parents were not confident enough with their own knowledge about math learning to stop a video and talk about its contents. Parents often commented on the fact that they didn't know how to talk to their children about math, and that math was always hard for them, or that they weren't sure what math would be right for a four-year-old. We also knew that telling parents *about* joint media engagement was not good enough, instead, we needed to *model*—through video and audio—what that looked like and what it sounded like. For this study, we created our own digital media (videos) designed to support and model better engagement for parents and children with the study resources.

Our findings provided several important insights tied to language development. First, children in the PBS KIDS math condition learned more math than those who were in the business-as-usual condition. Second, parents tended to view the parent tip videos only one time, even though they were available throughout the study's 12-week period. Third, even though parents spent very little time viewing the parents' tips (between 15 and 20 minutes total during the study), they reported that they changed their behavior with regard to talking with their children. Significantly, higher numbers of parents expressed confidence in talking with their child about math and stated they engaged in joint media viewing with their child, when compared to the business-as-usual parents. We were surprised to see such substantial shifts in communication behavior resulting from such brief moments of modeling. Clearly, parents needed some information about how to better engage with their children, but the time and effort to support this was quite small compared to the potential benefit.

Looking to the Future

It is our hope that the children's media field is contributing to a future where videos, games, and apps designed for early learners recognize and embrace the benefits of exposing children to new concepts and vocabulary while giving them opportunities to hear dialogue and to see it modeled. These moments help build foundational background knowledge that children can draw on for later interactions with adults, peers, and the academic and social worlds in which they must thrive. In this future, devices and content are designed with the assumption that use will take place in social settings where children and adults communicate both with and without digital devices, and where adults feel the support and confidence needed to make use of digital media in ways that engage their child in learning on and off-screen.

The CPB-PBS Ready To Learn Initiative continues to expand and support the development of high-quality children's digital media content. And, as Lund, Duke, and Greenwald describe in Chapter 12, the initiative is poised to address a new area of focus that is a natural extension of oral language development: informational text. We're looking ahead to designing new studies to examine the effects of information text-rich public media resources on young children's early literacy development and skill. There, too, we'll be attending to opportunities children and adults will have to speak with one another. When children talk about their world, when they listen to others talk about what they are doing or seeing, when they ask and answer questions, they are engaging in activities that foster an understanding of their world. Through this process, children can learn how to access, critique, and author their own informational texts for their own purposes.

References

Anderson, D. R., Bryant, J., Wilder, A., Santomero, A., Williams, M., & Crawley, A. M. (2000). Researching *Blue's Clues*: Viewing behavior and impact. *Media Psychology, 2*(2), 179–194.

Barr, R., Lauricella, A., Zack, E., & Calvert, S. L. (2010). Infant and early childhood exposure to adult-directed and child-directed television programming: Relations with cognitive skills at age four. *Merrill-Palmer Quarterly, 56*(1), 21–48.

Crawley, A. M., Anderson, D. R., Santomero, A., Wilder, A., Williams, M., Evans, M. K., & Bryant, J. (2002). Do children learn how to watch television? The impact of extensive experience with *Blue's Clues* on preschool children's television viewing behavior. *Journal of Communication, 52*, 264–280.

Fernald, A., Marchman, V. A., & Weisleder, A. (2013). SES differences in language processing skill and vocabulary are evident at 18 months. *Developmental Science, 16*(2), 234–248.

Gola, A. A. H., Richards, M. N., Lauricella, A. R., & Calvert, S. L. (2013). Building meaningful parasocial relationships between toddlers and media characters to teach early mathematical skills. *Media Psychology, 16*(4), 1–22.

Hurwitz, L. (2018). Getting a read on Ready To Learn media: A meta-analysis review of effects on literacy. *Child Development, 1*, 1–18.

Justice, L. M., Mashburn, A. J., Hamre, B. K., & Pianta, R. C. (2008). Quality of language and literacy instruction in preschool classrooms serving at-risk pupils. *Early Childhood Research Quarterly, 23*(1), 51–68.

Kearney, M. S., & Levine, P. B. (June 2015). Early childhood education by MOOC: Lessons from Sesame Street. *NBER Working Paper No. w21229.*

Kirkorian, H. L., Pempek, T. A., Murphy, L. A., Schmidt, M. E., & Anderson, D. R. (2009). The impact of background television on parent–child interaction. *Child Development, 80*(5), 1350–1359.

Lavigne, H. J., Hanson, K. G., & Anderson, D. R. (2015). The influence of television coviewing on parent language directed at toddlers. *Journal of Applied Developmental Psychology, 36*, 1–10.

McCarthy, B., Li, L., & Tiu, M. (2012). *PBS KIDS transmedia mathematics suites in preschool homes. A report to the CPB-PBS Ready To Learn Initiative.* San Francisco, CA: WestEd.

Nathanson, A. I. & Rasmussen, E. E. (2011). TV viewing compared to book reading and toy playing reduces responsive maternal communication with toddlers and preschoolers. *Human Communication Research, 37*(4), 465–487.

National Institute for Literacy. (2005). *Developing early literacy. A report of the national early literacy panel* (p. 188). Washington, DC: National Institute for Literacy, https://lincs.ed.gov/publications/pdf/NELPReport09.pdf.

Neuman, S., & Dwyer, J. (2009). Missing in action: Vocabulary instruction in Pre-K. *The Reading Teacher, 62*(5), 384–392.

Pasnik, S. & Llorente, C. (2013). *Preschool teachers can use a PBS KIDS transmedia curriculum supplement to support young children's mathematics learning: Results of a randomized controlled trial. A report to the CPB-PBS Ready To Learn Initiative.* Waltham, MA and Menlo Park, CA: Education Development Center, Inc., and SRI International.

Pasnik, S., Moorthy, S., Llorente, C., Hupert, N., Dominguez, X., & Silander, M. (2015). *Supporting parent-child experiences with PEG + CAT early math concepts: Report to the CPB-PBS Ready To Learn Initiative.* New York and Menlo Park, CA: Education Development Center, Inc., and SRI International.

Pasnik, S., Penuel, W. R., Llorente, C., Strother, S., & Schindel, J. (2007). *Review of research on media and young children's literacy: Report to the Ready To Learn Initiative.* New York and Menlo Park, CA: Education Development Center, Inc., and SRI International.

Pempek, T. A., Kirkorian, H. L., & Anderson, D. R. (2014). The effects of background television on the quantity and quality of child-directed speech by parents. *Journal of Children and Media, 8*(3), 211–222.

Pempek, T. A. & Lauricella, A. R. (2018). The effects of parent-child interaction and media use on cognitive development in infants, toddlers, and preschoolers. In Fran C. Blumberg & Patricia J. Brooks (Eds.), *Cognitive development in digital contexts* (pp. 53–74).

Penuel, W. R., Pasnik, S., Bates, L., Townsend, E., Gallagher, L. P., Llorente, C., & Hupert, N. (2009). *Preschool teachers can use a media rich curriculum to prepare low income children for school success: Results of a randomized controlled trial.* New York and Menlo Park, CA: Education Development Center, Inc., and SRI International.

Silander, M., Grindal, T., Hupert, N., Garcia, E., Anderson, K., Vahey, P., & Pasnik, S. (2018). *What parents talk about when they talk about learning: A national survey about young children and science.* New York and Menlo Park, CA: Education Development Center, Inc., and SRI International.

Takeuchi, L. & Stevens, R. (2011). *The new coviewing: Designing for learning through joint media engagement.* New York: Joan Ganz Cooney Center at Sesame Workshop.

Troseth, G. L., Saylor, M. M., & Archer, A. H. (2006). Young children's use of video as a source of socially relevant information. *Child Development, 77*(3), 786–799.

12

INFORMATIONAL TEXT ADVENTURES WITH *MOLLY OF DENALI*

Nell K. Duke, Carol Greenwald, and Anne E. Lund

Introduction

In 2015, the Corporation for Public Broadcasting (CPB) and Public Broadcasting Service (PBS) were awarded a five-year grant as part of the Ready To Learn Initiative focused on supporting children's learning in the areas of literacy and science. One goal outlined in the CPB-PBS joint grant proposal was to support literacy skills through informational text. This chapter explores the process behind developing *Molly of Denali*, a new PBS KIDS multi-platform literacy property and action-adventure comedy that follows the adventures of feisty and resourceful ten-year-old Molly Mabray, an Alaska Native girl. The following is a conversation between Carol Greenwald, Senior Executive Producer and Director of Children's Media at WGBH Boston (with contributions from the *Molly* writing and production team), Nell Duke, University of Michigan Professor of Education and informational text advisor for *Molly*, and Anne Lund, Director of Curriculum and Content at PBS KIDS. In it, we learn more about the development of this new property, its informational text curriculum, and the world, characters, and the Alaska Native culture that makes *Molly* special.

Why Informational Text and How We Got Started

1. What is informational text and why is it an important area for early learning?

Nell Duke: Informational text has as its primary purpose to convey information (Duke, 2000). Informational text comes in many forms. Written text can be informational but so can oral texts (e.g., interviews, presentations), visual texts (e.g., photographs, illustrations, videos), and texts that include a combination of written, oral, and visual elements (as in informational websites).

There are many types of informational text. Table 12.1 describes five types of informational text addressed in *Molly of Denali.*

Informational text is involved in many aspects of daily life, and most jobs and careers require interaction with informational text. Likewise, accessing and producing informational text is important to active citizenship. School success also entails skill with informational text, not only in English Language Arts or literacy classes, but in science, social studies, and mathematics. All of these domains are heavily mediated by informational text.

Unfortunately, U.S. students do not, on average, reach the same level of achievement with informational text as students in some other countries (e.g., Warner-Griffin, Liu, Tadler, Herget, & Dalton, 2017). One contributor to this situation is that informational text has received limited attention in early schooling and in many homes (e.g., Jeong, Gaffney & Choi 2010; Pentimonti, Zucker, Justice & Kaderavek, 2010; Yopp & Yopp, 2006). In part, the Common Core State Standards have responded to this situation by calling for

TABLE 12.1 Five types of informational text addressed in *Molly of Denali*

Type of Informational Text	Purpose	Examples
Informative / Explanatory	To convey information about the natural or social world	Information books about science and social studies topics (e.g., frogs, Egypt); reference books such as atlases and field guides; some website and apps; some magazine articles; some pamphlets; some posters.
Procedural or How-to	To teach someone how to do something	Text on how to carry out a scientific investigation; text on how to make something, such as an entrée or craft; text on how to navigate to a particular place; text on how to administer first aid; and so on.
Biographical	To interpret and share the experience of a real person	Profiles of individuals (e.g., on the web, on television); books that are biographies.
Nonfiction Narrative	To interpret and share the story of a real event	The true story of a specific historical event; the history of a nation's development.
Functional	To support the carrying out of everyday tasks	Schedules, weather charts, list, forms, basic, labels, signs.

the ability to understand and produce informational text, with support, beginning in kindergarten (National Governors Association Center for Best Practices & Council of Chief State School Officers, 2010). However, many educators and families are unprepared to make this shift. *Molly of Denali* is designed to help support families and educators in exposing children to informational text and beginning to teach the specific knowledge, skills, and dispositions needed to interact with such texts.

2.   What are some of the foundational informational text skills and understandings needed by children ages four- to eight-years-old?

Nell Duke: Children in this age range should begin to learn why people use informational texts. Most fundamentally, people use informational texts they access and/or create to meet their needs and wants. For example, they use informational texts to help solve real-world problems, such as to learn how to improve water quality in a community. People also use informational texts to take advantage of opportunities, such as communicating about a community tradition, as well as satisfying their curiosity, teaching others, and accomplishing a variety of tasks. Related to this, academic standards expect that children determine the purpose and topic of informational texts and how people might use the texts to access or convey information. For example, children might recognize that a particular informative/explanatory text, such as a field guide, has the purpose of teaching about the different types of birds and how that text could be used to identify a bird that is nesting near their home. Similarly, children might realize that a particular procedural or how-to text, such as a recipe, has the purpose of teaching someone how to make maple syrup and how that text could be used to make maple syrup themselves (with adult assistance, of course).

Even with preschoolers and early elementary students, it is possible to engage with multiple informational texts on a particular topic. Many "standards" documents expect young children to begin to learn to compare texts and to integrate information across multiple textual sources. We can accomplish this by drawing upon young children's interests and invoking age-appropriate topics and situations. For example, in one episode of *Molly*, Molly and her friend Tooey use multiple sources to ascertain that there are no polar bears near where they live, reassuring Trini, a new neighbor from Texas who is afraid of polar bears. For their informational writing, many standards documents expect that children will begin to learn to draw on multiple sources of information as well as their personal experiences. For example, Molly could write a set of instructions (procedural text) for protecting a plant from the cold, drawing on tips she found online as well as personal experience. In considering the use of a source, it is also important for young children to begin to develop the disposition that texts are fallible—sometimes texts are poorly written, ill-suited to their purpose, or outright wrong—because they are out of date, because the source is not sufficiently knowledgeable, or even because the source is deliberately misleading.

During the process of reading or listening to informational text, education experts hope that children engage in certain habits of mind, including:

- Paying attention to whether what they are reading is making sense and, if it isn't, employing strategies, such as rereading, to fix the situation;
- "Reading between the lines" of text, generating inferences that are important to constructing meaning with text but aren't explicitly stated;
- Asking themselves and others questions as they read or listen to text, using question words including *how* and *why*;
- Generating mental pictures;
- Identifying how a text is organized to convey information;
- Using strategies to figure out the meanings of unfamiliar words, including saying the word aloud, examining written context and/or graphics around the word, and perhaps looking at word parts or drawing on cognates;
- Determining the main idea as well as key details in a text, in some cases resulting in a summary of what has been read or listened to.

Similarly, while writing or orally presenting informational text, experts hope that young children develop related dispositions: paying attention to whether what they are writing is making sense and employing strategies such as revising to fix the situation as needed; organizing their text to help convey information effectively; thinking about questions their audience might ask, using detailed descriptions in writing; and making informational texts they are writing or presenting better (e.g., by adding detail, by clarifying) to most effectively convey information to the audience. Other foundational informational text skills and understandings are discussed in the following response.

3. Why is informational text particularly important to the CPB-PBS Ready To Learn Initiative and its work on behalf of children in low-income, underserved communities?

Nell Duke: Informational text is particularly important to the CPB-PBS Ready To Learn Initiative because it is one of many areas in which children have different levels of preparedness. Some children come from homes in which they routinely hear information books read to them, observe adults using a variety of informational texts for a variety of purposes, and are encouraged to write their own informational texts, such as instructions for how to play a game or labels on a drawing they have made of a favorite animal. Other children do not have these experiences but, through *Molly*, will be exposed to informational text in an engaging action-adventure context.

The CPB-PBS Ready To Learn Initiative has a particular commitment to supporting the development of children from low-income, underserved communities. On average, students of low socioeconomic backgrounds perform worse on tests of informational reading and writing (e.g., Warner-Griffin, Liu, Tadler, Herget, & Dalton, 2017), underscoring the value of a program such as *Molly* in the PBS KIDS line-up. In addition to foundational informational text skills and understandings discussed in response to the previous question, *Molly* also provides an opportunity for children to learn about the specific features of informational text that aid in conveying information. Ages four to eight are key years for learning about these features (which vary depending upon the type of informational text). These features include, but are not necessarily limited to:

- **Language features:** definitions, explanations, description, denotative language, new terms/vocabulary.
- **Navigational features:** tables of contents, indexes, headings and subheadings, search boxes, electronic menus.
- **Structural features:** introductions, conclusions, glossaries, titles, materials, specific text structures; in procedural or how-to texts, materials, numbered steps.
- **Graphical features:** photographs and illustrations, captions, labels, diagrams, tables, charts, graphs, maps, bold print.

Molly encounters many of these features and uses them to accomplish her purposes. For example, an index helps Molly and her friend Tooey find a much-needed homemade mosquito repellent. Our emphasis is always on how these features can help access or convey information in everyday life.

4. Why did PBS KIDS and CPB choose informational text as a literacy priority for the 2015–2020 Ready To Learn Television Grant Program?

Anne Lund: After learning that literacy was one of the curricular areas of focus for the 2015–2020 Ready To Learn Television Grant Program, the PBS-CPB Ready To Learn team began looking at the current PBS KIDS programming line-up and digital media assets to identify gaps in coverage of literacy skills for the target age group of two to eight years. Informational text was an area of literacy not directly addressed by any current PBS KIDS television series and had very limited coverage on any other media platforms. We were also unaware of any other children's media companies directly tackling this curriculum through programming and/or digital games. And there was an additional benefit that informational text is an integral part of the other curriculum focus of the Ready To Learn Television Grant Program: science.

The team also considered the Common Core State Standards which, as Nell mentioned, called for an increase in children's exposure to and skills with informational text (Common Core State Standards, 2010). Since the Ready To Learn Initiative's target audience comprises children from high-need homes and communities, and these children are less likely to have access to or spend time with these texts (Duke, 2000; Jeong, Gaffney & Choi, 2010; Pentimonti, Zucker, Justice & Kaderavek, 2010; Yopp & Yopp, 2006), this particular area of literacy became an important focus of the grant proposal.

5. What is the PBS KIDS Literacy-English Language Arts (ELA) Learning Framework and how does it support informational text learning?

Anne Lund: The Literacy-ELA Learning Framework (see Figure 12.1) is an important resource created to support producers, advisors, and the CPB-PBS Ready To Learn team, helping ensure consistent and thorough integration of the curriculum into content created within and across literacy-focused properties, including *Molly*. This Framework outlines age-appropriate foundational skills and learning progressions in literacy and English Language Arts for the PBS KIDS target audience of two- to eight-year-olds. The Framework, in its current form, was first developed in 2011 as part of the CPB-PBS 2010–2015 Ready To Learn Initiative, with guidance from a team of early childhood literacy advisors, some with children's educational media experience. This foundational document was crafted to align with national and state standards including the Common Core State Standards for English Language Arts (National Governors Association Center for Best Practices & Council of Chief State School Officers, 2010) and the Head Start Early Learning Outcomes Framework (U.S. Department of Health and Human Services, 2015). It also considers current understandings, pedagogy, and evidence-based research in early literacy education and media, as well as position statements and guidelines from foundations such as the National Childhood Early Literacy Panel.

   With our new focus on informational text, we invited Nell to join the Framework's advisory group to help with revisions specifically focused on informational text goals. Also providing input for the revised Framework, Universal Design for Learning (UDL) advisors and partners were there to ensure that all children have opportunities to learn, and early childhood educators to provide a classroom practitioner perspective. (See Chapter 14 for more details about UDL priorities for the CPB-PBS Ready To Learn Initiative.)

6. What did the effort to find a new children's series on informational text entail and what were the major priorities?

Anne Lund: The process from proposal to greenlighting *Molly* for series production took over 19 months. After CPB-PBS was awarded the grant, the PBS Children's Programming team, with guidance from Nell, began the process of writing the request for proposals (RFPs) to solicit proposals for an original or

Ready To Learn

PBS KIDS Literacy-English Language Arts (ELA) Learning Framework
Preschool through Grade 2

Foundational Reading Skills

Print Concepts
Knowing about print and books and how they are used.

Book Parts and Features	Print Conventions	Role of print in the world

Phonological Awareness
The understanding that spoken language is made up of individual and separate sounds (phonemes) and that phonemes work together to make words.

Rhyming	Alliteration	Phoneme Awareness	Blending & Segmentation	Phoneme Manipulation

Phonics and Word Recognition
Connecting the sounds of spoken language to the letters and spellings that represent those sounds in written language.

Letter and Letter-Sound Knowledge	Decoding	Spelling	High Frequency & Irregularly Spelled Word Recognition	Advanced Word Recognition Strategies

Fluency with Connected Text
Ability to read text accurately with appropriate pacing and understanding.

Reading with Accuracy	Reading with Appropriate Rate and Prosody (Expression)

Reading Comprehension: Literary and Informational Texts

General Reading Comprehension Strategies
Strategies to read with purpose and understanding

Comprehension of Literary Texts
Understanding the meaning of literary texts

Characteristics of Literary Texts	Understanding Key Ideas and Details	Integrating Knowledge and Ideas Within and Across Texts

Comprehension of Informational Texts
Understanding the meaning of Informational texts

Characteristics of Informational Texts	Understanding Key Ideas and Details	Integrating Knowledge and Ideas Within and Across Texts	Evaluation

Language, Speaking & Listening

Vocabulary
Learning the meaning of words and appropriate word usage in a variety of contexts.

Acquisition and Determining Meaning	Relationship Among Words	Nuances and Figurative Language	Categorization

Conventions of Standard English
The conventions of standard English grammar (including syntax) and usage when writing or reading.

Using Correct Grammar	Using Correct Capitalization, Punctuation, and Spelling

Speaking and Listening
The language of talking and listening; in contrast to written language, which is the language used in writing and reading.

Follow Verbal Instructions	Comprehension and Collaboration	Presentation of Knowledge and Ideas

Writing (Composition)

Composition
Knowing how to express experiences or ideas and convey meaningful information in writing

Composing Narrative Texts	Composing Opinion Pieces and Informational/Explanatory Texts

Revising, Editing & Publishing Compositions
Using strategies to improve one's own writing, often in preparation for publication

FIGURE 12.1 Cover page of the PBS KIDS Literacy-English Language Arts (ELA) Learning Framework

book-based multi-platform property for children ages four to eight. Key requirements that we highlighted for creators/producers to consider when responding to the RFP included:

- Through the property, kids should grow familiar with the purposes and features of different informational texts in a variety of contexts. Thought should be given to how characters might model comprehension skills and strategies and how they might convey information to others. The ultimate goal should be to introduce and reinforce key literacy skills through engaging characters and narratives, compelling purposes for informational text reading and writing, and innovative designs and aesthetics.
- Though the core curriculum focus for the property is centered on informational texts, there should also be a focus on science and/or social studies as key contexts, illustrating how informational texts add to our understanding of the world around us and how they can be used for further inquiry and exploration.
- Content should be appropriate and relevant for low-income and minority audiences.
- Content should consider Universal Design for Learning (UDL) principles to reach the needs of a broad and diverse audience.

After receiving 59 proposals, we began a multi-step review process, narrowing down to the top five submissions. The remaining proposals were reviewed by members of the PBS Children's Media and Education Core Matrix team, representatives from CPB, members of the PBS Programmer Advisory Board, and Nell, with a goal of identifying one or two pilots for development. After this commissioning round, we decided to take two properties, including *Molly*, to pilot development and production. Once delivered, both pilots were focus-group tested with a diverse group of children in the target age group and their caregivers, who were representative of the target audience for the Ready To Learn Initiative. After a review of the testing results, we determined that the pilot for *Molly* had best met the goals as outlined in the RFP. The show was greenlit as a new PBS KIDS series and multi-platform property. At the time of this writing, *Molly* is in series production and scheduled to premiere in summer 2019.

Bringing Informational Text to Life with *Molly of Denali*

7. How did WGBH's efforts to create a compelling world complete with dynamic characters, exciting storylines, and best practices in informational text learning lead you to the development of *Molly of Denali*?

Carol Greenwald: Based on our experiences with popular and award-winning PBS KIDS projects, including *Curious George, Arthur, Between the Lions*, and *The Ruff Ruffman Show*, the WGBH Children's Media and Education team knew that curriculum and learning goals must be embedded into an engaging narrative, with strong characters that children will relate to, and stories that resonate with young viewers. Drawing on our knowledge of how to seamlessly incorporate literacy, STEM, social studies, and social-emotional skills into an entertaining television series, we recognized that the use of informational texts would best be presented as authentic adventures. The storylines, told with humor and purpose, would involve the characters using those texts to help solve real-world problems, satisfy their curiosity, and to accomplish tasks in their daily lives.

As we brainstormed possibilities, our team came up with the idea of setting the show in Alaska. Rather quickly, the setting inspired the creation of our main character: Molly, a ten-year-old Alaska Native girl, whose parents run a trading post in the fictional village of Qyah (see Figures 12.2 and 12.3). Once we placed the show in that environment, with those characters, we saw that there was an opportunity to showcase children from rural and indigenous communities, specifically the Alaska Native population—children who are typically underrepresented in media. In addition to making sure that the show would appeal to all children, the setting would also be ideal for supporting children's exploration of nature and other STEM topics. From the very beginning, we understood that we needed input from the communities we intended to serve and solicited help from Alaska Native advisors. This led to expanding the series' goals to provide authentic cultural awareness.

8.   What is your team learning about informational text as *Molly of Denali* is developed into a multi-platform media property?

Carol Greenwald: Nell's in-depth scholarship informs the series in every way. With her as our curriculum advisor, we have extended and expanded our initial

FIGURE 12.2 Image from an episode of *Molly of Denali*; Molly (left) and her mom, Layla, a bush pilot (right)

(Courtesy of WGBH Educational Foundation © 2018)

FIGURE 12.3 Image from an episode of *Molly of Denali;* Molly's parents manage the Denali Trading Post in Qyah, Alaska
(Courtesy of WGBH Educational Foundation © 2018)

knowledge about informational text, including the understanding that all informational text is not equal. Some types, such as informative/explanatory texts, are more important than others for children's academic success. Our priority in the series, therefore, is to feature the forms of informational text that all young children, especially the Ready To Learn audience, often struggle with (see Table 12.1). In addition, digital games, hands-on activities for families, and PBS LearningMedia resources for educators—intrinsic components of the series—are being developed concurrently, as part of a cohesive whole. Those teams also have Nell as an advisor and thus are well-versed in the curriculum.

9. How is the team's understanding of informational text shaping the current development and design of *Molly of Denali*?

Carol Greenwald: Throughout the series, we use all forms of informational text: print, oral, audio, visual, and digital. With Nell consulting on scripts and game development, we ensure that Molly and her friends and family use the texts in a real-world context. Because the curriculum was developed simultaneously with the series and its other components, it's been a very organic process. We rely on three core concepts—accessing informational texts, conveying information, and using informational texts for authentic purposes—as well as 15 specific informational text learning goals to shape each script or asset, but we also never lose sight of the importance of making Molly and her world appealing, interesting, and enjoyable.

10. How do the needs of the Ready To Learn Initiative's target audience
     figure into the production equation as you balance the need to support all
     children, while also ensuring that the content meets the engagement and
     learning needs of underserved children?

Carol Greenwald: While the Ready To Learn Initiative strives to reach all
children, we are also driven by the initiative's goal to support kids from high-
need communities who may not have access to high-quality resources or
enriching educational experiences. This includes children living in rural communities who represent a significant segment of the U.S. population. In fact,
one in six students attend rural schools, with a significant number being
children of color (Showalter, Klein, Johnson & Hartman, 2017). Research has
shown that children who grow up in these areas often lag behind their non-
rural peers in educational achievement (Lee & Burkam, 2002; Miller, Votruba-
Drzal & Setodji, 2013). Since *Molly* focuses on daily life in a rural community,
the series offers skill-building opportunities for children from low-income,
high-need communities who will readily relate to the setting. *Molly* also fills
an important gap in children's media with its culturally authentic depiction of
an Alaska Native community.

Because of Molly's relationships with her friends and family, and the situations she encounters, her experiences as a ten-year-old will be familiar to most
children, whether they live in urban, suburban, or non-Native rural communities. Deftly told with humor and compassion, the scripts encompass issues and
incidents that all children deal with, such as getting along with friends, meeting
new people, and mastering new skills. The setting emphasizes the importance of
the natural world and people as stewards of that world, a concept that has been
shown to be beneficial for children no matter where they live.

11. What is the role of testing—particularly with underserved children—and
     how does early formative research contribute to your production process?

Carol Greenwald: The testing of story outlines was essential in forming and
informing the characters, narratives, and curriculum for the series. We tested two
outlines at Title 1 schools in Washington, DC, to measure not only the appeal of
the *Molly of Denali* characters, setting, and stories, but also whether the informational texts were integrated in a meaningful way and presented at an age-
appropriate level. The early results were positive: Children liked the characters
and the stories, recognized that Qyah, despite being different, was a community
like theirs, and they understood what was being conveyed through informational
texts (Rockman et al., 2018). We will continue testing with formative research
among Alaska Native children and other rural populations as the series develops.

Testing has been equally important throughout the development of the
digital games and apps. The digital team is creating the assets through an

iterative process, with several rounds of prototype testing at Title 1 schools and afterschool programs, usually with children on a one-on-one basis. Further testing, conducted by Ready To Learn research partners, will take place at key milestones in game development with children in high-need, low-income communities, and with children representing a range of disabilities and learning challenges. This research helps us determine how to create online and mobile games and apps that will appeal to young audiences from all backgrounds, are fun to play, and meet the educational goals of the series.

12.   How do the digital games, episodes, and informational text curriculum relate to one another?

Carol Greenwald: Our goal is to create a Playful Learning Experience (PLE), in which games, videos, and interactive activities are all in one place. Children, who may or may not be able to read proficiently, will likely be playing the games on their own, without an adult. Our mission is to create a game that a child will be eager to play and complete while helping develop his or her informational text skills. It's the kind of challenge we relish! Whereas the show can model using informational text, we can give children the opportunity to actually practice their skills and put their knowledge into action. As we have done when developing previous PBS KIDS games, the digital and production teams will work together to maintain the "look," tone, and personality of the show. Games will reflect the episodes in the series by presenting a task or dilemma that Molly and her family and friends might do or care about. From game developers to designers, all members of the digital team know and understand the curriculum and the learning goals for the series.

13.   How do you envision real-world, hands-on informational text learning experiences based on *Molly of Denali* will be crafted and used in home, school, and out-of-school settings by children living in high-need communities?

Anne Lund: All PBS KIDS properties, especially those created for the Ready To Learn Initiative, have the goal of reaching children anytime, anywhere by focusing on all aspects of a child's learning ecosystem. *Molly* will be no exception, with the creation of a variety of rich educational television and digital media resources for a child to access at home on their own, with a sibling or parent, with a teacher in school, or at a local PBS station family or community learning event. We hope these resources will inspire children to notice and explore informational texts for a variety of purposes in their home, communities, and the greater world around them. Complementary offline supplemental materials, thoughtfully connected through story and curriculum, will also be produced for use by families, educators, and PBS stations to further extend the learning with informational texts. For example, innovative, interactive lesson plans on PBS

LearningMedia for use by Grade K–1 teachers will incorporate video from the show to provide students with a hands-on, media-rich learning experience.

Carol Greenwald: As we develop these materials, we will engage in a human-centered design approach, helping us listen to and understand the needs of our audience. This approach provides an inclusive and iterative framework for solving problems. It is a method that generates solutions from within, rather than imposing solutions on those we are seeking to serve. For this reason, input from partners, including those in rural, high-need communities, will be crucial.

14.   What aspects of Molly's Alaska Native culture and her geographic surroundings lend themselves to stories and games that are ripe for informational text learning, and how do you go about ensuring cultural accuracy and authenticity?

Carol Greenwald: Less than one percent of characters in children's cartoons are Native American. Perhaps more devastating are the media's inaccurate and negative depictions of Native Americans. This takes a toll: The most common tropes have harmful impacts on Native American children and their academic success (Leavitt et al., 2015).

We began our work on *Molly* with a two-day summit in Alaska, which evolved into an Alaska Native Advisory Group. This group is integral to the series development, as is our Creative Producer, Princess Daazhraii Johnson, a member of the Gwich'in Nation. Princess Johnson has been part of every aspect of production, including a review of scripts and digital content. To provide cultural authenticity and support for social-emotional learning and growth, we will incorporate Alaska Native values into the storylines (see Figure 12.4). The character Molly is voiced by Sovereign Bill who is Tlingit (an Alaska Native group) and Muckleshoot. Two of the show's writers are Alaska Natives and we are recruiting other indigenous talent as directors, designers, and animators. In addition, the interstitials—short, live-action videos that appear between the two animates—will be filmed in Alaska by local production teams.

Nell Duke: Molly lives in a setting with a lot of communication within the family and among members of the community. There is significant expertise in her family: of her mother, a bush pilot; her father, a wilderness guide; her grandfather, a volcanologist; and so on. There is also deep indigenous knowledge among members of the community, from woodworking to geology to canoeing to fishing and more. The local library is a popular destination, and Molly's family's trading post is visited by local community members as well as tourists from around the world—scientists, birders, and others. This setting provides so many opportunities for conveying and accessing information through oral, written, and visual informational texts.

Molly's world is one of tremendous beauty, with diverse plant and animal life and interesting land features, including forests, mountains, volcanoes, lakes,

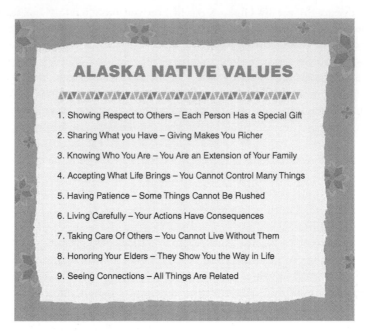

FIGURE 12.4   List of Alaska Native values incorporated into *Molly of Denali* storylines (Written text from the Alaska Native Knowledge Network, 2006)

and others. This environment provides many opportunities to read, write, listen to, present, view, and visually represent informational texts about the natural world, such as field guides, Internet sites with animal webcams, and so on.

Discoveries and Aspirations

15.   What are you learning or discovering as you produce *Molly of Denali*?

Carol Greenwald: Creating *Molly* has been an amazing experience. In addition to learning about different ways of thinking about informational text, we are exploring and absorbing the diversity, culture, language, values, and needs of the Alaska Native people and environment. A gift of that collaboration has been learning to stop talking and just listen. For many of us, this has been as much a life lesson as it is part of the fabric of the show.

   Nell Duke: We are learning how, in a fun and accessible way, to develop engaging content that puts it all together: presenting engaging stories and characters; developing informational text knowledge, skills, and dispositions; building content knowledge in science and social studies; and conveying a sense of the diversity, culture, and values of Alaska Native groups.

16.   As you work on bringing this original property to life, what aspirations do you have for *Molly of Denali* and informational text learning?

Carol Greenwald: We are eager for children and their families to fall in love with Molly and her world! We also look forward to having Native children and those living in rural communities see themselves portrayed in a positive way on screen. We are excited to show the wonders and beauty of the natural Alaskan world to children around the country. And, as we model for younger children the importance, variety, and usefulness of informational text in the series, we hope to build essential literacy skills, especially for those who need them most, in an innovative and appealing way.

Nell Duke: To add to Carol's comments, I hope we develop resources that educators will embrace to support them in developing young children's knowledge, skills, and dispositions with informational text, which, as noted earlier, is an area of instruction that is still relatively new and challenging to many teachers. I hope we are also able to highlight for families the role that informational texts play or can play in everyday life so that they might take advantage of other opportunities to interact with informational text.

Anne Lund: I echo Carol and Nell's aspirations and add my excitement for bringing Molly and her world to the millions of children around the country who might never experience Alaska or the adventures *Molly* takes them on firsthand. Through *Molly*, I hope they will gain background knowledge about the wider world and develop a passion for sharing what they know and learn about their own environments and communities. I also hope that our commitment to building literacy skills through informational text will help move the needle for children who would not otherwise have consistent opportunities to access and gain the knowledge, skills, and dispositions with these important texts to help them succeed in school and life.

Acknowledgments

We would like to recognize the members of the WGBH Children's Media and Education team who made significant contributions to Carol Greenwald's commentary in this chapter, including Melissa Carlson, Senior Digital Producer; Dorothea Gillim, Executive Producer, *Molly of Denali*; Marcy Gunther, Director of Media Development, Senior Producer, *Molly of Denali*; Mary Haggerty, Director of First 8 Labs and Media Engagement; Cyrisse Jaffee, Editorial Project Manager, Education; and Bill Shribman, Senior Executive Producer and Director of Digital Partnerships.

References

Alaska Native Knowledge Network. (2006). *Alaska native values for curriculum*. Fairbanks, AK: ANKN. Retrieved from www.ankn.uaf.edu/ANCR/Values/.

Duke, N. K. (2000). 3.6 minutes per day: The scarcity of informational texts in first grade. *Reading Research Quarterly*, 35(2), 202–224.

Jeong, J., Gaffney, J. S., & Choi, J. (2010). Availability and use of informational texts in second-, third-, and fourth-grade classrooms. *Research in the Teaching of English*, 44(4), 435–456.

Leavitt, P. A., Covarrubias, R., Perez, Y. A., & Fryberg, S. A. (2015). Frozen in time: The impact of native American media representations on identity and self-understanding. *Journal of Social Issues*, 71(1), 39–53.

Lee, V. E. & Burkam, D. T. (2002). *Inequality at the starting gate: Social background differences in achievement as children begin school*. Washington, DC: Economic Policy Institute.

Miller, P., Votruba-Drzal, E., & Setodji, C. M. (2013). Family income and early achievement across the urban–rural continuum. *Developmental Psychology*, 49(8), 1452-1465.

National Governors Association Center for Best Practices & Council of Chief State School Officers. (2010). *Common core state standards for English language arts & literacy*. Washington, DC: National Governors Association Center for Best Practices & Council of Chief State School Officers.

Pentimonti, J. M., Zucker, T. A., Justice, L. M., & Kaderavek, J. N. (2010). Informational text use in preschool classroom read-alouds. *The Reading Teacher*, 63(8), 656–665.

Rockman et al. (2018, March). *Molly of Denali storybook testing with in-school and after-school focus groups–summary report*. Bloomington, IN: Rockman et al.

Showalter, D., Klein, R., Johnson, J., & Hartman, S. L. (2017). *Why rural matters 2015–2016: Understanding the changing landscape*. Washington, DC: The Rural School and Community Trust.

U.S. Department of Health and Human Services (USDHHS), Administration for Children and Families, Office of Head Start. (2015). *Head start early learning outcomes framework: Ages birth to five*. Washington, DC: USDHHS.

Warner-Griffin, C., Liu, H., Tadler, C., Herget, D., & Dalton, B. (2017). *Reading achievement of U.S. Fourth-grade students in an international context: First look at the progress in international reading literacy study (PIRLS) 2016 and ePIRLS 2016 (NCES 2018-017)*. Washington, DC: U.S. Department of Education, National Center for Education Statistics. Retrieved June 6, 2018 from https://nces.ed.gov/pubsearch.

Yopp, R. H. & Yopp, H. K. (2006). Informational texts as read-alouds at school and home. *The Reading Teacher*, 38(1), 37–51.

13

BUILDING COMMUNITY PARTNERSHIPS TO SUPPORT FAMILY LEARNING

Aaron Morris, Devon Steven, and Kea Anderson

> Creating the conditions where families have the time, space, and resources to hang out, play, and learn with one another is a big deal. If we really want to impact parents' confidence and ability to support their kids' learning, then there is incredible value in creating the conditions where they can try it out for themselves in a safe and fun context.
>
> *Aaron Morris, PBS*

Introduction: A New Approach to Community Engagement

On a Thursday evening after a long day, Ava walks into the multipurpose room of her daughter's school, her younger son in tow. She greets her daughter as the room fills with other families also coming to participate in the third workshop of a PBS KIDS Family & Community Learning series hosted by the local PBS station and a parent advocacy organization. Two weeks earlier, at the first workshop, she was cautious and quiet, not sure what she'd got into. Tonight, she chats comfortably with other parents she has got to know: "It's great to have a night off from cooking and dishes and just focus on being there with the kids."

Scenes like this are taking place in 16 communities around the country where public media stations have initiated a new model for partnering with organizations such as local schools, libraries, housing authorities, and cultural organizations that also serve local families. "Ava" is a composite of an experience hundreds of parents have had in these communities in the last two years. The Corporation for Public Broadcasting (CPB) and the Public Broadcasting Service (PBS) fund the community partnerships through the Ready To Learn Initiative, a long-running federal program that aims to improve children's school readiness and success (see Chapter 1 for a description of the initiative's history). Public media stations have sought to serve as community partners since the Public Broadcasting Act of 1967 described stations as "valuable local community resources for utilizing electronic media to address national concerns and solve local problems through community programs and outreach programs." This new model, called Community Collaboratives for Early Learning & Media, builds on this tradition while innovating in three key ways.

First, the Collaboratives seek to foster mutually beneficial relationships among a network of community partners that leverages the expertise and resources of all participants, rather than an older hub-and-spoke model, with the station at the center providing resources to various partners who were not necessarily connected to one another. Each Collaborative focuses its joint activity in a well-defined community where at least one partnering organization has established relationships, usually a neighborhood or school feeder pattern. This approach enables Collaboratives to serve the same families in multiple settings throughout the year, creating the potential for deeper engagement, while presenting a new way for public media stations to respond to communities' most pressing needs.

Leveraging the expertise of relevant local partners and maintaining a sustained presence in specific neighborhoods enables the second innovation, a new approach to family learning. A centerpiece of the Collaboratives' activities is PBS KIDS Family & Community Learning, a multi-generational model of family engagement, which aims to help parents, and other caregivers, especially those in under-resourced communities, support their young children's learning (see Figures 13.1–13.5 for pictures of workshop participants). Each Family & Community Learning series is designed to involve eight to ten families across four, two-hour workshops. At each workshop, participants share a meal, explore STEM and literacy concepts via PBS KIDS digital media and related hands-on activities, and reflect on their experiences. (Collaboratives also offer child-focused versions of the curriculum as out-of-school-time camps.) Tasha Weinstein, Manager of Educational Outreach at WFSU in Tallahassee, FL, compared the model's more intensive eight hours of programming to prior public media family engagement efforts:

> The purpose of the new work remains the same as earlier family engagement efforts: to use media to turn any time into learning time and to turn PBS resources into immersive learning experiences that blend online components with hands-on collaborative curiosity and exploration. [. . .] It's different in that it provides for a much deeper experience where parents and kids collaborate together. [. . .] We give them the power of engaging with media and show them how to stop and engage with their kids. And four times—hopefully, that's enough to establish some new patterns.

FIGURE 13.1 Picture of participants at a PBS KIDS Family & Community Learning with *ScratchJr* workshop
(Courtesy of Kentucky Educational Television)

FIGURE 13.2 Picture of participants at a PBS KIDS Family & Community Learning with *Ruff Ruffman* workshop
(Courtesy of WQED Multimedia, Pittsburgh, PA)

Echoing this distinction, Cindy Putman, Ready To Learn Project Manager at WCTE in Cookeville, TN, called the new approach "a buffet rather than a drive-thru window." CPB and PBS posited that the higher dosage and depth of the four workshops would promote stronger family engagement and the potential for deeper learning gains for both parents and children.

FIGURE 13.3 A picture of participants at a PBS KIDS Family & Community Learning with *Ruff Ruffman* workshop

(Courtesy of WQED Multimedia, Pittsburgh, PA)

FIGURE 13.4 A picture of participants at a PBS KIDS Family & Community Learning with Play and Learn Science workshop

(Courtesy of Kentucky Educational Television)

The third innovation is the robust infrastructure that links the 16 Collaboratives into a national network and supports continuous improvement of their activities. PBS KIDS develops the Family & Community Learning workshops and related camp experiences centrally, then trains all Collaboratives on the new

FIGURE 13.5 Picture of participants in a PBS KIDS Family & Community Learning with *ScratchJr* workshop
(Courtesy of WFSU, Tallahassee, FL)

curriculum at one- to two-day training workshops, during which participants work with other Collaboratives to walk through the new materials and discuss how the resources will work with their families. CPB and PBS also develop comprehensive guides for educators containing the pedagogical rationale, step-by-step curriculum, and reflection tools to support implementation. Along with the training workshops and guides, CPB and PBS established a professional learning community on the Basecamp platform to help Collaboratives ask questions and share their experiences. The Basecamp community is active year-round and particularly so during the earliest implementations of new workshops, as station staff share detailed descriptions of successes, challenges, and changes they have made. Stations also provide detailed information about the workshops and camps they host (e.g., participation data, adaptations made) in event-specific and monthly reporting to CPB. Evaluators from the Education Development Center (EDC) and SRI International (SRI) further assist stations in using national measures to generate overall insights into implementation and impact of the experiences.

Collaboratives' formative input on new resources at training meetings, ongoing conversation on Basecamp, station reports to CPB, and evaluation findings all provide data used to continuously improve the learning experiences and accompanying guidance, and also are the data sources for this chapter. As we—representing PBS, CPB, and the evaluation team—prepare to onboard

14 new Collaboratives in fall 2018, we share what we have learned from the first 16 about (1) generating high family engagement, (2) building the capacity of workshop facilitators, and (3) supporting high-quality adaptation of the workshop model. First, we describe the purpose of the workshop model and its place in the Collaboratives' activities and in the Ready To Learn Initiative more broadly.

Why Family & Community Learning

To fulfill the Ready To Learn Initiative's goal of improving outcomes for children, especially children from under-resourced communities, the Collaboratives seek to build the capacity of the parents and other adults who support them. As discussed in more detail in Chapter 3, research suggests that parental involvement can play a key role in supporting early learning and reducing achievement gaps in early grades (Bassok et al., 2016; Burgess, Hecth, & Lonigan, 2002; Dearing et al., 2004; Niklas et al., 2016; Sénéchal & LeFevre, 2002; Skwarchuk, Sowinski, & LeFevre, 2014). A recent national survey conducted by the EDC and SRI found that nearly all parents, including low-income parents, want to help their children learn, but many feel they lack the content knowledge or confidence to do so, or simply do not know where to begin (Silander et al., 2018). The Collaboratives, through Family & Community Learning and other experiences, use PBS KIDS media to help parents move beyond these barriers.

Media can offer an appealing gateway for helping parents support their children's learning. Research has shown that when parents and children use media together, sometimes called joint media engagement, the experience has the potential to support increased learning among children (Fisch et al., 2008; Takeuchi & Stevens, 2012). Further, high-quality, evidence-based media such as the PBS KIDS content created under the Ready To Learn Initiative can support learning across the whole family (McCarthy et al., 2015; Pasnik et al., 2015). However, as Barron and Levinson (2018) note, "There are few resources available to systematically guide parents who want to know more about how to productively harness media for their children." To address this gap, they call for "design work that can help families explore resources and approaches to using media," including "social learning opportunities in places where families spend time [such as] schools, libraries, museums, and workplaces." The Family & Community Learning workshops offer such opportunities, in the context of partnerships formed among organizations that already serve families. Based on a family engagement model developed at the MIT Media Lab by Ricarose Roque, and in alignment with the Ready To Learn Initiative's goals for 2015–2020, workshops aim to positively influence parents':

• Attitudes toward, understanding of, and practices in early STEM and literacy;

- Confidence related to helping their children learn, by providing them with strategies, vocabulary, and experiences that can be transferred beyond the workshops into the home and community; and
- Understanding of how media and technology can be used to support learning.

As of May 2018, four workshop series have been developed, and a fifth is underway. Targeting families with children ages five to eight or ages three to five, they use content from PBS KIDS properties including *The Ruff Ruffman Show*, *The Cat in the Hat Knows a Lot About That!*, and *Ready Jet Go!* (All workshop materials are publicly available at https://pbslearningmedia.org/collec tion/pbs-kids-family-community-learning.) The successes and lessons learned from Collaboratives implementing the workshops are relevant for any high-touch family engagement effort centered on building parent and educator capacity to help improve young children's learning, as well as more broadly for community partnerships.

Getting Families to Come and Come Again

In under-resourced communities, convincing parents that the workshops are indeed for them—and not just their children—can be the first hurdle. Parents may not feel comfortable or may feel ill-prepared to participate, especially if they do not already have a relationship with one of the partnering organizations. Many Collaboratives were initially concerned that not enough families would come. As author Aaron Morris recalls, "A surprising number of people told me that families would never show up for four Family & Community Learning workshops, four weeks in a row—it was way too much to ask of busy, stressed families." In fact, participation at many Collaboratives has exceeded expectations.

In the most recent implementation of the Family & Community Learning with *Ruff Ruffman* series across all 16 Collaboratives, each site hosted between 4 and 19 families, at locations such as their children's elementary school or a community center in their neighborhood or housing complex. Approximately 130 total families—comprising about 140 children ages five to eight, about 130 parents and other caregivers, and about 90 siblings and cousins—attended at least part of the series. Three Collaboratives reported that all participating families attended all four workshops, while five noted that nearly all did (e.g., 9 of 11 families, 18 of 19 families). Three shared that about half of families attended all workshops.

The most notable successes occur where stations have worked hand-in-hand with their partners and have been attentive and responsive to the families themselves. In Jackson, MS, for example, the Collaborative has seen high partici-pation from the start, thanks in part to families' established relationships with both Mississippi Public Broadcasting and partner Springboard to Opportunities, a non-profit that supports residents of affordable housing. Even with strong relationships in place, it is easy to underestimate the care and planning that enable such high participation and completion. We describe a few critical factors below.

Trust, Location, Time, and Language

Offering the workshops at sites where and when families spend time has been critical—for example, at the afterschool program at 5:30 p.m., when parents normally come to pick up their children, or at the community center of an apartment complex when families are typically home. The Collaboratives have also worked to accommodate local families' needs when selecting workshop dates and times, which has meant scheduling around weeknight church services, youth sports, and other family commitments.

To ensure that recruited families attend all workshops, Collaboratives have used a variety of strategies, including sending text message reminders, offering completion certificates and/or ceremonies, offering PBS KIDS goodie bags, and gifting PBS KIDS Playtime Pad tablets to families at the last workshop. One Collaborative had families attending one workshop series choose the dates for the next series, ensuring a second experience with the same group of families. Having workshop leaders (facilitators) who speak the preferred language of English-learner parents has also helped those parents participate fully in the experience and shifted the burden of interpreting away from the children. As we describe above, when Collaboratives create the conditions in which families can easily attend, families do so, often attending all four workshops in a series. Parents who complete a series convey a sense of accomplishment and gratitude for opportunities they do not otherwise have with their children. Janelle Eastland, a 1st-grade teacher and parent participant in a Family & Community Learning series hosted by Vegas PBS and its partners, shared:

> The hug I got from my son—and I don't want to cry but—it was, like, amazing, because I got to do it with him—the whole entire four times— and he was like, "Mommy, I love you so much."

The opportunity for parents to learn alongside one child can be even more elusive in families with multiple children. To make participation feasible for parents and children in the target age range, Collaboratives must also accommodate other family members.

Welcoming the Whole Family

Partners must familiarize themselves with local families' needs, which can vary greatly. In some instances, families have had more children in the age range than parents attending, and twice as many siblings and cousins outside of the target age range. In other instances, two parents have attended for every child, with low sibling participation. These differences have implications for the number of facilitators and other staff needed, the skills those staff need, and possibly the need to adapt offerings to incorporate or otherwise accommodate siblings; discovering families' needs in planning stages has been critical. Several Collaboratives provide on-site child care for younger siblings. Collaboratives have also given older siblings roles, such as helping parents and younger siblings use devices, reading aloud, and taking pictures to document the experience.

Building Facilitator Capacity

Improving parents' confidence and knowledge to help their children learn requires training educators and other partner organization staff to effectively support parents and model skills for them. Training is particularly vital in cases where facilitators have little experience with two-generation programs as intensive as Family & Community Learning. Some of the partner organization staff who lead and assist with the workshops (for example, from housing authorities or community centers) may not have experience as educators, much less as educators of both parents and children. Further, some facilitators are volunteers rather than staff and maybe stepping in with little time to prepare. In surveys, one or more facilitators from every Collaborative reported needing more training in the relevant content areas and/or in using media and technology to support learning (EDC & SRI, 2017a). CPB and PBS had substantial training and guidance in place from the start, combined with feedback loops to enable ongoing support and improvement; however, as CPB and PBS have learned more about facilitator backgrounds and needs, they continue to develop a broader array of training resources:

- Facilitators requested *at-a-glance versions of each guide* for just-in-time help.
- Collaboratives report that *pictures and videos* are useful in supporting both facilitator training and the uptake of the program with other potential partners and funders. CPB and PBS have plans underway for videos that will show what high-quality Family & Community Learning looks like in action.
- Collaboratives have also shared a need for a *professional development workshop* modeled on the ones Collaborative leaders attend, to enable them to train others in their communities. In March 2018, CPB and PBS began piloting a professional learning series, Playful Learning for Educators, designed to create for educators the same types of playful, media-integrated experiences that Family & Creative Learning provides for families.

These three types of resources make guidance more accessible and flexible and, in the case of the new professional development workshop, support the Collaboratives' ability to train others.

In the new resources as well as in yet-to-be-developed workshops and guides, we especially aim to address two critical areas. First, many facilitators are new to the workshops' guided-play pedagogy. Guided play scaffolds learners' pursuit of goals through structured yet learner-led processes (Weisberg, Hirsh-Pasek, & Golinkoff, 2013). Facilitators need to see this pedagogy modeled at training workshops and in videos, and most importantly need opportunities to practice it themselves. Just-in-time guidance can feature question prompts to encourage facilitators' own exploration of guided-play pedagogy while familiarizing themselves with the content and available resources. Facilitators also need help supporting adult learning. The workshop model calls for more direct interaction with the parents than with children, but teachers and others trained to support children can find it difficult to focus first on the parents and other caregivers during workshops. In contrast, some Collaboratives, including PBS SoCal, have successfully leveraged the expertise of station staff, school community engagement managers, parent advocacy organization staff, or others experienced in supporting adults to address this challenge.

PBS SoCal has honed its parent engagement approach through efforts such as its STEM Parent Academy, which it has offered for several years to parents of children ages two to five. In the Academy, participating parents learn age-appropriate STEM concepts and how they can engage their children in STEM learning and exploration using PBS KIDS educational media. Many parents who now participate in PBS SoCal's Family & Community Learning workshops are STEM Academy graduates; the workshops provide opportunities for these parents to use their new skills and confidence alongside their children. Susie Grimm, Early Learning Manager at PBS SoCal, observed that some "parents have more trepidations—they are less certain, less empowered, and less likely to engage" in the workshops when they do not have the foundation in media literacy or science learning that the STEM Parent Academy provides. The STEM Parent Academy also helps prepare PBS SoCal and its Collaborative partners to lead the new workshops. Grimm reports that facilitator roles shift between the two experiences, from mainly providing instruction during the Academies to more of a supporting role in the workshops as the families begin to teach and learn from one another, an exciting progression for families and facilitators alike.

Supporting High-Quality Adaptation

While CPB and PBS develop the workshops and camps centrally, the learning experiences are designed for implementation in vastly different local contexts, which introduces a seemingly infinite range of local adaptations. Collaboratives may modify the experiences in response to community needs or for a host of other reasons. Adaptations come about as Collaboratives navigate requirements associated with other funding streams, integrate the new experiences with existing programming or partner offerings, or take advantage of other local opportunities. Stations have reported integrating field trips and hosting visits from the local fire department. One station reported that a local farmer brought a cow and did a milking demonstration as part of a camp. Some Collaboratives kick-off workshops with a more intensive introductory phase only for parents, while others skip a parent-focused introduction altogether due to time constraints. The more information we can gather from Collaboratives about the changes they make and why, the better we can support them in making high-quality modifications to ensure the workshops' potential for building parent capacity can be realized in these highly varied contexts.

One example of a substantive adaptation comes from WQED and its Collaborative partners around Pittsburgh, PA. The Collaborative is serving the nearby suburbs of Allegheny County, where suburban poverty is part of an often overlooked but unfortunately growing national trend (Kneebone, 2017). This trend is of particular concern because suburban areas often lack accessible, visible supports to families who live at or below the poverty line. Partnering with a local elementary school, two libraries, and the South Hills Interfaith Movement (South Hills), the Collaborative began to infuse gardening and related science concepts into its activities, giving children a hands-on opportunity to grow their own food and donate fresh produce to a pantry operated by South Hills. This led to the realization that families whose children attend the partnering school could benefit from the workshops as well as from partner services such as the pantry. One family began using the pantry after learning of it from a flyer their child brought home from a camp offered by the Collaborative.

The station has now been funded by the Jefferson Regional Foundation, a local health-focused non-profit, to develop and pilot new Family & Community Learning-style workshops on health science for families in low-income communities in and around Pittsburgh. If the most beneficial learning experiences combine CPB and PBS's nationally developed models and materials with the responsiveness to local needs illustrated by the Pittsburgh-area Collaborative's early successes, these adaptations and opportunities also complicate the evaluation's effort to interpret and report on the impact of this work both locally and nationally.

To some degree, adaptation is inherent in the design of the experiences. CPB and PBS encourage a sense of ownership of the model, recognizing that the Collaboratives will be able to sustain the work beyond the 2015–2020 funding cycle only as it continues to prove feasible and to align with partners' goals and organizational missions. Encouraging ownership has meant using the Collaboratives' input to improve the resources and also passing creative control to the stations themselves. The two newest workshop series were developed by the education staff at WQED and Vegas PBS. PBS SoCal also has a new workshop series in progress. As we are still reflecting on how best to develop guidance to support high-quality adaptations, we also find ourselves exploring how best to support scaling the Family & Community Learning workshop model as we see it and the camp models expanding beyond the Collaboratives earlier than we anticipated.

Scaling Planned and Spontaneous

CPB and PBS had planned to work toward scaling the new learning experiences nationally by first adding 14 new Collaboratives in fall 2018 to the current 16, and then supporting the network of 30 Collaboratives in sharing the learning experiences with other organizations beyond their partnerships. However, in early 2018, Collaboratives began fielding requests from local organizations outside their partnerships for training on the Family & Community Learning model.

Seven of eight Collaboratives we contacted about expansion in their communities for this chapter reported receiving requests about the model from more than one other organization in their state. News of the model is spreading among organizations with which stations already partner in another capacity, at early learning and family engagement meetings where stations share their Collaborative work, and by sheer word of mouth. Stations reported responding to requests for training from school and district leaders in neighboring areas, an early learning coalition, a local housing authority, statewide conferences, a family shelter, the director of a makerspace, youth development organizations, a children's museum, and a hospital foundation. Considering that the Collaboratives themselves have used the model for less than two years, we find this range of interest remarkable.

How stations respond to these requests depends on staff capacity and how an organization is interested in using the model. Cindy Putman, the Ready To Learn Project Manager at WCTE in Appalachian Tennessee, has presented on the model at a statewide family engagement conference, at the conference's request. She also plans to train staff and volunteers at other organizations in the area who have requested training, including:

- A group of school family engagement coordinators, at the request of a local school;
- 40 volunteers from the local housing authority that runs a summer meals program, with a focus on engaging families; and
- Members of a local Rotary International club that secured a grant to offer Family & Community Learning workshops as a service project.

WFSU, in Tallahassee, FL, similarly reports requests for training from all over the state. WFSU is working with a statewide early learning coalition to integrate workshop materials into kits for teachers for use in seven counties, and is working with the Title I director in another county, all beyond the station's traditional service area. WVIZ/PBS ideastream in Cleveland, OH, reports that a Vice President from the Head Start early learning program requested a proposal to replicate the workshop program in all 13 Head Start centers in the area. The spontaneous expansion in the communities around the current Collaboratives is an encouraging sign for the model's potential sustainability while making thoughtful guidance for high-quality adaptation all the more urgent.

Early Indications of Benefits for Families and Partners

At least within the Collaboratives and ideally beyond them as well, new versions of the workshops will maintain and improve on early signs of the workshops' benefits for participating families and partners emerging in national evaluation findings, as well as in testimonials in station reports, proof-of-performance videos, and informal conversation.

Learning Outcomes for Parents and Children

In the implementation study of the first series of workshops (PBS KIDS *ScratchJr*), the EDC and SRI found early evidence that participation in the workshops can increase parent confidence in supporting their children's learning, as well as in skills related to the workshops' focal content—in this case using technology, and helping their children use technology to create something (EDC & SRI, 2017b). These benefits reflect the experience of Mauro Reyes, a father who participated in a Family & Community Learning with PBS KIDS *ScratchJr* series; as he stated,

> At first I was kind of nervous. I didn't really know how to understand it, but as soon as they started doing the instructions, I started catching up to it. [. . .] I feel proud that I came here to learn something that I could teach them in the house, you know, something educational.

Most parents also reported that the workshop helped them think in a new way about science, engineering, and/or technology. Nearly all parents reported that the workshop led them to try new learning activities at home with their children (EDC & SRI, 2017b).

Parents Develop a Sense of Belonging

We have also identified promising signs that the workshops create opportunities for parents and children to connect with one another and also with other families, and that sustained participation promotes a sense of belonging and community for parents. Parenting can be busy and isolating—even more so for parents in under-resourced communities. The stresses of finances, employment, food, and housing can hinder parents' opportunities to connect with others in their community. Testimonials suggest that the workshops provide a trusted environment where parents and other caregivers can engage their children in fun learning activities while also building connections with other families that may last beyond the last workshop. Nichole, a mother of twins and participant in multiple workshop series through KBTC in Tacoma, WA, described the workshop atmosphere:

> It's like a community within itself; you come to eat, you talk, you get to know people, you learn, and you walk away going, 'Wow, that was really fun!' I think as a single mom it's really important to have that connection and to feel like it's not just me doing it, but other people out there can help me do it too.

In addition, as this mother implies, by participating, parents may learn of and realize they could benefit from other services offered by partner organizations, such as food pantries, job training, or counseling.

Benefits to Partners

Community Collaboratives are designed to be more intensive and more mutually beneficial partnerships than public media stations had commonly had in the past. This begins with a needs assessment conducted prior to the start of a Collaborative's work and continues with partners' inclusion in training meetings for each new workshop series. Through their input in front-end and implementation stages, partners contribute to the design and development of the workshops. We observe that in many Collaboratives, partners' visibility as facilitators and conveners increases as they grow more comfortable with the model and resources. Partners also appreciate the opportunity to network nationally with other partnerships, as noted by a participant in the training workshop held in Cleveland, OH, in June 2016:

> The organization [of the training meeting] helped to get us into the content, but also see the bigger picture of what was trying to be accomplished. We appreciated being able to both learn about what was coming with Ruff Ruffman (and get excited about the content) and provide input as it was being developed. It was also good to network with the other groups and get ideas about how they were implementing the work.

Analyzing station staff and partner organization staff surveys from 13 of 16 Collaboratives from 2017, the EDC and SRI found that members of all reporting Collaboratives think the partnership increases their organization's capacity and visibility in the community, including among local schools and families. Partners reported valuing the collaboration: Respondents from 10 of 13 Collaboratives spoke highly of support from station staff. Similarly, partners in

11 of 13 Collaboratives reported positive views of the workshops' PBS KIDS-based resources. And nearly all partner respondents felt that Collaborative activities align with their organization's mission (EDC & SRI, 2017a). Remarks from Jim Tackett of the Appalachian Renaissance Initiative, a Kentucky Educational Television (KET) Collaborative member, reflect this view:

> Equipping our children and families for the future is one of the greatest responsibilities we have as educators. [The focus on] early childhood and family engagement aligns so nicely with many of our partners' missions, including KET's Ready To Learn work. By collectively providing the knowledge, skills, and networks for our families and communities, rural lives are being transformed stronger than ever.

We will look to findings from the 2017–2018 evaluation data, the first full year of data from more than one event, for more in-depth, national-level insights into families' experiences and Collaboratives' partnership strength and visibility.

Looking Ahead: Supporting New Collaboratives and Ongoing Expansion

While the Collaboratives have encountered unexpected successes, such as high family participation and completion of the workshops, they have also raised a number of challenges we are seeking to address, including facilitator needs and the need for guidance to support high-quality adaptation. We aim to use Collaboratives' input to improve the learning experiences and related supports to flatten the learning curve of the 14 new Community Collaboratives who will join the current 16 in fall 2018—through mechanisms such as providing best-practice guidance and pairing new Collaboratives with older ones to form mentoring relationships.

Given the expansion of the model beyond the Collaboratives, we are also beginning to track how, where, and among what types of organizations this expansion is happening, for example by updating surveys to systematically capture data on Collaboratives' training activities. It will also be valuable to capture who is accessing workshop materials online beyond the Collaboratives (and, ideally, their plans for using them) and how many families are being reached, while also encouraging broader use of the measures designed by the EDC and SRI. Noting that high-quality facilitation is vital to changing parents' attitudes and practices—and thereby to improve outcomes for children—we will also use survey findings and other input about the professional development workshop series that select Collaboratives are currently piloting, as well as some of their own early training efforts to improve success in the train-the-trainer approach.

Lastly, while early indications suggest that the Family & Community Learning model within the context of the Collaborative work has the potential to achieve the goals that we identified for participants, additional research is needed. It will be important to reconnect at later points with families who have attended workshops, particularly those who participate in more than one series, to evaluate the longer-term impact of their shared family experiences. Relatedly, checking back in with the Collaboratives over time will provide insights into how their shared effort implementing the workshops and other joint work supported by the Ready To Learn Initiative impact their relationships with one another and the communities they serve moving forward.

References

Barron, B. & Levinson, A. M. (2018). Media as a catalyst for children's engagement in learning at home and across settings. In E. Gee, L. Takeuchi, & E. Wartella (Eds.), *Children and Families in the Digital Age: Learning Together in a Media Saturated Culture.* New York, NY: Routledge, 17–36.

Bassok, D., Finch, J. E., Lee, R., Reardon, S. F., & Waldfogel, J. (2016). Socioeconomic gaps in early childhood experiences: 1998 to 2010. *AERA Open, 2*(3), 1–22.

Burgess, S. R., Hecth, S. A., & Lonigan, C. J. (2002). Relations of the home literacy environment (HLE) to the development of reading-related abilities: A one-year long-itudinal study. *Reading Research Quarterly, 37*(4), 408–426.

Dearing, E., McCartney, K., Weiss, H. B., Kreider, H., & Simpkins, S. (2004). The promotive effects of family educational involvement for low-income children's literacy. *Journal of School Psychology, 42*(6), 445–460.

EDC & SRI. (2017a). *Community Collaboratives for Early Learning & Media: A National Picture of CC-ELM Results, 2016–2017.* New York, NY and Menlo Park, CA: Education Development Center and SRI International.

EDC & SRI. (2017b). *Ready to Learn Research: PBS KIDS ScratchJr Family Creative Learning Workshop Implementation Study.* New York, NY and Menlo Park, CA: Education Development Center and SRI International.

Fisch, S. M., Akerman, A., Morgenlander, M., McCann Brown, S. K., Fisch, S. R., Schwartz, B. B., & Tobin, P. (2008). Coviewing preschool television in the U.S.: Eliciting parent-child interaction via onscreen prompts. *Journal of Children and Media, 2*(2), 163–173.

Kneebone, E. (2017). The changing geography of U.S. poverty: Testimony before the house ways and means committee, subcommittee on human resources. February 15. Available at https://waysandmeans.house.gov/wp-content/uploads/2017/02/20170215HR-Testimony-Kneebone.pdf.

McCarthy, B., Li, L., Tiu, M., Atienza, S., & Sexton, U. (2015). *Learning with PBS KIDS: A Study of Family Engagement and Early Mathematics Achievement.* San Francisco, CA: WestEd.

Niklas, F., Nguyen, C., Cloney, D. S., Tayler, C., & Adams, R. (2016). Self-report measures of the home learning environment in large scale research: Measurement properties and associations with key developmental outcomes. *Learning Environments Research, 19*(2), 181–202.

Pasnik, S., Moorthy, S., Llorente, C., Hupert, N., Domínguez, X., & Silander, M. (2015). *Supporting Parent-Child Experiences with PEG+CAT Early Math Concepts: Report to the*

CPB-PBS Ready to Learn Initiative. New York, NY and Menlo Park, CA: Education Development Center and SRI International.

Sénéchal, M., & LeFevre, J. A. (2002). Parental involvement in the development of children's reading skill: A five-year longitudinal study. *Child Development, 73*(2), 445–460.

Silander, M., Grindal, T., Hupert, N., Garcia, E., Anderson, K., Vahey, P., & Pasnik, S. (2018). *What Parents Talk about When They Talk about Learning: A National Survey about Young Children and Science*. New York, NY and Menlo Park, CA: Education Development Center and SRI International.

Skwarchuk, S. L., Sowinski, C., & LeFevre, J. A. (2014). Formal and informal home learning activities in relation to children's early numeracy and literacy skills: The development of a home numeracy model. *Journal of Experimental Psychology, 121*, 63–84.

Takeuchi, L., & Stevens, R. (2012). *The New Coviewing: Designing for Learning Through Joint Media Engagement*. New York, NY: Joan Ganz Cooney Center at Sesame Workshop.

Weisberg, D. S., Hirsh-Pasek, K., & Golinkoff, R. M. (2013). Guided play: Where curricular goals meet a playful pedagogy. *Mind, Brain, and Education, 7*(2), 104–112.

14

HOW READY TO LEARN IS BRINGING INCLUSIVE DESIGN TO PBS KIDS

Jennifer Rodriguez and Michael Conn-Powers

Introduction

With the support of the U.S. Department of Education's Ready To Learn television Grant Program, and in collaboration with partners at the Corporation for Public Broadcasting (CPB), the Public Broadcasting Service (PBS) has developed educational content over the past decade that has helped close achievement gaps in literacy and math among children ages three to eight (Hurwitz, 2018; Moorthy et al., 2014). Although successful at improving skills among children from low-income communities, past Ready To Learn–funded content has not typically addressed the wider variation in abilities and experiences among the children who watch, play, and learn from PBS KIDS. That changed with the 2015–2020 federal grant solicitation and its specific invitational priority to develop personalized and adaptive learning experiences supportive of all learners. Energized by this opportunity to expand inclusive design practices at PBS KIDS, the project team evolved its understanding, operations, and culture, applying principles of Universal Design for Learning (UDL) to create media that embrace user diversity and reduce barriers.

The co-authors of this chapter are both instructional designers who approach inclusive design with varied background experiences: one from academia with a focus on special education and assessment and the other from the kids' media and educational technology industry. Although very different, we consider ourselves advocates for inclusively designed experiences and have relied upon the principles of UDL to guide the making of Ready To Learn–funded content. In this chapter, we describe the iterative nature of inclusive design and examine: (1) the institutional levers needed to support it; (2) specific lessons learned from educational game and story development; and (3) the role gameplay data and formative testing can play in measuring the impact of UDL features on learning and engagement. Although ambitious, the potential for public media to make contributions to the field of UDL research is significant because of its commitment to high-quality learning and its reach (over 8 million monthly unique visitors to pbskids.org). We close the chapter with a brief discussion of future UDL experiments the project team is contemplating.

Early Notions of Inclusion and Building a Theory of Change

PBS KIDS producers are a talented group of creators who share a common philosophy about child-centered design informed by user testing. A subset of producers have developed content that accommodates special populations (e.g., a game for children with autism about recognizing emotions, Spanish-translated content, keyboard-enabled games for children with low-vision), but their efforts have been more grassroots than system-wide. Before this Ready To Learn grant cycle, the tendency at PBS KIDS was to address audience variation by assigning learners to age/grade ranges, (e.g., two–three years, PreK–K, and K–2nd) or by developing products for specific populations. Retrospectively, both of these approaches reflect early (and limited) thinking about variation; if our team was to be successful in meeting the needs of all learners, we would have to be inclusive of a broader range of experiences, backgrounds, and abilities, and we would have to be more systematic than we had been previously.

In January 2016, PBS and CPB first discussed the grant's focus on personalized and adaptive learning with its project producers and partners. Joining in the conversation were expert designers of inclusive content who introduced the UDL framework created by the Center for Applied Special Technology (CAST, 2018).

The UDL framework takes the position that many learning experiences are developed from the limited perspectives of designers and their notions of a typical learner. As a result, most content is not fully usable or beneficial to the wide range of children that exist, leading to a mismatch between the designed world and an individual's preferences and strengths (Inclusive Design Research Centre, 2018). The UDL framework considers the means by which *all* or at least most learners might best acquire information and demonstrate competence. It relies on three guiding principles for creating flexible, accessible, and engaging content:

1)   Provide multiple means of representation (the "what" of learning).
2)   Provide multiple means of engagement (the "why" of learning).
3)   Provide multiple means of action and expression (the "how" of learning).

Figure 14.1 conveys PBS KIDS vision for how UDL can help reach all or most learners. The image is based on a popular meme used by equity practitioners and the Interaction Institute for Social Change (IISC, 2016).

As a consequence of the framework discussions and the decision to embrace UDL principles, the project team established a theory of change to guide the development of media products for the 2015–2020 Ready To Learn Television Grant Program:

> If PBS KIDS producers apply the principles of UDL to the development of educational content, then the content will provide learning experiences that engage and positively impact more children.

Operationalizing Universal Design for Learning

Because the theory of change requires the successful application of UDL principles by PBS KIDS producers, the project team worked together to develop documents and supports to scaffold producer efforts. Our goal was to operationalize inclusive design and UDL principles for the producer community. As a result, over the past two years, the project team employed continuous quality-improvement strategies: written UDL guidelines; consultative support by UDL experts; simplified UDL guidelines and inclusive design concepts; and the inclusion of children with disabilities in content testing and evaluation.

A First Step: Written Guidelines

The Ready To Learn project team began by developing and sharing written UDL guidelines that adopted the taxonomy of CAST's three organizing principles, embedding them into the PBS KIDS Science Learning Framework

FIGURE 14.1 PBS KIDS UDL meme

(Courtesy of PBS based on designs created by the Interaction Institute for Social Change as interpreted by artist, Julie Maski)

(see Chapter 9 for a description of the framework). The guidelines provided examples for television and digital producers in relatable and concise terms and were shared at an inaugural meeting of the Ready To Learn Television Grant Program. The project team encouraged producers to integrate them into their design work.

Retrospectively, while the PBS KIDS UDL guidelines were intended to raise awareness about inclusive design and UDL in the producer community, their placement near the end of a dense curriculum document limited discovery. For producers who engaged with the guidelines, some found them practical, but their presentation in a text-heavy table with little context left some uninspired or uncertain how to go about applying them.

Advisors to Make Practical Sense of the Guidelines

As important as the written guidelines were, many new and seasoned developers needed support in applying them. The project team matched each Ready To Learn–funded production with a UDL expert to provide just-in-time feedback and suggestions throughout the design and development process. This integration of personalized support worked out well in digital production with members of the CAST team engaged in brainstorming and reviews of game documents and builds.

The same support strategy, however, proved more challenging in broadcast production due to the fast-paced, 48-hour review turnarounds required for scripts and storyboards. Also, advisors struggled to limit their suggestions to a number that producers could implement. While UDL advisors have adapted to the pace and context of media design and development (e.g., suggesting minor script changes or changes to the order of concepts presented), it is still challenging to prioritize inclusive design efforts alongside other production realities (e.g., broadcast premiere and launch dates as well as budgets that drive the allocation of available time and resources).

Simplifying the UDL Guidelines, Adding Practical Checkpoints

After two years of sharing written materials and assigning UDL advisors to production teams, it became clear that the PBS KIDS UDL framework was not a turnkey approach. To expand and sustain inclusive design efforts, the project team needed to provide guidelines that were simple enough to be taken up with or without the support of an embedded UDL advisor. At the time of writing, the co-authors of this chapter are working on a concise set of checkpoints written as questions that can activate inclusive design mindsets and practices among producers. The questions below can be adapted for any media format but are framed to be most useful for digital producers. The current (until further testing) questions include:

- What are the intended learning goals of the activity?

  ○ How much variation in the difficulty of those goals does the activity support?

- How will this activity interest, motivate, and challenge children?

  ○ Is the activity fun, familiar, and authentic for a wide range of children?
  ○ How (if at all) does the activity provide supports for self-reflection, struggle, or optimizing challenge?
  ○ What options does the activity provide for different aspects of executive function (goal-setting, progress monitoring, time management, and planning)?

- How will this activity ensure that children receive and understand the information they need?

  ○ Does the activity provide information in multiple ways (words, pictures, cues), clarify vocabulary, and highlight critical features for children?

- How will the child interact with the activity and demonstrate what they know?

  ○ Does the activity support children's fine motor interactions?
  ○ Does the activity provide options, so everyone can create/learn/share?
  ○ Does the activity support fluency and generalization?

- Whom are you including and excluding with this decision? (Design decisions about excluding children should be made consciously.)

The new UDL Checkpoints have only been used for one PBS KIDS series, and they will not likely remain the same. One change under consideration is to turn these questions into a formal rubric for producers to use (e.g., checkboxes to rate how and how well each of the UDL criteria is met).

UDL in Action

The PBS KIDS UDL guidelines and expert support contributed to the design and continuous improvement of one major product: WGBH Educational Foundation's *The Ruff Ruffman Show's* digital game, "Fish Force." Below is a description of what our project team learned in the development of that game as well as two other products, Random House's *The Cat in the Hat Builds That* game app and Wind Dancer Entertainment's *Ready Jet Go!* television series.

Case #1: UDL and **Ruff Ruffman's** *"Fish Force"* Game

WGBH was the first PBS KIDS producer to develop grant-funded educational games and stories with the PBS KIDS UDL guidelines and embedded UDL advisor support. One of their games, "Fish Force," is a leveled physics simulation designed for children ages four to eight that enables learners to experiment with altering force magnitude and the direction of force to achieve the goal of sliding an object across an icy surface to a target. Chapter 15 offers a detailed case study of this particular game, and this narrative mostly focuses on two specific inclusively designed features: the user interface that represents force magnitude or the "force slider" as it is referred to below, and the addition of an on-demand hint feature. We encourage readers to consider these questions from the UDL Checkpoints as a method of interrogating the example that follows:

How does the activity provide supports for self-reflection, struggle, or optimizing challenge?
How do we ensure that children receive and understand the information they need?
Does the activity provide information in multiple ways (words, pictures, cues), clarify
  vocabulary, and highlight critical features for children?

Focus on Force Slider, Version 1

The force slider is the control panel of the game containing most of the mechanics and buttons that enable learners to interact with the simulation. The slider conveys critical information about the amount of force being applied in the simulation and enables players the ability to finely calibrate it. The journey the game designers took to get to the current implementation involved many hours of playtesting with earlier versions that are not represented in this narrative. Some of these include vertically oriented sliders and user interfaces that incorporated buttons instead of a slider. The design of the force slider involved an iterative process spanning almost eight months that had the production team at WGBH and our content experts grappling with issues of perception. The changes made at the outset were modest efforts toward inclusive design; further into the process, the game producers made significant breakthroughs as a result of playtesting, UDL advisor guidance, and the production team's creativity.

Although there were many iterations of the force slider before the version represented in Figure 14.2, for the sake of expediency, Version 1 represents an early approach that included a number of buttons for projectile selection (e.g., fish, snowball, and rope), a force magnitude adjustment meter, an activation button labeled "go," and a "replay" button enabling players to watch instant replay footage of their last shot and reflect on the results.

Playtesting of Version 1 that PBS KIDS Digital did with a diverse group of children from elementary schools in Boston and Washington, DC, yielded these

FIGURE 14.2   Image of the first version of the force slider from the "Fish Force" game (Courtesy of PBS and WGBH Educational Foundation TM/© 2017)

findings: Children understood and used the orange "go" button, however, several children were confused by the number of buttons available. Only a third of participants noticed the "replay" button, and even they were not inclined to use it more than once or with a clear purpose. Another version was needed to address these problems and better highlight critical features.

Force Slider, Version 2

Based on playtesting results, the production team identified the need for three changes in Version 2 (see Figure 14.3). First, the projectile selector was simplified to include only one option: the frozen fish. Second, the slider labels were changed to clarify key vocabulary associated with the science concepts (e.g., use of the word "force" on the meter and "push" instead of "go" on the orange button). In addition, a slight color gradation on the meter was added to highlight critical information (i.e., change in greater or lesser magnitude). Finally, a camera tool was substituted for the "replay" button to provide an iconic approach to better support non-readers.

The production team initiated another round of playtesting with Version 2. Results from this testing indicated that learners began to use key language more than in previous testing, such as: "I need more/less *force*" (PBS KIDS Digital, 2017). The team also learned that children infrequently engaged with the replay button and were reluctant to interrupt play to watch videos of their performance. Based on this cycle of playtesting, the producers decided to simplify the

FIGURE 14.3   Image of the second version of the force slider from the "Fish Force" game (Courtesy of PBS and WGBH Educational Foundation TM/© 2017)

design by omitting the replay button and providing on-demand support for learners needing additional assistance.

Force Slider, Version 3

Retrospectively, the quality-improvement cycle that yielded Version 3 signaled a leap forward in inclusive design. In building the game, the lead developer had assigned numerical values to sections of the force meter as part of the level design process and recognized an opportunity to reveal that information to players. The ability to communicate force as a more exact number would be helpful for fine-tuning adjustments. At the same time, the production team's UDL advisor from CAST suggested adding sound to make the game more engaging and accessible, to better highlight the amount of force selected by the child, and to provide additional cues concerning the type of material being struck. As a result, the designers added a subtle sound effect to the force meter that changed frequency as the player moved up and down the slider. See Figure 14.4 depicting Version 3 of the slider.

A second modification integrated into Version 3 involved removing the little-used camera button and replacing it with an instant visual hint that exposed a guideline showing the likely path of the projectile and the path of the stationary object once it collided with the projectile (see Figure 14.5).

Playtesting of Version 3 revealed new developments in the fluency learners expressed as they set up, ran, and reflected on the physics simulation. The numerical values on the force meter gave some children a new way to express their thinking: "That went too fast! I had it at 54!" or "I'm going to aim it this way and go to 65" (PBS KIDS, 2017). The on-demand visual hint helped some learners calibrate their settings without giving the answer away. To ensure players were not over-relying on the hint guide, game designers decided to make it disappear once the player was in active play. A "hint" button was later added to the far left of force slider.

The project team launched Version 3 to the public in September 2017 and is actively analyzing gameplay data to inform future iteration cycles. One thing it is paying close attention to is the discoverability and use of the on-demand hint feature.

FIGURE 14.4 Image of the third version of the force slider from the "Fish Force" game (Courtesy of PBS and WGBH Educational Foundation TM/© 2017)

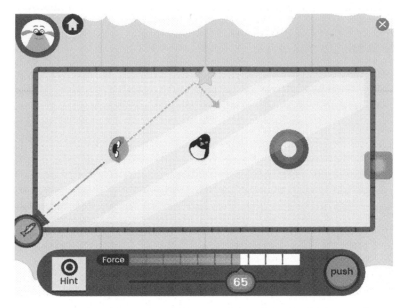

FIGURE 14.5 Image of the on-demand hint guideline from the "Fish Force" game (Courtesy of PBS and WGBH Educational Foundation TM/© 2017)

These three force slider options—in reality, the team developed and tested more than 20 versions—illustrate how intentional the project team was in providing options for perception. Despite our efforts, the "final" slider did not as fully support options for physical action beyond the tappable (touchscreen) or clickable (mouse and keyboard) user interface. At the time of this writing, the project team is experimenting with a tappable version of the force slider mechanic and launcher to enable children with less fine motor control to play the game more easily. Although previous study cycles did not include children with motor challenges, future playtesting will.

Case #2: UDL and the Cat in the Hat Builds That *Game, "Slidea-Ma-Zoo"*

Another game-based learning experience supported by the Ready To Learn Television Grant Program is Random House's *The Cat in the Hat Builds That* multi-game preschool app available in English and Spanish. In the app, children are presented with multiple opportunities to learn and practice new skills in Seussian worlds (see Chapter 9 for examples) and in the authentic backyard environment that is home to characters Nic and Sally.

Similar to iteration efforts described above in the "Fish Force" game, the game, "Slidea-ma-zoo," in *The Cat in the Hat Builds That* app, prompted improvement cycles that focused on a number of features. We highlight two inclusive design features; the first one focuses on multiple ways to represent information, and the second supports multiple ways a learner can engage with the content.

As before, we encourage readers to consider these questions from the UDL Checkpoints as a method of interrogating the descriptions that follow:

How do we ensure that children receive and understand the information they need? Does the activity provide information in multiple ways (words, pictures, cues), clarify vocabulary, and highlight critical features for children?

How will the child interact with the activity and demonstrate what they know? Does the activity provide options, so everyone can create, learn, and share? Does the activity support fluency and generalization?

In the game "Slidea-ma-zoo," children are asked to raise or lower the height of a slide so that Nic and Sally can go faster (or slower or the same) as Thing 1 and Thing 2. Earlier designs representing the heights of two slides in "Slidea-ma-zoo" relied too heavily on the learner's ability to visually size up the slides, and playtesters (including a child with low-vision) struggled to figure out which one was taller or shorter (see Figure 14.6). As a result of this study cycle, formative

FIGURE 14.6 Image from an early build of the "Slidea-ma-zoo" game

(Derived and adapted from the Series *The Cat in the Hat Knows a Lot About That!*) Courtesy of © Penguin Random House and Dr. Seuss Enterprises, LP. 2018. Used with Permission.; Dr. Seuss Books and Characters TM & © 1957–1958 Dr. Seuss Enterprises, L.P. All Rights Reserved.; and PBS)

researchers from Rockman et al recommended adding blocks to represent the number of rungs needed to climb up to the top), and later added numbered units to each rung. By giving learners multiple ways to understand the slide's height and by removing distracting information (e.g., canopies) the result was a more usable experience for all players (see Figure 14.7; Rockman et al., 2018).

The second example of inclusive design in "Slidea-ma-zoo" addresses how children can experience both guided and open-ended play around the same concepts. In the game, children are gradually introduced to key science concepts that support their investigations of the impact of height and texture on the speed Nic and Sally travel down the slide (as compared with Things 1 and 2). After completing approximately eight rounds of play in any game, children are redirected to the backyard to "unlock" a free play simulation (i.e., enabling kids to build and explore freely and in a manner guided by their own goals). This feature provides all learners the opportunity to practice and apply newly learned skills in a new context. It also provides children with a fun and familiar context to motivate their continued engagement.

FIGURE 14.7   Image from the final build of the "Slidea-ma-zoo" game

(Derived and adapted from the Series *The Cat in the Hat Knows a Lot About That!*) Courtesy of © Penguin Random House and Dr. Seuss Enterprises, LP. 2018. Used with Permission.; Dr. Seuss Books and Characters TM & © 1957–1958 Dr. Seuss Enterprises, L.P. All Rights Reserved.; and PBS)

Case #3: UDL and the **Ready Jet Go!** *Broadcast Series Interstitials*

The CPB-PBS supported series *Ready Jet Go!* is the subject of this third and final case. Each episode in the series comprises animated stories and 90-second live-action segments. The latter are the focus of this section. Bear in mind that opportunities to iterate within broadcast formats are more costly and limited and, therefore, rarer than with digital content. We encourage the reader to consider this question from the UDL Checkpoints as a way to critically examine this unique example:

How will we interest, motivate, and challenge children? Is the activity fun, familiar, and authentic for a wide range of children?

The first season of the *Ready Jet Go!* series produced by Wind Dancer Entertainment was developed before the 2015–2020 Ready To Learn grant was awarded to the CPB-PBS Ready To Learn Initiative. As a result, the Season One work did not benefit from the cultural and structural shifts described earlier in the chapter that helped producers gain awareness about and apply UDL principles. In Season Two, inclusive design principles were seeded throughout the series, and their influence was very powerful in refining the 90-second live-action segments featuring Amy Mainzer as the adult scientist host ("Astronomer Amy Mainzer") talking about astronomy, space, and scientific phenomena. These segments, referred to as "interstitials" by industry insiders, had the feel of unscripted mini-documentaries (see Figure 14.8). In formative testing done by Rockman et al., researchers noted that the Season One interstitials confused some children and parents who

FIGURE 14.8 Image from *Ready Jet Go!* Season two interstitial (Photo courtesy of PBS and Jet Propulsion, LLC)

perceived them to be unrelated to the previous animated stories and described them as similar to advertisements in their form, although they were non-commercial. The researchers also noted that younger viewers thought the interstitials must be for parents or older kids. They observed several instances where kids disengaged with the show during these segments (e.g., looking around the room or talking with parents or members of the evaluation team). Children seemed to be more interested in these segments when Amy was showing or doing something interesting, rather than talking to other adults (Rockman et al., 2016).

Focusing on the UDL principle of providing multiple, fun, and authentic ways to motivate learners, the production team worked to make the content more child-centered and to bring appealing and familiar visual aspects of the animated stories into the live-action formats. For example, they scripted inter-actions to ensure concepts and vocabulary included curriculum relatable to even the youngest viewers in the target audience. They also placed the live-action host in the animated environment of the series using green-screen technology. Finally, they provided additional information and cues through overt messaging with intro and outro features that would explicitly prepare kids for the transitions. These transitions featured the principle animated character, Jet, introducing the live-action host: "And now, here's my friend, Astronomer Amy Mainzer!"

Once this production work was complete, another round of formative testing was done on the improved interstitials, and it yielded these findings: children kept watching and, when prompted, many recalled the live-action host, Amy Mainzer. Their recall of specific content was better after inter-stitials that had relatable aspects, such as a project-based segment where Amy made ice cubes from different substances and another segment where she referred to Jupiter's moon, Io, as the "pizza planet." Some participants learned that "not everything freezes like water, [for example] chocolate syrup or ketchup" (Rockman et al., 2018). These findings validated the production team's effort to make more inclusive educational content.

Measuring the Implementation and Impact of UDL Efforts

Within Ready To Learn, the project team is attempting to measure the implementation and impact of UDL on children's engagement and learning through frequent playtesting with children of diverse abilities and back-grounds. We have been successful in recruiting children from low-income communities but have struggled to include children with a range of learning abilities (aside from dual language learners). As a result, we are establishing new relationships with local entities (e.g., public school special education programs) to recruit diverse playtesting groups. Consequently, we have learned that problems encountered in playtesting and gameplay data generally reside in the design of products and not the makeup of the child. This awareness has impacted research design, more broadly, and we have been more sensitive to include, rather than exclude, children previously perceived as statistical outliers.

In addition to field research, we also have focused on the possible role of gameplay data in providing some basis of empirical evidence validating UDL's benefits. Drawing on Min Wook Ok et al.'s work, we have considered these particular issues:

1. "Although UDL has an intuitive appeal and a conceptually sound basis as a framework that supports inclusive education, the promise of UDL as an instructional equalizer will remain unfulfilled until a base of empirical evidence validates UDL's benefits for diverse students and identifies specific practices that have a positive impact on student outcomes."
2. "Although the UDL guidelines provide a menu of options for designing instruction that addresses learner variability, researchers have not validated how UDL principles can be 'mixed and matched' and which guidelines and myriad checkpoints should be applied to design effective instruction for all" (2016).

From a practical standpoint, since the launch of "Fish Force" in September 2017, PBS KIDS began collecting anonymous gameplay data-capturing engagement (e.g., average session times and return traffic). We are presently analyzing the data in ways that could help answer the first call for empirical evidence of UDL practices and their impact on learning with large sample sizes powered by the 8 million unique visitors a month to pbskids.org. We are exploring two questions with "Fish Force" gameplay data: (1) How might on-demand hints correlate with engagement and learning? (2) Does the availability of different ways to engage with content, through playing a leveled game or creating an open-ended sandbox, influence engagement and learning? Chapter 16 provides specific examples and describes a variety of analytical approaches being taken by project researchers.

Future Frontiers in Universal Design for Learning

Embracing the tenets of inclusive design and the guidelines offered by UDL has been a challenging journey for the PBS KIDS project team and its partners. Committing to active and strategic experimentation with UDL principles has required institutional-level changes in expanding conceptions about learner variation based solely on chronological age to more purposefully including children from diverse backgrounds who represent a range of abilities and individual learning needs. The seeds of awareness are germinating, and some of the fruits of these efforts are emerging (e.g., 30+ minutes of focused, purposeful play in "Fish Force" or the improved retention of concepts and information from the revised *Ready Jet Go!* interstitials), but there is more yet to do to test the project team's theory of change; namely, "If PBS KIDS producers applied the principles of UDL to the development of content, this process could result in educational experiences that could lead to more engaged learners and, consequently, more impactful outcomes for more children" (Rockman et al., 2016, 2017).

As we await summative and empirical results from these initial efforts, the team will continue to deepen its commitment to inclusive design practices and consider new tools and trends, including but not limited to these initiatives: (1) expanding the availability of closed captions to games (not just videos) available in the PBS KIDS Games app; (2) building smarter translation and localization supports in the PBS KIDS publishing platforms to increase the availability of multi-language content; (3) providing more accommodations in the way content is presented (i.e., font size and color customization and keyboard input alternatives); and (4) experimenting with innovative tools such as voice skills technologies similar to those available on smart speakers. At the time of writing, the PBS KIDS products team is conducting a literature review and competitive scan to better understand its affordances and limitations, bearing in mind the need to keep PBS KIDS a safe and trusted environment for all children.

References

Center for Applied Special Technology (CAST) (2018). Universal Design for Learning Guidelines Version 2.2. Wakefield, MA: CAST. Retrieved from http://udlguidelines.cast.org.

Hurwitz, L. B. (2018, February 19). Getting a Read on Ready to Learn Media: A Meta-analytic Review of Effects on Literacy. *Child Development*, doi: 10.1111/cdev.13043.

Inclusive Design Research Centre. (2018). What is Inclusive Design? Toronto, Canada: IDRC. Retrieved from https://idrc.ocadu.ca/about-the-idrc/49-resources/online-resources/articles-and-papers/443-whatisinclusivedesign.

Interaction Institute for Social Change. (2016). "Equality vs. Equity" Meme. Boston, MA: IISC. Retrieved from http://interactioninstitute.org/illustrating-equality-vs-equity/.

Moorthy, S., Hupert, N., Llorente, C., & Pasnik, S. (2014). *PEG+CAT Content Study: Report to the CPB-PBS Ready To Learn Initiative.* New York and Menlo Park, CA: Education Development Center and SRI International.

Ok, M. W., Kavita, R., Bryant, B. R., & McDougall, D. (2016). Universal Design for Learning in Pre-K to Grade 12 Classrooms: A Systematic Review of Research. *Exceptionality*, 25(2), 116–138.

PBS KIDS Digital Play Testing Team. (2017, May). *Hoffman Boston School Play Testing Topline Findings.* Crystal City, VA: Rockman et al., Inc.

Rockman et al., Inc. (2016, April). *Ready, Jet, Go!* A Report on Findings from Family Feedback Sessions. San Francisco, CA: Rockman et al., Inc.

Rockman et al., Inc. (2017, July). "Fish Force." Evaluation Report. San Francisco, CA: Rockman et al., Inc.

Rockman et al., Inc. (2018, January). *Cat in the Hat.* Playtesting Report. San Francisco, CA: Rockman et al., Inc.

15

ADAPTIVE AND PERSONALIZED EDUCATIONAL GAMES FOR YOUNG CHILDREN

A Case Study

Jennifer Rodriguez, Dylan Arena, and Jeremy D. Roberts

Introduction

Since 1997, the Public Broadcasting Service (PBS) has developed digital content that builds on and enhances the educational goals of its children's television series. Its digital presence has evolved from a desktop-only website to the desktop- and mobile-friendly pbskids.org and over 45 PBS KIDS apps. Although the PBS KIDS games inventory includes bleeding-edge experiments with augmented reality and gestural games, its recipe for game design has largely centered on the following formal features: character hosts, customization opportunities, leveled and sandbox play, in-game incentives (e.g., stickers and badges), and simple hard-coded or randomized leveling schemas. More importantly, games were mostly designed to meet the needs of average, "typically developing" children.

In 2015, with support from the U.S. Department of Education's Ready To Learn Television Grant Program, PBS joined its partners at the Corporation for Public Broadcasting (CPB) to initiate an ambitious effort to make personalized and adaptive educational content that would go beyond the idea of an "average" learner by supporting individual variation to better serve all children. In September 2017, the project team launched its first personalized and adaptive game, "Fish Force," and leveraged Universal Design for Learning (UDL) and Bayesian Item Response Theory to keep learners of varied abilities and backgrounds in an optimal state of engagement—in the Zone of Proximal Development (ZPD) (Vygotsky, 1978) or in a "flow" state (Csikszentmihalyi, 1990).

This case study reflects on lessons learned from formative research and gameplay data and describes successes, challenges, and opportunities. The co-authors, who come from diverse backgrounds in instructional design, game design, educational psychology, and software development, argue for the promise of the aforementioned adaptive approaches, citing findings from early research on "Fish Force" and other games developed under the grant. The chapter closes by acknowledging the need for empirical research that can further inform personalized and adaptive learning game design, preparing the reader for a deeper discussion of measurement and evaluation in the closing chapter of this book.

Making Personalized and Adaptive Learning Games at PBS KIDS

Prior to "Fish Force," PBS KIDS had defined personalization as a form of creative customization wherein an individual might "personalize" something like an avatar to satisfy a need or want. During the game's production, the project team worked with UDL advisors from the Center for Applied Special Technology (CAST) to expand its definition of "personalization" to include pedagogical approaches that focused on learner-led options for challenge and support. This shift from considering personalization as a purely affect-driven engagement mechanism to considering it as an affective, recognitive, and strategic approach evolved from literature reviews that included CAST's *Theory and Practice* and Todd Rose's *The End of Average*, whose evidence-based arguments urge designers to design for individuals rather than a mythical mean (Meyer, Rose, & Gordon, 2014; Rose, 2016). With this new perspective, the team redefined "personalized" as *learner-led* approaches with options for challenges and supports that individuals can activate, and "adaptive" as *system-led* responses to individual learner inputs, usually in the form of an intelligent tutor that can guide each child to the best next level. As the project team developed "Fish Force," it tested and further refined these definitions. Through this exercise, the project team discovered the complementary nature of these approaches and how both could be applied to keep learners in their ZPD. The ZPD is defined by Lev Vygotsky as "the distance between the actual developmental level as determined by independent problem-solving and the level of potential development as determined through problem-solving under adult guidance, or in collaboration with more capable peers" (Vygotsky, 1978). In this case, the "adult guidance" is instantiated in the game's artificial intelligence.

Adapting Content with Bayesian Item Response Theory

Since 1997, PBS KIDS has developed hundreds of digital games with a mix of level design approaches including random, fixed sequence, and "smart" levels, which get harder as the player shows increased ability (by having 0–1 errors per round). Once a player achieves the highest level, those questions cycle indefinitely. This paradigm has limitations. First, it orients the design of game levels toward players of average ability rather than offering a broader range of levels that anticipate less and more skilled learners. Second, once this "smart" leveling algorithm is set and launched to the public, it never changes. Third, no data (anonymous or associated with a user account) is collected on individual or aggregate learner abilities or on how well the smart algorithm meets individual learner abilities. And, finally, no empirical evidence is gathered about the accuracy of the original difficulty ratings for game levels as set by the game designer. The constraints of this approach to adaptive leveling motivated the project team to engage adaptive learning experts who could support a greater range than "average" ability. In this chapter, we focus on Kidaptive's proprietary Adaptive Learning Platform, which uses Bayesian Item Response Theory to equip game designers with the observations (i.e., measurements) and interventions (i.e., adaptive responses) needed to support learner variation. In so doing, it enabled us to deliver individualized support for each player, something no PBS KIDS game had done before.

The Case of "Fish Force"

"Fish Force" was produced by the WGBH Educational Foundation simulta-neously with related videos and activities from the series, *The Ruff Ruffman Show*, designed for children ages four to eight. "Fish Force" is a physics simulation wherein players shoot frozen fish from a cannon with varying levels of force to recover a toy from an ice rink while avoiding obstacles. Its purpose is to teach concepts of force and motion: how pushes can have different strengths and cause objects to move in various directions, and how objects can push one another when they touch or collide. The game is available at pbskids.org/ruff/sports/game or in the PBS KIDS games app. Additionally, the game supports children in practicing inquiry skills such as making and testing predictions, planning and conducting simple investigations, and engaging in cause-and-effect observations. Key game features include:

- A skippable character-led introduction.
- A core game loop: cycles of adjusting force magnitude and direction to achieve the goal of launching a projectile at a stationary object to move the object to a target location (see Figure 15.1).
- A core "create-a-level" loop: Players can create their own levels by dragging game objects onto a blank ice rink. They can play, edit, and save levels for others to play.
- Levels 1–10 (tutorial) are designed to teach game skills and foundational science concepts (see Figure 15.2). These levels introduce basic skills like tapping "push" to launch the projectile (Level 1) and more complex skills like moving the launcher to set up shots and avoid obstacles (Level 4).

Core Game Loop

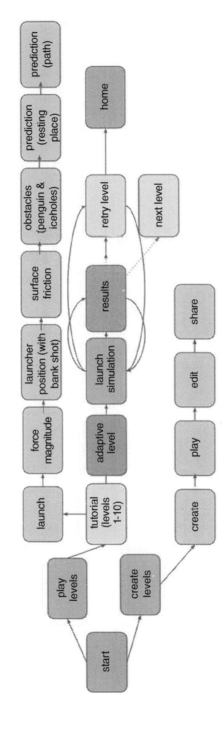

FIGURE 15.1 "Fish Force" game core loop diagram
(Courtesy of PBS)

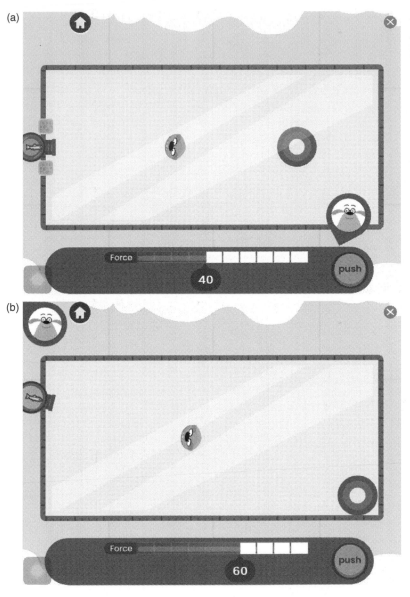

FIGURE 15.2 Images of the "Fish Force" game's tutorial levels (a) Level 2 – force slider intro (b) Level 3 – launcher position intro (c) Level 6 – obstacle intro: ice hole (d) Level 7 – obstacle intro: moving penguin

(Courtesy of PBS and WGBH Educational Foundation TM/© 2017)

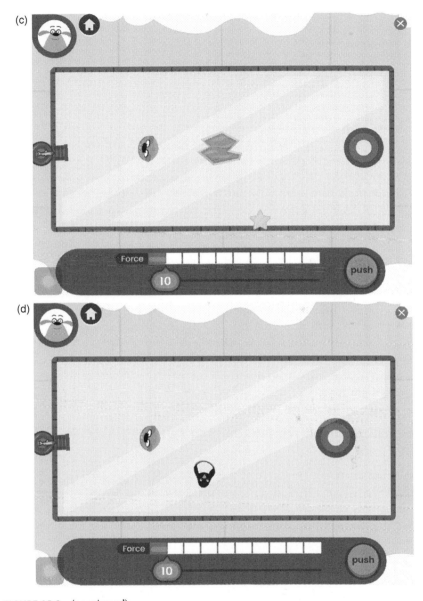

FIGURE 15.2 (continued).

These levels also engage players in using inquiry practices like making predictions. Below are snapshots of key game skills introduced in a step-by-step progression.

- Levels 11 and beyond are all adaptive, which means that different learners may see different challenges as their 11th, 12th, 13th, etc. level. (See below for further elaboration on this point.)

- In addition to the ten tutorial levels, the game's 256 gameplay levels include 128 performance levels (in which the goal is to push the toy to the destination) and 128 prediction levels (of which there are two types: predict the toy's path, or predict where the toy will end up).

- The Kidaptive platform continuously estimates each player's ability as he/she plays. It also empirically ranks levels by difficulty using gameplay data from PBS KIDS' audience (8 million unique visitors per month according to an internal Google Analytics report). With knowledge of the learner's ability and the difficulty level for each of the available 256 challenges in the "Fish Force" game, the game can choose a next level that keeps learners in flow, potentially leading to improved engagement and learning outcomes.

- As for the number of levels generated, the goal is to ensure that learners at all levels of proficiency receive an adequate supply of distinct challenges. That means something different in each supported context and in fact, the team does not yet know whether 256 is too many, not enough, or just the right number of levels/challenges in "Fish Force." The team's theory is that having an abundance of levels/challenges from the start is a strength for the game.

Personalized and Adaptive Learning Design Features in "Fish Force"

In this chapter we put the UDL Checkpoints that Rodriguez and Conn-Powers introduce in Chapter 14 into practical use, providing a holistic view of "Fish Force" and its personalized and adaptive features. Our responses to the checkpoint questions serve as a self-assessment; they indicate the accomplishments of "Fish Force" as well as areas of further opportunity.

UDL Checkpoints Question: What are the intended learning goals of the activity? How much variation in the difficulty of those goals does the activity support?

The 256 levels are meant to ensure that learners at all levels of proficiency receive an adequate supply of distinct challenges; each player's experience is unique and informed by his or her dynamic abilities. Ability estimates are initially based on the learner's tutorial performance and then adjust with each new level attempted. The adaptive algorithm uses the player's ability estimate to determine which level to present next. Below is a snapshot and description of the adaptive experiences of two young learners of different abilities, a child of age four ("Sam") and another age eight ("Sophia"). To better understand how adaptive leveling works, it is best to play "Fish Force" to the 20th level or beyond.

Sam and Sophia play levels 1–10 (the tutorial sequence) and encounter the very same challenges but perform differently. Sam, a less experienced gamer, plays through the tutorial and struggles with positioning the launcher to align with the target and with setting up a bank shot. As he attempts prediction levels in the tutorial, he is uncertain about what a "prediction" is (even though the voiceover defines it). He takes a full minute longer to get through the tutorial than Sophia, a more experienced gamer. Below is an adaptive level that is served up to each player: the images represent a thin slice of the game, but they illustrate how each "next" level is different and informed by the player's abilities.

Sam's level 12 is a prediction level that involves a fixed launcher position, one stationary penguin, and a star on the rink indicating the trajectory of the plush toy. Sophia's is also a prediction level with a fixed launcher position and a stationary penguin, but the demands are greater due to the additional presence of a moving penguin that might deflect the plushie from its path. Her level does not include a star on the rink or any other form of help.

Learner ability guides level selection as seen in Figure 15.3. Figure 15.4 presents a conceptual design for a reporting feature that shows how learner abilities are dynamically tracked. Ability estimates are distributed normally and centered at the mean for the target population; the estimate for this learner starts at the mean and descends as the system observes his or her performance.

UDL Checkpoints Question: How will we interest, motivate, and challenge children? Is the activity fun, familiar, and authentic for a wide range of children?

PBS KIDS worked with its research partners and the firm Rockman et al to test a beta build of the game with children ages four to eight (most of whom were in the series "sweet spot" of age six). Rockman et al conducted formative research to test the appeal, usability, and learning potential of "Fish Force." Its findings suggest even broader potential appeal beyond the core target age group (four to eight). According to Rockman et al's formative research, "A few siblings tried the game, and we found that three-year-olds were still able to get the basics (and could be successful with some help from a caregiver), and a ten-year-old also found the game to be engaging too!"

UDL Checkpoints Question: How (if at all) does the activity provide supports for self-reflection, struggle, or optimizing challenge?

"Fish Force" primarily prompts self-reflection in contextual and graduated voiceover feedback. Learners can tap the character host to hear these prompts repeated:

- "What does this patch of sand do [to the toy's trajectory]?" (prediction prompt)
- "I wonder if more force would do it." (investigation prompt)

FIGURE 15.3 Images from the "Fish Force" game showing a comparison of adaptive level 12 for two players of different ability. (a) Level 12 – Sam, age 4 (b) Level 12 – Sophia, age 8

(Courtesy of PBS and WGBH Educational Foundation TM/© 2017)

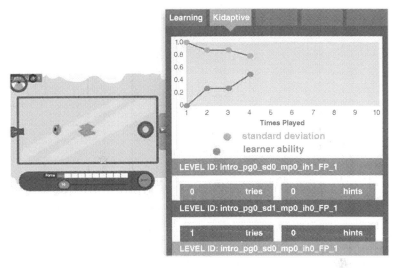

FIGURE 15.4 Image of "Fish Force" and corresponding conceptual design for learner ability estimate interface

(Courtesy of PBS and WGBH Educational Foundation TM/© 2017)

- "You used just the right amount of force to push the plushie to the target." (observation prompt)
- "Was that the right amount of force?" (reflection prompt)

One limitation of this approach is that it is audio-driven and, although captions are available, there are no visual cues to prompt self-reflection.

The availability of an on-demand hint feature (described in detail in Chapter 14) provides a temporary marker that shows the path of the projectile and the plushie it collides with. This hint offers another way to support learners when they struggle.

The game also gives learners the opportunity to "retry" or move on to the "next" level as a way to optimize challenge. This gives learners the ability to self-reflect and retry or seek more challenge.

UDL Checkpoints Question: How do we ensure that children receive and understand the information they need? Does the activity provide information in multiple ways (words, pictures, cues), clarify vocabulary, and highlight critical features for children?

The force slider mechanic as pictured in Figure 15.5 provides learners with multiple ways to understand the key concept of force magnitude: (1) visual: a color gradient that brightens with increasing magnitude; (2) quantitative: a number value assigned to the force slider dial to support learners' emerging sense of number to more finely tune and calibrate the force "units"; (3) audial:

FIGURE 15.5 Image of "Fish Force" game slider mechanic
(Courtesy of PBS and WGBH Educational Foundation TM/© 2017)

a sound effect upon dragging the force slider that increases in pitch with increasing magnitude. This multiple-representation feature fits well into the category of learner-led "personalization" because it allows learners to choose their preferred representation (or to combine several).

UDL Checkpoints Question: What options does the activity provide for different aspects of executive function (goal-setting, progress monitoring, time management, and planning)?

The absence of a clear progress indicator proved frustrating to most children. From the Rockman et al formative research, the project team learned:

> Some responses regarding re-playability and some specific suggestions for potential improvements centered on a clearer progression of levels. One of the kids actually suggested this. Some thought there weren't many levels, whereas others realized that the levels were just going on indefinitely. Players want to feel that they have completed something or that they are making progress.

Although this finding has not been applied to "Fish Force," the project team has applied it to other Ready To Learn games using progress monitoring meters, including "Bridge-a-rama," appearing in Figure 15.7.

UDL Checkpoints Question: Does the activity support children's fine motor interactions?

"Fish Force" is available on desktop and touch-enabled devices, and most interactions involve dragging a fingertip or mouse cursor across the screen—both were conventional interactions for most of the children who playtested the game. However, none of the testers who played the game had fine motor issues, and the project team overlooked the challenge that drag-enabled user interfaces present to children with, for example, cerebral palsy. The project team is revisiting the "Fish Force" user interface design to support tap-enabled play.

UDL Checkpoints Question: Does the activity provide options, so everyone can create, learn, and share?

Learners have the option to play the leveled experience or to create a level. The create mode supports sharing and social learning opportunities by enabling children to save and edit their levels for another individual to play. In playtesting done by PBS KIDS Digital, one 2nd-grade tester tried to create a level that would be "easy enough for my four-year-old sister to play."

The game also gives learners two ways to make predictions about the simulation: (1) predicting the resting place of the toy after the projectile collides with it, and (2) predicting the path the toy will take after the projectile collides with it (see Figure 15.6). In testing, some learners appreciated the novelty of looking at prediction-making in more than one way, while others (especially those struggling with basic game skills) found the prediction tasks disruptive.

UDL Checkpoints Question: Does the activity support fluency and generalization?

Learners who participated in PBS KIDS Digital playtesting commented throughout gameplay using the language of inquiry modeled in the game: for example, "I *wonder* what happens if I push it all the way to 100!" And some actively connected gameplay with their lived experiences building on intuitions about force and motion, such as one learner who thought she could overcome the ice hole obstacle by ramping up the force slider to 100. Her hypothesis was based on a real-life experience where she got a ball to move out of a hole by putting enough speed on it to overcome a shallow dip. In these ways, learners communicated how they were intentionally thinking about what they were doing in the game and how it related to real life.

UDL Checkpoints Question: Whom are you including and excluding with this decision? (Design decisions about excluding children should be made consciously.)

Although "Fish Force" is not available in multiple languages, the game scaffolds more academic language by providing definitions and labels for key terms and uses Spanish friendly cognates (such as "observe," which is very similar to "observar" in Spanish) to support a dominant language minority. Testing "Fish Force" with dual-language learners showed that the simulation could be easily understood and intuited because of how visual and immediate the feedback is. Still, some testers felt it would benefit them to be able to switch from English to Spanish.

Taking this into account, the project team is making content from *Ready Jet Go!* and *The Cat in the Hat Knows a Lot About That!*, two other programs supported through Ready To Learn, available in Spanish. PBS KIDS is also updating digital product features globally to support greater multi-language localization.

Also excluded from playing were learners with motor issues (an unintentional exclusion that is being addressed, as discussed above). Finally, "Fish Force" provides captioned text for all game voiceover to support deaf learners and alt-text on the related home site where the game appears, but it does not include keyboard inputs or descriptive audio to help blind children participate. At the time of this writing, PBS KIDS and producing partner WNET are working with Bridge Multimedia, a partner in developing universally accessible media, to launch its first game with a learner-controlled accessibility console;

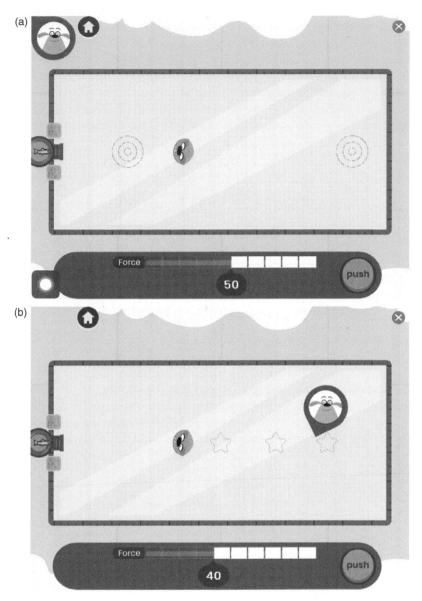

FIGURE 15.6 Images of "Fish Force" game prediction mechanics (a) Prediction mechanic – bullseye (b) Prediction mechanic – star path

(Courtesy of PBS and WGBH Educational Foundation TM/© 2017)

this console can serve as a prototype for standard accessibility features in PBS KIDS games.

Measuring the Potential of Personalized and Adaptive Learning Strategies

"Fish Force" is unlike any game PBS KIDS had launched before, and there is great curiosity about how successfully it engages learners, sustains their interest, and supports their individual needs. PBS KIDS worked with the firm Rockman et al to test a beta build of the game with children ages four to eight (most of whom were in the game's "sweet spot" of age six). Key formative research findings included:

- Participants stayed engaged for 30 minutes and described the leveling as "not too hard" and "not too easy."
- Children who tried the "hint" button were generally able to understand its function and seemed to find it helpful.
- Some participants struggled to gather a sense of their progress and wondered what they had achieved and when they would reach the end of the game. Some participants thought there were not many levels because they got levels that felt very similar, whereas others realized that the levels were just going to go on and on indefinitely.
- If children picked "create" before they tried the regular levels, they got confused about what they were trying to do. In response, we made "create" mode available only after a child completed the ten tutorial levels and the ten game levels. Researchers found that children who created levels after they had learned and played the game liked "create" mode: Some added hundreds of things to the screen, creating impossible levels, but others purposefully designed levels they thought would be challenging but "beatable" (and, without prompting, invited other kids to try out the levels they had created, resulting in an impromptu co-play condition where kids would each design levels and then swap devices).
- Prediction levels did not seem as intuitive and posed challenges for some players, especially given that sometimes they were being asked to pick the predicted landing spot for the plushie, and sometimes they were being asked to pick stars along the predicted path.

Findings from the Rockman et al formative research cited above indicate that an adaptive leveled game can keep children engaged in focused play for more than 30 minutes. That said, the number of times children are willing to play a game in a controlled setting (with no other options available) is considerably greater than when they are playing at home and can choose from a larger inventory. Gameplay data for "Fish Force" on pbskids.org shows average session times closer to typical times for popular games on the site (approximately five minutes). Although formative testing indicates that "Fish Force" can engage children for longer, focused play, when positioned alongside other options, many learners might not stick with it long enough to actually get to adaptive levels. Knowing that average play sessions in the real world are often much shorter than in the research lab, future personalized and adaptive learning games should incorporate engagement strategies that incentivize account creation and replay (reward systems, customization, etc.). They should also consider introducing adaptive leveling sooner, even in tutorial levels, so that more learners experience all those benefits.

As instructive and influential as the formative research findings are, the project team recognizes that they represent only the start of what can be discovered about this game. We are eager to analyze anonymous gameplay data and summative findings to better understand whether and how specific game features influence learning.

Applying Personalized and Adaptive Learning Lessons in New Games

Some of the lessons learned from "Fish Force" were applied to the second personalized and adaptive learning game developed with the Kidaptive platform, "Bridge-a-rama," from the app *The Cat in the Hat Builds That*, which incorporates an anonymous save-slot system that enables players to save progress and rewards them with in-game stickers and unlockable content.

Visualizing Mastery and Progression in Adaptive Experiences

Although "Fish Force" provides graduated and contextual feedback for each level, it does not provide a view into overall progress. Players cannot choose levels from a fixed level map, and each "next level" varies for each player. For similar reasons, tying a global incentive system to an adaptive game also proved challenging because children might reach mastery of concepts or practices at different levels. Formative testing demonstrated that players sought feedback on their progress, an important consideration for future personalized and adaptive learning games. The project team concluded that future and improved global incentive systems could directly reward achievements of mastery regardless of when or where they occur. This lesson was applied to "Bridge-a-rama," where learners can visualize progress along a path to a castle destination as shown in Figure 15.7.

Offering Multiple Modes of Engagement (Guided and Free Play) With Possible Recommendations for Sequencing

"Fish Force" was the first PBS KIDS game to study very similar-leveled and free-play modes alongside each other (see Figure 15.8). The team learned that children were more purposeful in how they approached the create mode once

FIGURE 15.7 Image of "Bridge-a-rama" game progress meter
(Derived and adapted from the Series *The Cat in the Hat Knows a Lot About That!* Courtesy of © Penguin Random House and Dr. Seuss Enterprises, LP. 2018. Used with Permission.; Dr. Seuss Books and Characters TM & © 1957–1958 Dr. Seuss Enterprises, L.P. All Rights Reserved.; and PBS)

they had learned the mechanics and key variables in the leveled game. This lesson was applied to the design of *The Cat in the Hat Builds That* app, wherein players unlock free-play experiences only after they complete guided levels.

Formalizing Practices into Game Mechanics

Finally, the difficulty some learners had with switching from performance to prediction tasks in "Fish Force" reappeared in a beta build of *The Cat in the Hat Knows All About That!* game titled "Bridge-a-rama." In this build of the game, predictions were argument-based and personified by the characters Nic and Sally (see Figure 15.9). Learners tapped on the character whose argument they agree with. This approach was modeled on the work of Page Keeley's formative assessments in *Uncovering Student Ideas* about science (Keeley, 2013). For example, consider the image below and the scripted audio:

SALLY SAYS: "I think it's strong enough because it's made of wood and is strong."
NIC SAYS: "It's not strong enough; it's too thin. it will break."

FIGURE 15.8 Screenshots of *The Cat in the Hat Builds That*. The image on top shows guided, leveled play. The image on the bottom shows open-ended play in Nic and Sally's backyard

(Derived and adapted from the Series *The Cat in the Hat Knows a Lot About That!* Courtesy of © Penguin Random House and Dr. Seuss Enterprises, LP. 2018. Used with Permission.; Dr. Seuss Books and Characters TM & © 1957–1958 Dr. Seuss Enterprises, L.P. All Rights Reserved.; and PBS)

FIGURE 15.9 Image of "Bridge-a-rama" game prediction mechanic
(Derived and adapted from the Series *The Cat in the Hat Knows a Lot About That!* Courtesy of © Penguin Random House and Dr. Seuss Enterprises, LP. 2018. Used with Permission.; Dr. Seuss Books and Characters TM & © 1957–1958 Dr. Seuss Enterprises, L.P. All Rights Reserved.; and PBS)

Formative research showed that learners cited different reasons for agreeing ("because it's strong") and disagreeing ("the thin end might break"), and one participant said she picked Sally because "I like her best." On the whole, participants tended to make correct predictions, but the potential for bias (simply choosing a favorite character) was detected. Consequently, the team is exploring a more neutral visual response input—thumbs up and down buttons—to predict the success or failure of the bridge. Nic and Sally will still model making arguments and opinions, but learners do not have to choose between them.

Conclusion: Researching PAL Approaches and Pushing Boundaries

At the time of writing, the project team is reflecting on lessons learned from the development and formative research of "Fish Force," PBS KIDS' first personalized and adaptive educational game. We also are seeking actionable insights from anonymous gameplay data (accruing since fall 2017) and anticipating results from forthcoming summative research studies. As we continue to develop similar content, we return often to these early findings and ideas:

(1) Personalized and adaptive learning games hold promise for keeping individual learners in their ZPD, as indicated by the 30+ minute sessions children of diverse abilities played the game in a focused manner.
(2) Tools like the UDL Checkpoints are helpful in creating an inclusive design mindset and in motivating content producers to actively evaluate their work along the three UDL dimensions. They are also useful in identifying game features based on UDL principles that can be evaluated. In this way, we can more systematically and effectively apply UDL features in games, study their impact, and contribute empirical evidence to the field.
(3) In these early stages of developing personalized and adaptive learning content, frequent playtesting is critical—and this testing should include individuals with diverse abilities and backgrounds. This serves as a necessary check on assumptions made by developers and designers and supports evaluation of systems that are intended to serve a wider variety of users.
(4) Producers must plan for iteration to achieve greater equity and inclusion in their content. This includes planning for post-launch iterations as research and gameplay data suggest improvements to products before, during, and after launch.

We have only just begun, but even at this early stage, our team can see the crest of a new wave of game-based learning that may get closer to helping map and tap human potential than ever before. It would be an understatement to say that we are excited. We are inspired and hope that you will be, too.

References

Csikszentmihalyi, M. (1990). Flow: The Psychology of Optimal Experience. *Journal of Leisure Research*, 24(1), 93–94.

Keeley, P. (2013). *Uncovering Student Ideas in Primary Science*. Arlington, VA: NSTA Press Book.

Meyer, A., Rose, D. H., & Gordon, D. (2014). *Universal Design for Learning: Theory and Practice*. Wakefield, MA: CAST.

Rose, T. (2016). *The End of Average*. New York, NY: HarperOne Publishing.

Vygotsky, L. (1978). *Mind in Society: The Development of Higher Psychological Processes*. Cambridge, MA: Harvard University Press.

16

INNOVATIONS IN EVIDENCE AND ANALYSIS

The PBS KIDS Learning Analytics Platform and the Research it Supports

Jeremy D. Roberts, Charles B. Parks, Gregory K. W. K. Chung, Flizabeth J. K. H. Redman, Katerina Schenke, and Cosimo Felline

Introduction

In 2015, the Corporation for Public Broadcasting (CPB) and Public Broadcasting Service (PBS) were awarded a five-year grant as part of the Ready To Learn Television Grant Program, a school readiness and educational media initiative funded by the U.S. Department of Education and Congress. As a part of this program, PBS KIDS is exploring new and innovative approaches to research related to engagement and learning with PBS KIDS media.

The U.S. Department of Education solicitation for the Ready To Learn Television Grant Program invited the creation of games that use analytics and embedded assessments, consistent with applicable privacy requirements, in order to (a) create personalized learning experiences that adapt as users progressively demonstrate competency or (b) provide useful and meaningful learning data to parents, caregivers, or educators. In collaboration with UCLA's National Center for Research on Evaluation, Standards, and Student Testing (CRESST), PBS KIDS has created the PBS KIDS Learning Analytics Platform to collect, store, and support the analysis of data gathered as children engage with media such as playing games and watching videos. Kids' safety and privacy are of the utmost importance to PBS KIDS, and the purpose of the PBS KIDS Learning Analytics Platform is to harness the power of technology and data to support kids' learning. Kids simply go about the business of being kids as they play PBS KIDS games and videos, but under the hood, a growing number of games (currently approximately 30) can use the PBS KIDS Learning Analytics Platform to gather anonymous information about gameplay. The granularity of the data collected by the PBS KIDS Learning Analytics Platform ranges from simple information about whether a game was played, or a video was watched, to very detailed information about user actions, the game's reactions, and the details of how things like puzzles and challenges change over time as kids play with them.

The authors of this chapter are a blended interdisciplinary team from PBS KIDS and UCLA CRESST that represent content, product, technology, science, education, and data analysis expertise. In this chapter, we describe several new and exciting lines of research, along with the data that are collected by the PBS KIDS Learning Analytics Platform to support it. To illustrate our points, we use examples from several games: (1) selections from the "Curious George Busy Day" game suite, (2) the "PBS KIDS Measure Up!" app, and (3) the *Ruff Ruffman* "Fish Force" game.

In a first example, we present evidence that gameplay can relate meaningfully to children's performance on standardized test items related to numbers and counting concepts. In a second example, we use gameplay data to help identify the specific interactions that promote learning involving measurement concepts. In a third example, we use gameplay data to power an individualized learning experience that adjusts difficulty to match a player's skill with force and motion concepts. And in a fourth example, we use gameplay data to identify problem areas that are decreasing player engagement, inform the design process, and improve gameplay.

The common theme across each of these examples is that high-value research supporting the goals of the Ready To Learn Television Grant Program is made possible by the new and detailed gameplay data gathered by the PBS KIDS Learning Analytics Platform. Preliminary research activities look promising and have led to increased confidence and investment in using data from the PBS KIDS Learning Analytics Platform. The data gathered from play is relevant to the study of how kids use PBS KIDS media, what kids can do, what they struggle with, what they are learning, and how the media can tailor itself to provide the best playful learning experience possible for each kid. Because of the experimental and promising nature of this work and its broader use within the Ready To Learn Television Grant Program, we highlight the kinds of questions we are exploring and the resulting insights that have been developed through the study of the PBS KIDS Learning Analytics Platform data.

Can We Create Quality Measures Using Gameplay Data?

To answer this question, CRESST created and tested measures that use gameplay data to predict scores on the Test of Early Mathematics Ability–Third Edition (TEMA-3; Ginsburg & Baroody, 2003). "Curious George's Busy Day" is a suite of 16 games that each target closely related numbers and counting skills for three- to five-year-olds (see Figure 16.1). CRESST first analyzed the games to describe the demands that gameplay makes of players, especially related to the

FIGURE 16.1 Screenshot of the "Curious George's Busy Day" home screen (Courtesy of PBS; The PBS logos and wordmarks are trademarks of the Public Broadcasting Service and used with permission.; and from *Curious George* by H. A. Rey. Copyright © 1941, renewed 1969 by Margaret E. Rey and H. A. Rey. Curious George®, including without limitation the character's name and the character's likenesses, are registered trademarks of Houghton Mifflin Harcourt Publishing Company. Reprinted by permission. All Rights Reserved)

targeted numbers and counting skills. Then CRESST specified a very detailed set of gameplay data that the team hypothesized would be relevant to engagement and learning outcomes. McCarthy, Li, & Tiu (2013) fielded a study where participants played selected games and were administered selected items from the TEMA-3. As kids played the games, the PBS KIDS Learning Analytics Platform gathered the specified gameplay data. For example, the information gathered from the "Meatball Launcher" game includes when the player starts the game, starts a round, adjusts an answer, submits a final answer, beats a round, and receives feedback or instruction (including the text transcript and the media type of the feedback), as well as the intended correct answer, and the correctness or incorrectness of all interim and final player answers. CRESST then created various measures and predictive capabilities based on the gameplay data. For each participant, the outputs from the various gameplay measures and predictors were then compared to the scores produced by the TEMA-3 items.

CRESST first compared gameplay measures to TEMA-3 scores by examining correlations. In a series of analyses, CRESST found that games that used game mechanics requiring players to choose among different math-related actions (judgment games) compared to games that only require non-math-related actions (exposure games) yielded measures that correlated better to TEMA-3 scores (Chung, 2015; Chung & Parks, 2015a). Statistically significant correlations between the gameplay measure and TEMA-3 measure were observed more often in judgment games, and those correlations were generally of higher magnitude. Chung and Parks speculated that the reason for this was that the cognitive demands in judgment games were higher: Judgment games required an explicit response from children, and the higher the cognitive demand, the higher the correlations.

In a second set of analyses, Chung and Parks (2015b) examined the relationship between gameplay measures and the TEMA-3 math outcomes in more detail using three games from the McCarthy et al. (2013) study. These games were judgment games where actions in the game could be evaluated as correct or incorrect. Chung and Parks conceptualized gameplay in terms of progress and performance, reasoning that these two dimensions have an extensive history in the measurement of human performance in the motor (e.g., Fitts & Posner, 1967) and cognitive (e.g., Anderson, 1982) domains.

The progress-based measures were mean level time and maximum number of rounds completed. The performance-based measures were related to correct and incorrect player choices. The third set of measures were a function of both time and performance and represented the angle and magnitude components of the vector formed by the time and performance variables (see Figure 16.2).

Chung and Parks (2015b) found the correlations between the progress-based measures and TEMA-3 scores to be game dependent, with measures from only some games showing significant correlations with the TEMA-3. There was some evidence that mean level time was negatively related to math knowledge, suggesting that students who were less skilled in counting and cardinality take longer to beat a level on average. There was clear evidence that performance-based measures were sensitive to TEMA-3 scores, across all three games. The strongest positive predictor of math knowledge was the number of correct first

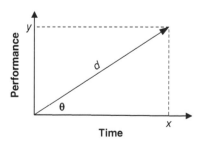

FIGURE 16.2   Components of vector measures, θ (angle) and d (magnitude) (Courtesy of CRESST)

attempts at a solution. The strongest negative predictor was the number of incorrect solution attempts. Finally, the angle-based measures that incorporated both progress and performance yielded the highest correlations with the TEMA-3, with significant correlations ranging from 0.4 to 0.6 across all three games (see Figure 16.3).

The second way CRESST compared gameplay to the TEMA-3 scores involved creating and training a neural network. The network was built in Python using the *PyBrain* library (Schaul et al., 2010). CRESST derived 1,702 indicators from the gameplay data of the selected games, reflecting in-game activity, such as rounds completed, mean round time, and number of times specific feedback was heard. The team provided the indicators to the trained neural net as inputs, and the network predicted TEMA-3 scores as output (see Figure 16.4). The neural network scores had a mean absolute error (MAE) of 6.74 out of 42 possible points from the actual TEMA-3 scores.

The team concluded that gameplay behavior in selected *Curious George* games could be used to predict TEMA-3 scores at a reasonable level of quality and confidence for low-stakes applications. This is a truly exciting finding. Gameplay from games that were not intentionally designed to be assessments show the potential to predict outcomes on validated standardized assessment items. The implication is that high-quality game-based assessments could provide a powerful foundation for effective individualized learning approaches.

Can We Use Gameplay Data to Evaluate Instructional Design?

To answer this question, the team is creating a model that connects gameplay data to learning outcomes by analyzing the contributions to learning that are made by various learning opportunities. In such a way, the team hopes to grow our understanding about the ways that media can be crafted to best promote learning. "PBS KIDS Measure Up!" is a tablet app for three- to five-year-olds that focuses on measurement concepts such as length and height, capacity, and weight by providing dozens of thoughtfully sequenced video clips, open-ended sandboxes, games, and milestone challenges as fun adventures that provide exposure to, exploration of, practice with, and assessment on learning goals (see Figure 16.5 for image of home screen).

CRESST is undertaking (as this chapter is being written) a study that uses pre- and post-test measures of targeted learning outcomes related to measurement concepts. The PBS KIDS Learning Analytics Platform data show exactly what kids do in the app, and CRESST is using that information to create a model that estimates the learning effects that are attributable to various in-app activities.

CRESST recruited four- and five-year-old study participants from three Title I public elementary schools and a childcare center affiliated with a community college. CRESST randomly assigned participants within site to

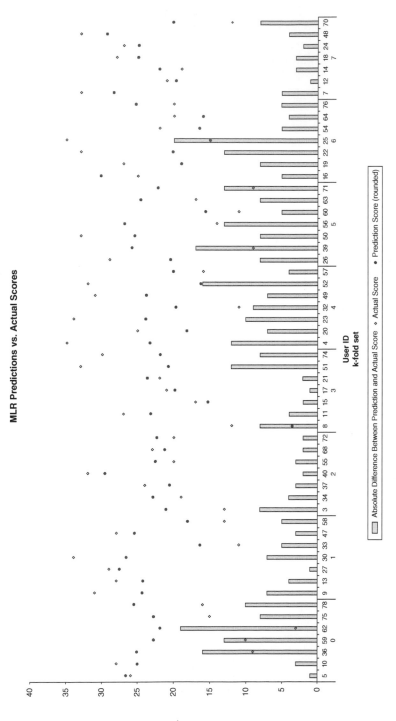

FIGURE 16.3 TEMA–3 predicted and actual scores—multiple linear regression (Courtesy of CRESST)

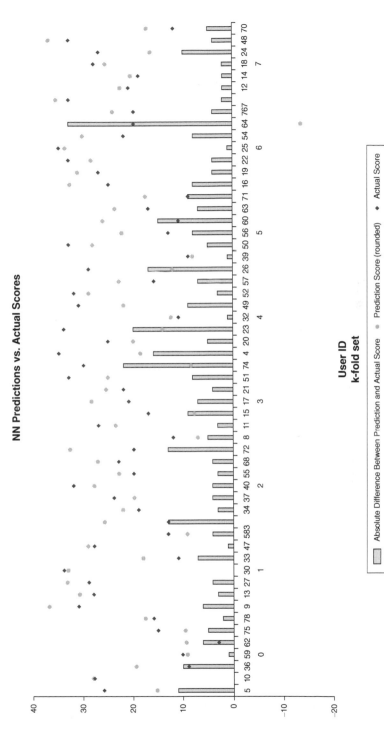

FIGURE 16.4 TEMA–3 predicted and actual scores—neural network (Courtesy of CRESST)

FIGURE 16.5 Screenshot of "PBS KIDS Measure Up!" home screen

(Courtesy of PBS; The PBS logos and wordmarks are trademarks of the Public Broadcasting Service and used with permission.; *Peg + Cat* © 2013 Feline Features, LLC, All Rights Reserved. *Odd Squad* © 2014 The Fred Rogers Company, All Rights Reserved; and ™& © 2018 The Jim Henson Company. *Dinosaur Train* and *Sid the Science Kid* marks, logos, characters and elements are trademarks of The Jim Henson Company. All Rights Reserved)

one of three conditions: (a) kids-app-only, in which children played "PBS KIDS Measure Up!" during class; (b) kids-app + parent-companion-app, where in addition to children playing "PBS KIDS Measure Up!" during class, parents were given a companion app to check their children's progress while they played during class; and (c) a control condition where children played literacy games on iPads. The main difference between the two treatment conditions was that parents in the kids-app + parent-companion-app condition were asked to check the companion app several times during the study. We present analyses only from children's gameplay in the "PBS KIDS Measure Up!" app. Children in the treatment conditions played "PBS KIDS Measure Up!" four days a week for 20–30 minutes a day in their classrooms. Children in the control condition played *Super Why!* (literacy) games during those times.

Children's knowledge of length and height, weight, and capacity was measured using a 20-item, researcher-administered assessment. The assessment was created by researchers at UCLA CRESST with some items adapted from the Child Math Assessment (CMA; Starkey, Klein, & Wakely, 2004) and some from the KeyMath-3 Diagnostic Assessment (Connolly, 2007). The creator of the CMA served as an expert reviewer, consulting on the creation of new items. The assessment items were administered using real-world objects, an iPad app that simulated a working pan balance, and images, all of which children could manipulate or point at to register their answers.

The PBS KIDS Learning Analytics Platform collected two streams of play data from the "PBS KIDS Measure Up!" app. The first stream of data is called activity data, which represents a high-level view of the ways a player engages with the "PBS KIDS Measure Up!" app. Activity data makes it easy to answer questions about which pieces of the content have been played, when, how often, and in what order. The second stream of data is called gameplay data, which represents very granular and detailed information about player activity inside games. For example, the information gathered from the "Cauldron Filler" game includes when the player starts and ends the game, adjusts or submits their answer (including all of their changes along the way), and receives feedback or instruction (including the text transcript and the media type of the feedback), as well as the intended correct answer, and the correctness or incorrectness of all interim and final player answers.

The team used the more granular gameplay data to determine how deeply a player engages with the individual games in the app. For example, the lowest level of engagement is when a player launches a game but then quits before doing anything meaningful. The second level of engagement is when a player launches a game, clicks on irrelevant objects, but does not succeed in activities that require knowledge of measurement concepts. The third level of engagement is when a player launches a game, succeeds at activities that require knowledge of measurement concepts but does not complete the game. Finally, the fourth level of engagement is when a player successfully completes the game.

Figure 16.6 illustrates the relative popularity of the individual games in the "PBS KIDS Measure Up!" app, and the drop-off across deeper levels of engagement when organized by game.

Figure 16.6 aggregates activity across all individuals in the study, but each individual's activity can also be visualized in a similar figure, giving a robust picture of each individual's engagement patterns.

With the activity and gameplay data, we can uncover many useful insights into how "PBS KIDS Measure Up!" is used. For example, of all the games that allow players to succeed and fail, "Mushroom Sorter" is the most popular. In 6.2% of game sessions, players exit the game without performing any click or other action; 8.8% of sessions end with the player performing some clicks, but not making any attempt at solving the level; 3.5% of sessions end with the player making some attempts, none of which are successful; 8.0% of sessions end with the player making some successful

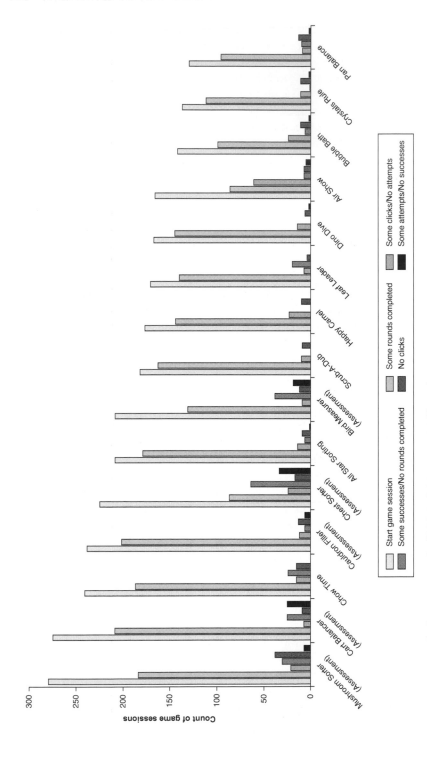

FIGURE 16.6 Level of engagement in "PBS KIDS Measure Up!" app by game
(Courtesy of CRESST)

attempts, but not completing a full challenge; and 73.4% of challenges end with the player completing some challenges.

Figure 16.7 illustrates engagement levels across games by individual. This is useful when trying to answer questions about the variability in engagement patterns that exists across a population.

With knowledge of the pre- and post-test scores collected as a part of the study, and with detailed knowledge of how each participant engaged with the "PBS KIDS Measure Up!" app, the CRESST research team is developing a diagnostic classification model (DCM; Rupp, Templin, & Henson, 2010) that relates gameplay to learning and engagement to outcomes.

The general form of the model is shown in Figure 16.8. The latent variable (ζ) represents a general factor associated with all the indicators measured by the game. The latent variables (x1, x2, x3,... xk) are binary latent variables that represent mastery/non-mastery of specific attributes in the model. A higher-order latent variable represents the association among the specific attributes. The indicators derived from gameplay data are represented by y1, y2, y3,... yi. The latent variables are based on the PBS KIDS Math Learning Framework (PBS KIDS, 2011), a framework that defines math-related learning goals and provides guidance for PBS KIDS media producers. These variables map to a set of expected learning and engagement constructs promoted by the "PBS KIDS Measure Up!" app. The indicators are derived from the gameplay data.

The use of DCMs extends beyond just the "PBS KIDS Measure Up!" app. They can be used across games and apps and make special use of the gameplay data collected by the PBS KIDS Learning Analytics Platform by imposing a theoretically driven statistical model to the data. When kids play a particular game or video, does it produce any effect? If so, how much play is required? And what design strategies do the effective media utilize? By connecting nuanced information about individual engagement with carefully crafted game-based indicators of individual knowledge and skill, along with detailed knowledge of each individual's results on each pre- and post-test item, the project team hopes to compare and compete models over time to promote our understanding of what "ingredients" produce desired learning and engagement outcomes.

Can We Use Gameplay Data to Improve Gameplay Itself?

To answer this question, the team is currently conducting and planning multiple studies (described below) of "Fish Force," a game from *The Ruff Ruffman Show* for four- to eight-year-olds about forces and motion. In the game, players try to use frozen herring to push a plushie across ice into a target and avoid different kinds of obstacles, while providing exposure to age-appropriate inquiry-related

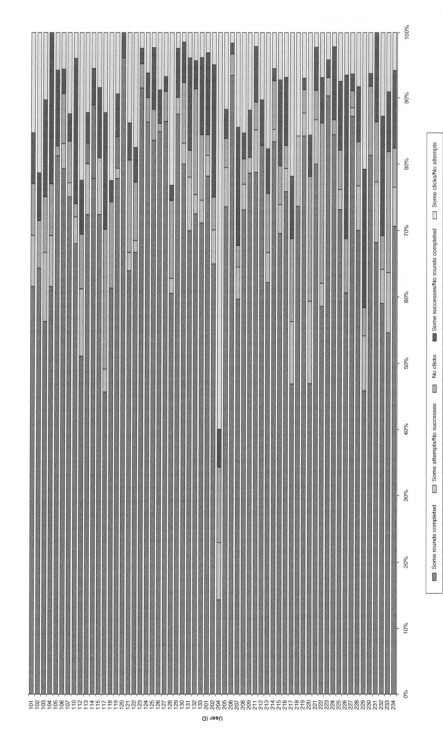

FIGURE 16.7 Engagement levels across games by individual player in "PBS KIDS Measure Up!" app (Courtesy of CRESST)

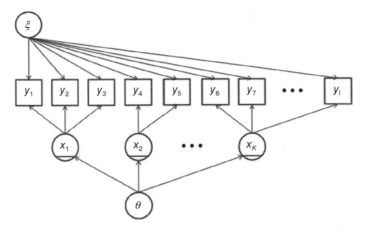

FIGURE 16.8 Diagnostic classification model—general form
(Courtesy of CRESST)

concepts in the process (see Figure 16.9 for the game's opening screen; also see Chapter 15 for a more detailed description of "Fish Force" overall). Players encounter different types of obstacles while attempting to push the plushie across the ice such as moving obstacles (penguins) and static obstacles (patches of sand to increase friction or ice holes players can fall into). The complexity of the obstacles on the rink forces players to use alternate methods of reaching the target such as using bank shots and incorporating timing into shots. "Fish Force" was designed to address force and motion topics as specified in the PBS KIDS Science Learning Framework (PBS KIDS, 2017; see Chapter 9 for a description of the development of the Framework). The four key concepts are (a) understand that pushes can cause objects to move; (b) understand that pushes can have different strengths and directions; (c) understand that pushing on an object can change the speed or direction of its motion and can start or stop it; and (d) understand that when objects touch or collide, they push on one another and can change motion.

Adaptivity Policy Study

CRESST is designing and will implement an experimental Adaptivity Policy Study to compare level-selection policies in the "Fish Force" game. The goal is to determine the effects that different level-selection policies have on player engagement and learning. The policies are (a) an adaptive sequencing policy using item response theory developed by a company called Kidaptive where level selection is individualized for each player based on real-time estimates of the player's ability and estimates of the difficulty of the available levels using data

FIGURE 16.9 Screenshot of the "Fish Force" game opening screen (Courtesy of WGBH Educational Foundation TM/© 2017)

from the PBS KIDS Learning Analytics Platform, (b) a policy with a fixed sequence of levels developed by the original game developer, and (c) a policy of sequencing levels that is randomized for each player.

CRESST will use learner outcomes that include measures of physics knowledge, and measures of engagement to examine the overall effectiveness of the different level-selection policies. The PBS KIDS Learning Analytics Platform will capture children's interaction with the game, including when the player starts the game, starts a round, adjusts their interim solution, submits a final solution, uses a hint, beats a round, and receives feedback or instruction (including the text transcript and the media type of the feedback), as well as rich detail about the outcomes of each solution attempt. It will also capture the specifics of the levels selected by each policy. The layouts of the challenges in "Fish Force" range from extremely simple (i.e., no obstacles) to very complicated (i.e., many obstacles, moving obstacles, patches of increased friction, bank shots required). Because of this, the platform will also capture the state of the rink at the beginning of the round, at the time of launch, and when objects come to rest. It also captures a list of objects that the plushie collided with to help determine what exactly happened during the course of an attempt.

The team will use this information to address questions about the impact of the different level-selection policies on children's interaction in the game, and their engagement and learning processes. For example, the team will measure children's engagement in terms of how long they spend playing the game and the number of challenges they complete. Researchers will measure learning in terms of success and error rates, degree of hint usage, successful or unsuccessful usage of various game controls (which presumably reflect the application of the targeted physics knowledge), as well as how children respond to the feedback and other instructional guidance provided by the game. By comparing the effects of the various level-selection policies, the team hopes to learn more about the potential for individualized learning approaches, such as Kidaptive's adaptive sequencing policy.

Population Data Studies

PBS KIDS will also use the PBS KIDS Learning Analytics Platform to gather data on how our audience plays "Fish Force" from the public PBS KIDS audience. "Fish Force" is live to the public, and has been played over 2 million times, which presents the opportunity to examine natural play patterns, engagement outcomes, and inferred learning outcomes across a large population. Using population data, we can answer questions relevant to instructional design. For example, asking a high-level question such as "Are any of the levels in the game too hard?" leads to more specific lower-level questions of the data: "During gameplay, which levels most often represent the last level played?" This question is important from a developer's perspective because it is informative for changing or creating levels that do not result in players discontinuing gameplay. In this example, we identified a particular level as clearly problematic due to an unusually high rate of players discontinuing gameplay. This resulted in close scrutiny of the level's design, the formation of new theories as to how to make improvements, and a plan to iterate the product and test the improvements.

The problematic level was the first level in the game that requires players to make a bank shot to successfully complete the challenge. Upon close scrutiny, it became clear that the level introduced the bank shot while also requiring a successful adjustment of the force meter as well as a successful adjustment of the position of the launcher. This suggests that the level is very difficult for many players and that difficulty could be why players are discontinuing gameplay. The team concluded we must scaffold the introduction of bank shots more, and more gradually introduce the concept of a bank shot. Modifications to the game are underway that include breaking that level into three separate levels: (1) Introduces bank, but does not require adjustments to force or launcher to succeed. Just click the launch button, observe bank, and succeed. (2) Requires a bank shot, and also requires adjustment to the force meter, but not to the position of the launcher. (3) Requires a bank shot and an adjustment to the force meter and to the launcher position. The team analyzed the data from the PBS KIDS Learning Analytics Platform to identify the problem and develop a theory. Once the modifications are launched to the public, the PBS KIDS Learning Analytics Platform will again support the team in quantifying and evaluating the effect of the changes.

Engagement Studies

The team will focus additional studies on player engagement in "Fish Force." The team defines engagement using flow theory (Csikszentmihalyi, 1990), in which engagement is viewed as a psychological state of optimal experience characterized by heightened, simultaneous experience of concentration, interest, and enjoyment (Shernoff, 2013).

In one study, CRESST will measure the player's self-reported in-the-moment engagement to understand to what extent adaptively selecting the game levels influences the time players spend on the game or their self-reported engagement during the game. CRESST will measure player engagement using experience sampling methods (Hektner, Schmidt, & Csikszentmihalyi, 2007). Experience sampling methods ask players to repeatedly respond to a short set of questions (such as: How fun is the game right now? How hard is this for you right now? How hard are you trying in the game right now? and How much do you want to keep playing this game right now?) with the ultimate goal of connecting players' responses to events that happen in the game as captured by the PBS KIDS Learning Analytics Platform.

In another planned study, the team will focus on creating gameplay-based measures of engagement. The study will examine the relationship between gameplay behavior and engagement using multiple, synchronized data streams. The data sources will include electroencephalography (also known as EEG, a method to collect and record players' electrical activity on the scalp during gameplay), gameplay telemetry, screen capture video, engagement questions posed at key points in the game (using the in-the-moment measures), and a comprehensive set of engagement questions posed at the end of the game. The EEG data will provide information on engagement states (e.g., periods of high engagement and periods of low engagement), and the screen capture video will be analyzed along with the gameplay data to develop algorithms that detect engagement levels using only gameplay data. The detectors will then be compared to the self-report engagement measures both in-the-moment and at the end of the game, as well as the EEG measures of engagement. The team will include these additional conceptualizations of engagement beyond what can be directly assessed using gameplay measures to validate the game-based measures and make claims about a player's cognition and emotion while playing the game. Thus, researchers are able to model changes in engagement or interest over time across many gaming contexts and use the self-reported measures as an anchor with which to validate measures derived from the player's in-game activity.

Combining multiple sources of information is key to being able to make claims about the player's learning and engagement from any one source. The hope is that engagement detectors based on gameplay telemetry will ultimately provide an unobtrusive and practical method to detect engagement.

Implications for the Future

The exploratory work described here is possible only through the availability of telemetry data on children's gameplay from the PBS KIDS Learning Analytics Platform. If PBS KIDS games demonstrate potential to provide high-quality, unobtrusive, low-stakes assessment of player knowledge, skills, and abilities, there are powerful implications for the future of educational technology. This capability could serve as the foundation for a library of games that react and adapt to each individual player's needs. Experiences that use gameplay data to adapt to individual player needs can potentially improve engagement and learning outcomes beyond what traditional game designs allow. Careful analysis of gameplay data may, in turn, give us a microscope that we can use to more accurately identify the specific "active ingredients" of effective media-based learning experiences. Gameplay data can also be used to understand exactly how a population is using educational technology, which can lead to improved products and design processes. Finally, new sources of information such as EEG look promising for use alongside gameplay to depict a more robust picture of how educational technology affects learning. In the final analysis, PBS KIDS believes this work represents a novel opportunity to increase the effectiveness of early childhood learning technology, and to translate that opportunity into impact for the millions of kids in the PBS KIDS audience by delivering playful learning experiences that help them build the skills they need for success in school and in life.

References

Anderson, J. R. (1982). Acquisition of cognitive skill. *Psychological Review*, 89(4), 369–406.

Chung, G. K. W. K. (2015). Guidelines for the design, implementation, and analysis of game telemetry. In C. S. Loh, Y. Sheng, & D. Ifenthaler (Eds.), *Serious games analytics: Methodologies for performance measurement, assessment, and improvement* (pp. 59–79). New York, NY: Springer.

Chung, G. K. W. K. & Parks, C. (2015a). *Feature analysis validity report (deliverable to PBS KIDS)*. Los Angeles, CA: UCLA, National Center for Research on Evaluation, Standards, and Student Testing.

Chung, G. K. W. K., & Parks, C. (2015b). *Bundle 1 computational model analysis report (deliverable to PBS KIDS)*. Los Angeles, CA: UCLA, National Center for Research on Evaluation, Standards, and Student Testing.

Connolly, A. J. (2007). *keymath-3 Diagnostic Assessment*. San Antonio, TX: Pearson.

Csikszentmihalyi, M. (1990). The domain of creativity. In M. A. Runco & R. S. Albert (Eds.), *Theories of creativity* (pp. 190–212). Newbury Park, CA: Sage.

Fitts, P. M. & Posner, M. I. (1967). *Human performance*. Belmont, CA: Brooks/Cole.

Ginsburg, H. P., & Baroody, A. J. (2003). *Test of early mathematics ability*. (3rd ed.) Austin, TX: ProEd.

Hektner, J. M., Schmidt, J. A., & Csikszentmihalyi, M. (2007). *Experience sampling method: Measuring the quality of everyday life*. Thousand Oaks, CA: Sage.

McCarthy, B., Li, L., & Tiu, M. (2013). *PBS KIDS Progress Tracker algorithm validation report*. San Francisco, CA: WestEd.

PBS KIDS (2011). *PBS KIDS Math Learning Framework*. Crystal City, VA: PBS.

PBS KIDS (2017). *PBS KIDS Science Learning Framework*. Crystal City, VA: PBS.

Rupp, A., Templin, J., & Henson, R. (2010). *Diagnostic measurement: Theory, methods, and applications*. New York, NY: Guilford.

Schaul, T., Bayer, J., Wierstra, D., Sun, Y., Felder, M., Sehnke, F., Ruckstieß, T., & Schmidhuber, J. (2010). *PyBrain*. *Journal of Machine Learning Research*, 11(February), 743–746.

Shernoff, D. J. (2013). *Optimal learning environments to promote student engagement*. New York, NY: Springer.

Starkey, P., Klein, A., & Wakely, A. (2004). Enhancing young children's mathematical knowledge through a pre-kindergarten mathematics intervention. *Early Childhood Research Quarterly*, 19(1), 99–100.

INDEX